Double Harness

by Anthony Hope

CHAPTER I
SOME VIEWS OF THE INSTITUTION

The house—a large, plain white building with no architectural pretensions—stood on a high swell of the downs and looked across the valley in which Milldean village lay, and thence over rolling stretches of close turf, till the prospect ended in the gleam of waves and the silver-grey mist that lay over the sea. It was a fine, open, free view. The air was fresh, with a touch of salt in it, and made the heat of the sun more than endurable—even welcome and nourishing. Tom Courtland, raising himself from the grass and sitting up straight, gave utterance to what his surroundings declared to be a very natural exclamation:

"What a bore to leave this and go back to town!"

"Stay a bit longer, old chap," urged his host, Grantley Imason, who lay full length on his back on the turf, with a straw hat over his eyes and nose, and a pipe, long gone out, between his teeth.

"Back to my wife!" Courtland went on, without noticing the invitation.

With a faint sigh Grantley Imason sat up, put his hat on his head, and knocked out his pipe. He glanced at his friend with a look of satirical amusement.

"You're encouraging company for a man who's just got engaged," he remarked.

"It's the devil of a business—sort of thing some of those fellows would write a book about. But it's not worth a book. A page of strong and indiscriminate swearing—that's what it's worth, Grantley."

Grantley sighed again as he searched for his tobacco-pouch. The sigh seemed to hover doubtfully between a faint sympathy and a resigned boredom.

"And no end to it—none in sight! I don't know whether it's legal cruelty to throw library books and so on at your husband's head——"

"Depends on whether you ever hit him, I should think; and they'd probably conclude a woman never would."

"But what an ass I should look if I went into court with that sort of story!"

"Yes, you would look an ass," Grantley agreed. "Doesn't she give you—well, any other chance, you know?"

"Not she! My dear fellow, she's most aggressively the other way."

"Then why don't you give her a chance?"

"What, you mean——?"

"Am I so very cryptic?" murmured Grantley as he lit his pipe.

"I'm a Member of Parliament."

"Yes, I forgot. That's a bit awkward."

"Besides, there are the children. I don't want my children to think their father a scoundrel." He paused, and added grimly: "And I don't want them to be left to their mother's bringing-up either."

"Then we seem to have exhausted the resources of the law."

"The children complicate it so. Wait till you have some of your own, Grantley."

"Look here—steady!" Grantley expostulated. "Don't be in such a hurry to give me domestic encumbrances. The bloom's still on my romance, old chap. Talking of children to a man who's only been engaged a week!" His manner resumed its air of languid sympathy as he went on: "You needn't see much of her, Tom, need you?"

"Oh, needn't I?" grumbled Courtland. He was a rather short, sturdily built man, with a high colour and stiff black hair which stood up on his head. His face was not wanting in character, but a look of plaintive worry beset it. "You try living in the same house with a woman—with a woman like that, I mean!"

"Thanks for the explanation," laughed Grantley.

"I must go and wire when I shall be back, or Harriet'll blow the roof off over that. You come too; a stroll'll do you good."

Grantley Imason agreed; and the two, leaving the garden by a little side gate, took their way along the steep road which led down to the village, and rose again on the other side of it, to join the main highway across the downs a mile and a half away. The lane was narrow, steep, and full of turns; the notice "Dangerous to Cyclists" gave warning of its character. At the foot of it stood the Old Mill House, backing on to a little stream. Farther on lay the church and the parsonage; opposite to them was the post-office, which was also a general shop and also had rooms to let to visitors. The village inn, next to the post-office, and a dozen or so of labourers' cottages exhausted the shelter of the little valley, though the parish embraced several homesteads scattered about in dips of the downs, and a row of small new red villas at the junction with the main road. Happily these last, owing to the lie of the ground, were out of sight from Grantley Imason's windows, no less than from the village itself.

"And that's the home of the fairy princess?" asked Courtland as they passed Old Mill House, a rambling, rather broken-down old place, covered with creepers.

"Yes; she and her brother moved there when the old rector died. You may have heard of him—the Chiddingfold who was an authority on Milton. No? Well, he was, anyhow. Rather learned all round, I fancy—Fellow of John's. But he took this living and settled down for life; and when he died the children were turned out of the rectory and took Old Mill House. They've got an old woman—well, she's not very old—with the uneuphonious name of Mumple living with them. She's been a sort of nurse-housekeeper-companion: a mixed kind of position—breakfast and midday dinner with the family, but didn't join his reverence's evening meal. You know the sort of thing. She's monstrously fat; but Sibylla loves her. And the new rector moved in a fortnight ago, and everybody hates him. And the temporary curate, who was here because the new rector was at Bournemouth for his health, and who lodged over the post-office, has just gone, and everybody's dashed glad to see the last of him. And that's all the news of the town. And, behold, Tom, I'm the squire of it, and every man, woman, or child in it is, by unbroken tradition and custom, entitled to have as much port wine out of my cellar as his, her, or its state of health may happen to require."

He threw off this chatter in a gay self-contented fashion, and Tom Courtland looked at him with affectionate envy. The world had been very good to him, and he, in return, was always amiable to it. He had been born heir and only child of his father; had inherited the largest share in a solid old-fashioned banking-house; was now a director of the great joint-stock undertaking in which the family business had consented to merge itself on handsome terms; had just as much work to do as he liked, and possessed, and always had enjoyed, more money than he needed. He was thirty-three now, and had been a social favourite even before he left school. If it was difficult to say what positive gain his existence had been to society, there was no doubt that his extinction would at any time have been considered a distinct loss.

"A country squire with a rosy-cheeked country girl for wife! That's a funny ending for you, Grantley."

"She's not rosy-cheeked—and it's not an ending—and there's the post-office. Go in, and be as civil as you can to Lady Harriet."

A smile of pity, unmistakably mingled with contempt, followed Courtland into the shop. The tantrums of other men's wives are generally received with much the same mixture of scepticism and disdain as the witticisms of other parents' children. Both are seen large, very large indeed, by sufferers and admirers respectively.

The obligation of being as civil as he could to his wife caused Courtland to take three or four minutes in framing his telegram, and when he came out he found Grantley seated on the bench that stood by the inn and conversing with a young man who wore a very old coat and rough tweed knickerbockers. Grantley introduced him as Mr. Jeremy Chiddingfold, and Courtland knew that he was Sibylla's brother. Sibylla herself he had not yet seen. Jeremy had a shock of sandy hair, a wide brow, and a wide mouth; his eyes were rather protuberant, and his nose turned up, giving prominence to the nostrils.

"No family likeness, I hope?" Courtland found himself thinking; for though Jeremy was a vigorous, if not a handsome, masculine type, the lines were far from being those of feminine beauty.

"And he's enormously surprised and evidently rather shocked to hear I'm going to marry his sister—oh, we can talk away, Jeremy; Tom Courtland doesn't matter. He knows all the bad there is about me, and wants to know all the good there is about Sibylla."

One additional auditor by no means embarrassed Jeremy; perhaps not a hundred would have.

"Though, of course, somebody must have married her, you know," Grantley went on, smiling and stretching himself luxuriously like a sleek indolent cat.

"I hate marriage altogether!" declared Jeremy.

Courtland turned to him with a quick jerk of his head.

"The deuce you do!" he said, laughing. "It's early in life to have come to that conclusion, Mr. Chiddingfold."

"Yes, yes, Jeremy, quite so; but——" Grantley began.

"It's an invention of priests," Jeremy insisted heatedly.

Courtland, scarred with fifteen years' experience of the institution thus roundly attacked, was immensely diverted, though his own feelings gave a rather bitter twist to his mirth. Grantley argued, or rather pleaded, with a deceptive gravity:

"But if you fall in love with a girl?"

"Heaven forbid!"

"Well, but the world must be peopled, Jeremy."

"Marriage isn't necessary to that, is it?"

"Oho!" whistled Courtland.

"We may concede the point—in theory," said Grantley; "in practice it's more difficult."

"Because people won't think clearly and bravely!" cried Jeremy, with a thump on the bench. "Because they're hidebound, and, as I say, the priests heaven-and-hell them till they don't know where they are."

"Heaven-and-hell them! Good phrase, Jeremy! You speak feelingly. Your father, perhaps——? Oh, excuse me, I'm one of the family now."

"My father? Not a bit. Old Mumples now, if you like. However that's got nothing to do with it. I'm going on the lines of pure reason. And what is pure reason?"

The elder men looked at one another, smiled, and shook their heads.

"We don't know; it's no use pretending we do. You tell us, Jeremy," said Grantley.

"It's just nature—nature—nature! Get back to that, and you're on solid ground. Why, apart from anything else, how can you expect marriage, as we have it, to succeed when women are what they are? And haven't they always been the same? Of course they have. Read history, read fiction (though it isn't worth reading), read science; and look at the world round about you."

He waved his arm extensively, taking in much more than the valley in which most of his short life had been spent.

"If I'd thought as you do at your age," said Courtland, "I should have kept out of a lot of trouble."

"And I should have kept out of a lot of scrapes," added Grantley.

"Of course you would!" snapped Jeremy.

That point needed no elaboration.

"But surely there are exceptions among women, Jeremy?" Grantley pursued appealingly. "Consider my position!"

"What is man?" demanded Jeremy. "Well, let me recommend you to read Haeckel!"

"Never mind man. Tell us more about woman," urged Grantley.

"Oh, lord, I suppose you're thinking of Sibylla?"

"I own it," murmured Grantley. "You know her so well, you see."

Descending from the heights of scientific generalisation and from the search after that definition of man for which he had been in the end obliged to refer his listeners to another authority, Jeremy lost at the same time his gravity and vehemence. He surprised Courtland by showing himself owner of a humorous and attractive smile.

"You'd rather define man, perhaps, than Sibylla?" suggested Grantley.

"Sibylla's all right, if you know how to manage her."

"Just what old Lady Trederwyn used to say to me about Harriet," Courtland whispered to Grantley.

"But it needs a bit of knowing. She's got the deuce of a temper—old Mumples knows that. Well, Mumples has got a temper too. They used to have awful rows—do still now and then. Sibylla used to fly out at Mumples, then Mumples sat on Sibylla, and then, when it was all over, they'd generally have a new and independent row about which had been right and which wrong in the old row."

"Not content with a quiet consciousness of rectitude, as a man would be?"

"Consciousness of rectitude? Lord, it wasn't that! That would have been all right. It was just the other way round. They both knew they had tempers, and Mumples is infernally religious and Sibylla's generous to the point of idiocy in my opinion. So after a row, when Sibylla had cheeked Mumples and told her to go to the devil (so to speak), and Mumples had sent her to bed, or thumped her, or something, you know——"

"Let us not go too deep into family tragedies, Jeremy."

"Why, when it had all settled down, and the governor and I could hear ourselves talking quietly again——"

"About marriage and that sort of question?"

"They began to have conscience. Each would have it borne in on her that she was wrong. Sibylla generally started it. She'd go weeping to Mumples, taking all her own things and any of mine that were lying about handy, and laying them at Mumples' feet, and saying she was the wickedest girl alive, and why hadn't Mumples pitched into her a lot more, and that she really loved Mumples better than anything on earth. Then Mumples would weigh in, and call Sibylla the sweetest and meekest lamb on earth, and say that she loved Sibylla more than anything on earth, and that she—Mumples—was the worst-tempered and cruellest and unjustest woman alive, not fit to be near such an angel as Sibylla. Then Sibylla used to say that was rot, and Mumples said it wasn't. And Sibylla declared Mumples only said it to wound her, and Mumples got hurt because Sibylla wouldn't forgive her, when Sibylla, of course, wanted Mumples to forgive her. And after half an hour of that sort of thing, it was as likely as not that they'd have quarrelled worse than ever, and the whole row would begin over again."

Grantley lay back and laughed.

"A bit rough on you to give your things to—er—Mumples?" suggested Courtland.

"Just like Sibylla—just like any woman, I expect," opined Jeremy, but with a more resigned and better-tempered air. His reminiscences had evidently amused himself as well as his listeners.

"Wouldn't it have been better to have a preceptress of more equable temper?" asked Grantley.

"Oh, there's nothing really wrong with Mumples; we're both awfully fond of her. Besides she's had such beastly hard luck. Hasn't Sibylla told you about that, Imason?"

"No, nothing."

"Her husband was sent to quod, you know—got twenty years."

"Twenty years! By Jingo!"

"Yes. He tried to murder a man—a man who had swindled him. Mumples says he did it all in a passion; but it seems to have been a cold sort of passion, because he waited twelve hours for him before he knifed him. And at the trial he couldn't even prove the swindling, so he got it pretty hot."

"Is he dead?"

"No, he's alive. He's to get out in about three years. Mumples is waiting for him."

"Poor old woman! Does she go and see him?"

"She used to. She hasn't for years now. I believe he won't have her—I don't know why. The governor was high sheriff's chaplain at the time, so he got to know Mumples, and took her on. She's been with us ever since, and she can stay as long as she likes."

"What things one comes across!" sighed Tom Courtland.

Grantley had looked grave for a moment, but he smiled again as he said:

"After all, though, you've not told me how to manage Sibylla. I'm not Mumples—I can't thump her. I should be better than Mumples in one way, though. If I did, I should be dead sure to stick to it that I was right."

"You'd stick to it even if you didn't think so," observed Courtland.

For a moment the remark seemed to vex Grantley, and to sober him. He spent a few seconds evidently reflecting on it.

"Well, I hope not," he said at last. "But at any rate I should think so generally."

"Then you could mostly make her think so. But if it wasn't true, you might feel a brute."

"So I might, Jeremy."

"And it mightn't be permanently safe. She sees things uncommonly sharp sometimes. Well, I must be off."

"Going back to Haeckel?"

Jeremy nodded gravely. He was not susceptible to ridicule on the subject of his theories. The two watched him stride away towards Old Mill House with decisive vigorous steps.

"Rum product for a country parsonage, Grantley."

"Oh, he's not a product; he's only an embryo. But I think he's a promising one, and he's richly amusing."

"Yes, and I wonder how you're going to manage Miss Sibylla!"

Grantley laughed easily. "My poor old chap, you can't be expected to take a cheerful view. Poor old Tom! God bless you, old chap! Let's go home to tea."

As they walked by the parsonage a bicycle came whizzing through the open garden-gate. It was propelled by a girl of fifteen or thereabouts—a slim long-legged child, almost gaunt in her immaturity, and lamentably grown out of her frock. She cried shrill greeting to Grantley, and went off down the street, displaying her skill to whosoever would look by riding with her arms akimbo.

"Another local celebrity," said Grantley. "Dora Hutting, the new parson's daughter. That she should have come to live in the village is a gross personal affront to Jeremy Chiddingfold. He's especially incensed by her lengthy stretch of black stockings, always, as he maintains, with a hole in them."

Courtland laughed inattentively.

"I hope Harriet'll get that wire in good time," he said.

No remark came into Grantley's mind, unless it were to tell his friend that he was a fool to stand what he did from the woman. But what was the use of that? Tom Courtland knew his own business best. Grantley shrugged his shoulders, but held his peace.

CHAPTER II

THE FAIRY RIDE

Courtland went off early next morning in the dog-cart to Fairhaven station—no railway line ran nearer Milldean—and Grantley Imason spent the morning lounging about his house, planning what improvements could be made and what embellishments provided against the coming of Sibylla. He enjoyed this pottering both for its own sake and because it was connected with the thought of the girl he loved. For he was in love—as much in love, it seemed to him, as a man could well be. "And I ought to know," he said, with a smile of reminiscence, his mind going back to earlier affairs of the heart, more or less serious, which had been by no means lacking in his career. He surveyed them without remorse, though one or two might reasonably have evoked that emotion, and with no more regret than lay in confessing that he had shared the follies common to his age and his position. But he found great satisfaction in the thought that Sibylla had had nothing to do with any of the persons concerned. She had known none of them; she was in no sense of the same set with any one of the five or six women of whom he was thinking; her surroundings had always been quite different from theirs. She came into his life something entirely fresh, new, and unconnected with the past. Herein lay a great deal of the charm of this latest, this final affair. For it was to be final—for his love's sake, for his honour's sake, and also because it seemed time for such finality in that ordered view of life and its stages to which his intellect inclined him. There was something singularly fortunate in the chance which enabled him to suit his desire to this conception, to find the two things in perfect harmony, to act on rational lines with such a full and even eager assent of his feelings.

He reminded himself, with his favourite shrug, that to talk of chance was to fall into an old fallacy; but the sense of accident remained. The thing had been so entirely unplanned. He had meant to buy a place in the North; it was only when the one he wanted had been snapped up by somebody else that the agents succeeded in persuading him to come and look at the house at Milldean. It happened to take his fancy, and he bought it. Then he happened to be out of sorts, and stayed down there an unbroken month, instead of coming only from Saturday to Monday. Again, Sibylla and Jeremy had meant to go away when the rector died, and had stayed on only because Old Mill House happened to fall vacant so opportunely. No other house was available in the village. So the chances went on, till chance culminated in that meeting of his with Sibylla: not their first encounter, but the one he always called his meeting with her in his own thoughts—that wonderful evening when all the sky was red, and the earth too looked almost red, and the air was so still. Then he had been with her in his garden, and she, forgetful of him, had turned her eyes to the heavens, and gazed and gazed. Presently, and still, as it seemed, unconsciously, she had stretched out her hand and caught his in a tight grip, silently but urgently demanding his sympathy for thoughts and feelings she could not express. At that moment her beauty seemed to be born for him, and he had determined to make it his. He smiled now, saying that he had been as impulsive as the merest boy, thanking fortune that he could rejoice in the impulse instead of condemning it—an end which *a priori* would have seemed much the more probable. In nine cases out of ten it would have been foolish and disastrous to be carried away in an instant like that. In his case it had, at any rate, not proved disastrous. From that moment he had never turned back from his purpose, and he had nothing but satisfaction in its now imminent accomplishment.

"Absolutely the right thing! I couldn't have done better for myself."

He stood still once in the middle of the room and said these words aloud. They exhausted the subject, and Grantley sat down at his writing-table to answer Mrs. Raymore's letter of congratulation. He had never been in love with Mrs. Raymore, who was his senior by ten years; but she was an old and intimate friend—perhaps his most intimate friend. She had been more or less in his confidence while he was wooing Sibylla, and a telegram apprising her of his success had called forth the letter to which he now owed a response.

"If I had been a poor man," he wrote in the course of his reply, "I wouldn't have married—least of all a rich wife. Even as a well-to-do man, I wouldn't have married a rich wife. You have to marry too much besides the woman! And I didn't want a society woman, nor anybody from any of the sets I've knocked about with. But I did want to marry. I want a wife, and I want the dynasty continued. It's come direct from father to son for five or six generations, and I didn't want to stand on record as the man who stopped it. I'm entirely contented, no less with the project than with the lady. It will complete my life. That's what I want—a completion, not a transformation. She'll do just this for me. If I had taken a child and trained her, I couldn't have got more exactly what I want; and I'm sure you'll think so when you come to know her. Incidentally, I am to acquire a delightful brother-in-law. He'll always be a capital fellow; but, alas, he won't long be the jewel he is now: just at that stage between boy and man—hobbledehoy, as you women used to make me so furious by calling me—breathing fury against all institutions, especially those commonly supposed to be of divine origin; learned in ten thousand books; knowing naught of all that falls under the categories of men, women, and things; best of all, blindly wrath at himself because he has become, or is becoming, a man, and can't help it, and can't help feeling it! How he hates women and despises them! You see, he has begun to be afraid! I haven't told him that he's begun to be afraid; it will be rich to watch him as he achieves the discovery on his own account. You'll enjoy him very much."

Grantley ended his letter with a warm tribute to Mrs. Raymore's friendship, assurances of all it had been to him, and a promise that marriage should, so far as his feelings went, in no way lessen, impair, or alter the affection between them.

"He's very nice about me," said Mrs. Raymore when she had finished reading; "and he says a good deal about the brother-in-law, and quite a lot about himself. But really, he says hardly one word about Sibylla!"

Now it was, of course, about Sibylla that Mrs. Raymore had wanted to hear.

Late afternoon found Grantley cantering over the downs towards Fairhaven. Sibylla had been staying the night there with a Mrs. Valentine, a friend of hers, and was to return by the omnibus which plied to and from Milldean. Their plan was that he should meet her and she should dismount, leaving her luggage to be delivered. He loved his horse, and had seized the opportunity of slipping in a ride. When she joined him he would get off and walk with her. As he rode now he was not in the calm mood which had dictated his letter. He was excited and eager at the prospect of meeting Sibylla again; he was exulting in the success of his love, instead of contemplating with satisfaction the orderly progression of his life. But still he had not, and knew he had not, quite the freedom from self-consciousness which marks a youthful passion. The eagerness was there, but he was not surprised, although he was gratified, to find it there. His ardour was natural enough to need no nursing; yet Grantley was inclined to caress it. He laughed as he let his horse stretch himself in a gallop; he was delighted, and a trifle amused, to find his emotions so fresh: none of the luxury, none of the pleasure-giving power, had gone out of them. He was still as good a lover as any man.

He was cantering over the turf thirty or forty yards from the road when the omnibus passed him. The driver cried his name, and pointed back with his whip. Grantley saw Sibylla a long way behind. He touched his horse with the spur, and galloped towards her. Now she stood still, waiting for him. He came up to her at full speed, reined in, and leapt off. Holding his bridle and his hat in one hand, with the other he took hers, and, bowing over it, kissed it. His whole approach was gallantly conceived and carried out.

"Ah, you—you come to me like Sir Galahad!" murmured Sibylla.

"My dear, Sir Galahad! A banker, Sir Galahad!"

"Well, do bankers kiss the hands of paupers?"

"Bankers of love would kiss the hands of its millionaires."

"And am I a millionaire of love?"

Grantley let go her hand and joined in her laugh at their little bout of conceits. She carried it on, but merrily now, not in the almost painful strain of delight which had made her first greeting sound half-choked.

"Haven't I given it all to you—to a dishonest banker, who'll never let me have it back?"

"We pay interest on large accounts," Grantley reminded her.

"You'll pay large, large interest to me?"

She laid her hand on his arm, and it rested there as they began to walk, the good horse Rollo pacing soberly beside them.

"All the larger if I've embezzled the principal! That's always the way, you know." He stopped suddenly, laughing, "It's quite safe!", and kissed her.

He held her face a moment, looking into the depths of her dark eyes. Now he forgot to be amused at himself or even gratified. If he was not as a boy-lover, it was not because he advanced with less ardour, but that he advanced with more knowledge; not because he abandoned himself less, but that he knew to what the self-abandonment was.

She walked along with a free swing under her short cloth skirt; evidently she could walk thus for many a mile with no slackening and no fatigue. The wind had caught her hair, and blew it from under, and round about, and even over the flat cap of red that she wore; her eyes gazed and glowed and cried joy to him. There under the majestic spread of sky, amid the exhilaration of the salt-tasting air, on the green swell of the land, by the green and blue and white of the sea, she was an intoxication. Grantley breathed quickly as he walked with her hand on his wrist.

"It's so new," she whispered in a joyful apology. "I've never been in love before. You have! Oh, of course you have! I don't mind that—not now. I used to before—before you told me. I used to be very jealous! I couldn't be jealous now—except of not being allowed to love you enough."

"When I'm with you I've never been in love before."

"I don't believe you ever have—not really. I don't believe you could—without me to help you!" She laughed at her boast as she made it, drumming her fingers lightly on his arm; his blood seemed to register each separate touch with a beat for each. "When we're married, Grantley, you shall give me a horse, such a good horse, such a fast horse—as good and as fast as dear old Rollo. And we'll ride—we'll ride together—oh, so far and so fast, against the wind, right against it breathlessly! We'll mark the setting sun, and we'll ride straight for it, never stopping, never turning. We'll ride straight into the gold, both of us together, and let the gold swallow us up!"

"A bizarre ending for a respectable West End couple!"

"No ending! We'll do it every day!" She turned to him suddenly, saying, "Ride now. You mount—I'll get up behind you."

"What? You'll be horribly uncomfortable!"

"Who's thinking of comfort? Rollo can carry us easily. Mount, Grantley, mount! Don't go straight home. Ride along the cliff. Come, mount, mount!"

She was not to be denied. When he was mounted she set her foot lightly on his, and he helped her up.

"My arm round your waist!" she cried. "Why, I'm splendid here! Gallop, Grantley, gallop! Think somebody's pursuing us and trying to take me away!"

"Must poor Rollo drop down dead?"

"No, but we'll pretend he will!"

Now and then he cried something back to her as they rode; but for the most part he knew only her arm about him, the strands of her hair brushing against his cheek as the wind played with them, her short quick breathing behind him. The powerful horse seemed to join in the revel, so strong and easy was his gait as he pulled playfully and tossed his head. They were alone in the world, and the world was very simple—the perfect delight of the living body, the unhindered union of soul with soul—all nature fostering, inciting, applauding. It was a great return to the earliest things, and nothing lived save those. They rode more than king and queen; they rode god and goddess in the youth of the world, descended from High Olympus to take their pleasure on the earth. They rode far and fast against the wind, against it breathlessly. They rode into the gold, and the gold swallowed them up.

The blood was hot in him, and when first he heard her gasp "Stop!" he would pay no heed. He turned the horse's head towards home, but they went at a gallop still. He felt her head fall against his shoulder. It rested there. Her breath came quicker, faster; he seemed to see her bosom rising and falling in the stress. But he did not stop. Again her voice came, strangled and faint:

"I can't bear any more. Stop! Stop!"

One more wild rush, and he obeyed. He was quivering all over when they came to a stand. Her hold round him grew loose; she was about to slip down. He turned round in his saddle and caught her about the waist with his arm. He drew her off the horse and forward to his side. He held her thus with his arm, exulting in the struggle of his muscles. He held her close against him and kissed her face. When he let her go and she reached earth, she sank on the ground and covered her face with both hands, all her body shaken with her gasps. He sat on his horse for a moment, looking at her. He drew a deep inspiration, and brushed drops of sweat from his brow. He was surprised to find that there seemed now little wind, that the sun was veiled in clouds, that a waggon passed along the road, that a dog barked from a farmhouse, that the old ordinary humdrum world was there.

He heard a short stifled sob.

"You're not angry with me?" he said. "I wasn't rough to you? I couldn't bear to stop at first."

She showed him her face. Her eyes were full of tears; there was a deep glow on her cheeks, generally so pale. She sprang to her feet and stood by his horse, looking up at him.

"I angry? You rough? It has been more than I knew happiness could be. I had no idea joy could be like that, no idea life had anything like that. And you ask me if I'm angry and if you were rough! You're opening life to me, showing me why it is good, why I have it, why I want it, what I'm to do with it. You're opening it all to me. And all the beauties come out of your dear hand, Grantley. Angry! I know only that you're doing this for me, only that I must give you in return, in a poor return, all I have and am and can be—must give you my very, very self."

He was in a momentary reaction of feeling; his earnestness was almost sombre as he answered:

"God grant you're doing right!"

"I'm doing what I must do, Grantley."

He swung himself off his horse, and the ready smile came to his face.

"I hope you'll find the necessity a permanent one," he said.

She too laughed joyfully as she submitted to his kiss.

It was her whim, urged with the mock imperiousness of a petted slave, that he should mount again, and she walk by his horse. Thus they wended their way home through the peace of the evening. She talked now of how he had first come into her life, of how she had begun to—— She hesitated, ending, "How I began first to feel you——" and of how, little by little, the knowledge of the feeling had disclosed itself. She was wonderfully open and simple, very direct and unabashed; yet there was nothing that even his fastidious and much-tested taste found indelicate or even forward. In glad confidence she told all, careless of keeping any secrets or any defences against him. The seed had quickened in virgin soil, and the flower had sprung up in a night—almost by magic, she seemed to fancy. He listened tenderly and indulgently. The flame of his emotion had burnt down, but there was an after-glow which made him delightfully content with her, interested and delighted in her, still more thoroughly satisfied with what he had done, even more glad that she was different from all the others with whom he had been thrown. While she displayed to him at once the joy and the spontaneity of her abandonment of her whole existence and self to him, she made him surer of his wisdom in taking her and all she offered, more convinced of the excellence of this disposition of his life. She could give him all he pictured as desirable—the stretches of tranquillity, the moments of strong feeling. She had it in her to give both, and she would give all she had to give. In return he gave her his love. No analysis seemed needful there. He gave her the love of his heart and the shelter of his arm; what more he could give her the afternoon had shown. But in the end it was all contained and summed up in a word—he gave his love.

They came to the crest of the hill where the road dipped down to Milldean, and paused there.

"What a wonderful afternoon it's been!" she sighed.

The enchantment of it hung about her still, expressing itself in the gleam of her eyes and in her restlessness.

"It's been a very delightful one," he leaned down and whispered to her. "It's given us something to look back on always."

"Yes, a great thing to look back on. But even more to look forward to. It's told us what life is going to be, Grantley. And to think that life used to mean only that!"

She waved her hand towards Milldean.

Grantley laughed in sheer enjoyment of her. Amusement mingled with his admiration. His balance had quite come back to him. A review of the afternoon, of their wild ride, made him give part of his amusement to his own share in the proceedings. But who expects a man, or need expect himself, to be wise when he is in love? If there be a chartered season for sweet folly, it is there.

"Can we always be careering over the downs in the teeth of the wind, riding into the gold, Sibylla?" he asked her in affectionate mockery.

She looked up at him, answering simply:

"Why not?"

He shook his head with a whimsical smile.

"Whatever else there is, our hearts can be riding together still."

"And when we're old folks? Isn't it only the young who can ride like that?"

She stood silent for a moment or two. Then she turned her eyes up to his in silence still, with the colour shining bright on her cheeks. She took his hand and kissed it. He knew the thought that his words had called into her mind. He had made the girl think that, when they were old, the world would not be; there would be young hearts still to ride, young hearts in whom their hearts should be carried still in the glorious gallop, young hearts which had drawn life from them.

They parted at the gate of Old Mill House. Grantley urged her to come up to his house in the evening and bring Jeremy with her, and laughed again when she said, "Bring Jeremy?" She was confused at the hint in his laughter, but she laughed too. Then growing grave, she went on:

"No, I won't come to-night. I won't see you again to-night. I want to realise it, to think it all over."

"Is it so complicated as that? You're looking very serious!"

She broke into a fresh laugh, a laugh of joyful confession.

"No, I don't want to think it over. I really want to live it over, to live it over alone, many, many times. To be alone with you again up on the downs there."

"Very well. Send Jeremy up. By now he must be dying for an argument; and he's probably not on speaking terms with Mrs. Mumple."

He gave her his hand; any warmer farewell there in the village street was quite against his ways and notions. He observed a questioning look in her eyes, but it did not occur to him that she was rather surprised at his wanting Jeremy to come up after dinner. She did not propose to spend any time with Jeremy.

"I'll tell him you want him," she said; and added in a whisper, "Good-bye, good-bye, good-bye!"

He walked his horse up the hill, looking back once or twice to the gate where she stood watching him till a turn of the lane hid him from her sight. When that happened, he sighed in luxurious contentment, and took a cigarette from his case.

To her the afternoon had been a wonder-working revelation; to him it seemed an extremely delightful episode.

CHAPTER III

THE WORLDLY MIND

For a girl of ardent temper and vivid imagination, strung to her highest pitch by a wonderful fairy ride and the still strange embrace of her lover, it may fairly be reckoned a trial to listen to a detailed comparison of the hero of her fancy with another individual—who has been sentenced to twenty years' penal servitude for attempted murder! Concede circumstances extenuating the crime as amply as you please (and My Lord in scarlet on the Bench had not encouraged the jury to concede any), the comparison is one that gives small pleasure, unless such as lies in an opportunity for the exercise of Christian patience. This particular virtue Jeremy Chiddingfold suspected of priestly origin; neither was it the strongest point in his sister's spiritual panoply. He regarded Sibylla's ill-repressed irritation and irrepressible fidgeting with a smile of malicious humour.

"You might almost as well come up to Imason's," he whispered.

"She can't go on much longer!" moaned Sibylla.

But she could. For long years starved of fruition, her love revelled luxuriantly in retrospect and tenderly in prospect; and she was always good at going on, and at going on along the same lines. Mrs. Mumple's loving auditors had heard the tale of Luke's virtues many a time during the period of his absence (that was the term euphemistically employed). The ashes of their interest suddenly flickered up at the hint of a qualification which Mrs. Mumple unexpectedly introduced.

"He wasn't the husband for every woman," she said thoughtfully.

"Thank heaven!" muttered Jeremy, glad to escape the superhuman.

"Eh, Jeremy?"

She revolved slowly and ponderously towards him.

"Thank heaven he got the right sort, Mumples."

"He did," said Mrs. Mumple emphatically; "and he knew it—and he'll know it again when he comes back, and that's only three years now."

A reference to this date was always the signal for a kiss from Sibylla. She rendered the tribute and returned to her chair, sighing desperately. But it was some relief that Mrs. Mumple had finished her parallel, with its list of ideal virtues, and now left Grantley out of the question.

"Why wasn't he the husband for every woman, Mumples?" inquired Jeremy as he lit his pipe. "They're all just alike, you know."

"You wait, Jeremy!"

"Bosh!" ejaculated Jeremy curtly.

"He liked them good-looking, to start with," she went on; "and I was good-looking." Jeremy had heard this so often that he no longer felt tempted to smile. "But there was more than that. I had tact."

"Oh, come now, Mumples! You had tact? You? I'm—well, I'm——"

"I had tact, Jeremy." She spoke with overpowering solidity. "I was there when he wanted me, and when he didn't want me I wasn't there, Sibylla."

"Didn't he always want you?" Brother and sister put the question simultaneously, but with a quite different intention.

"No, not always, dears.—Is that your foot on my table? Take it off this instant, Jeremy!"

"Quite a few thousand years ago there was no difference between a foot and a hand, Mumples. You needn't be so fussy about it."

Sibylla got up and walked to the window. From it the lights in Grantley's dining-room were visible.

"I haven't seen him for ten years," Mrs. Mumple went on; "and you've known that, my dears, though you've said nothing—no, not when you'd have liked to have something to throw at me. But I never told you why."

Sibylla left the window and came behind Mrs. Mumple, letting her hand rest on the fat shoulder.

"He broke out at me once, and said he couldn't bear it if I came to see him. It upset him so, and the time wouldn't pass by, and he got thinking how long the time was, and what it all meant. Oh, I can't tell you all he said before he was stopped by the—the man who was there. So I promised him I wouldn't go any more, unless he fell ill or wanted me. They said they'd let me know if he asked for me and was entitled to a visit. But word has never come to me, and I've never seen him."

She paused and stitched at her work for a minute or two.

"You must leave men alone sometimes," she said.

"But, Mumples, you?" whispered Sibylla.

Mrs. Mumple looked up at her, but made no answer. Jeremy flung down his book with an impatient air; he resented the approaches of emotion—especially in himself.

"He'll be old when he comes out—comes back—old and broken; they break quickly there. He won't so much mind my being old and stout, and he won't think so much of the time when I was young and he couldn't be with me; and he'll find me easier to live with: my temper's improved a lot these last years, Sibylla."

"You silly old thing!" said Sibylla.

But Jeremy welcomed a diversion.

"Rot!" he said. "It's only because you can't sit on us quite so much now. It's not moral improvement; it's simply impotence, Mumples."

Mrs. Mumple had risen in the midst of eulogising the improvement of her temper, and now passed by Jeremy, patting his unwilling cheek. She went out, and the next moment was heard in vigorous altercation with their servant as to the defects of certain eggs.

"I couldn't have done that," said Sibylla.

"Improved your temper?"

"No, stayed away."

"No, you couldn't. You never let a fellow alone, even when he's got toothache."

"Have you got it now?" cried Sibylla, darting towards him.

"Keep off! Keep off! I haven't got it, and if I had I shouldn't want to be kissed."

Sibylla broke into a laugh. Jeremy relit his pipe with a secret smile.

"But I do call it fine of Mumples."

"Go and tell her you've never done her justice, and cry," he suggested. "I'm going up to Imason's now, so you can have it all to yourselves."

"I don't want to cry to-night," Sibylla objected, with a plain hint of mysterious causes for triumph.

Jeremy picked up his cap, showing a studious disregard of any such indications.

"You're going up the hill now? I shall sit up for you."

"You'll sit up for me?"

"Yes. Besides I don't feel at all sleepy to-night."

"I shall when I come back."

"I shan't want to talk."

"Then what will you want? Why are you going to sit up?"

"I've ever so many things to do."

Jeremy's air was weary as he turned away from the inscrutable feminine. While mounting the hill he made up his mind to go to London as soon as he could. A man met men there.

No air of emotion, no atmosphere of overstrained sentiment, hung, even for Jeremy's critical eye, round Grantley Imason's luxurious table and establishment. They suggested rather the ideal of comfort lovingly pursued, a comfort which lay not in gorgeousness or in mere expenditure, but in the delicate adjustment of means to ends and a careful exclusion of anything likely to disturb a dexterously achieved equipoise. Though Jeremy admired the absence of emotion, his rough vigorous nature was challenged at another point. He felt a touch of scorn that a man should take so much trouble to be comfortable, and should regard the achievement of his object as so meritorious a feat. In various ways everything, from the gymnastic apparatus in the hall to the leg-rest in front of the study fire, sought and subserved the ease and pleasure of the owner. That, no doubt, is what a house should be—just as a man should be well dressed. It is possible, however, to be too much of a dandy. Jeremy found an accusation of unmanliness making its way into his mind; he had to banish it by recalling that, though his host might be fond of elegant lounging, he was a keen sportsman too, and handled his gun and sat his horse with equal mastery. These virtues appealed to the English public schoolboy and to the amateur of Primitive Man alike, and saved Grantley from condemnation. But Jeremy's feelings escaped in an exclamation:

"By Jove, you are snug here!"

"I don't pretend to be an ascetic," laughed Grantley, as he stretched his legs out on the leg-rest.

"Evidently."

Grantley looked at him, smiling.

"I don't rough it unless I'm obliged. But I can rough it. I once lived for a week on sixpence a day. I had a row with my governor. He wanted me to give up—— Well, never mind details. It's enough to observe, Jeremy, that he was quite right and I was quite wrong. I know that now, and I rather fancy I knew it then. However, his way of putting it offended me, and I flung myself out of the house with three-and-six in my pocket. Like the man in Scripture, I couldn't work and I wouldn't beg, and I wouldn't go back to the governor. So it was sixpence a day for a week and very airy lodgings. Then it was going to be the recruiting-sergeant; but, as luck would have it, I met the dear old man on the way. I suppose I looked a scarecrow; anyhow, he was broken up about it, and killed the fatted calf—killed it for an unrepentant prodigal. And I could do that again, though I may live in a boudoir."

Jeremy rubbed his hands slowly against one another—a movement common with him when he was thinking.

"I don't tell you that to illustrate my high moral character—as I say, I was all in the wrong—but just to show you that, given the motive——"

"What was the motive?"

"Pride, obstinacy, conceit—anything you like of that kind," smiled Grantley. "I'd told the fellows about my row, and they'd said I should have to knuckle down. So I made up my mind I wouldn't."

"Because of what they'd say?"

"Don't be inquisitorial, Jeremy. The case is, I repeat, not given as an example of morality, but as an example of me—quite different things. However, I don't want to talk about myself to-night; I want to talk about you. What are you going to do with yourself?"

"Oh, I'm all right!" declared Jeremy. "I've got my London B.A. (It didn't run to Cambridge, you know), and I'm pegging away." A touch of boyish pompousness crept in. "I haven't settled precisely what line of study I shall devote myself to, but I intend to take up and pursue some branch of original research."

Grantley's mind had been set on pleasing Sibylla by smoothing her brother's path. His business interest would enable him to procure a good opening for Jeremy—an opening which would lead to comfort, if not to wealth, in a short time, proper advantage being taken of it.

"Original research?" He smiled indulgently. "There's not much money in that."

"Oh, I've got enough to live on. Sibylla's all right now, and I've got a hundred a year. And I do a popular scientific article now and then—I've had one or two accepted. Beastly rot they have to be, though."

Grantley suggested the alternative plan. Jeremy would have none of it. He turned Grantley's story against him.

"If you could live on sixpence a day out of pride, I can live on what I've got for the sake of—of——" He sought words for his big vague ambitions. "Of knowledge—and—and——"

"Fame?" smiled Grantley.

"If you like," Jeremy admitted with shy sulkiness.

"It'll take a long time. Oh, I know you're not a marrying man; but still, a hundred a year——"

"I can wait for what I want."

"Well, if you change your mind let me know."

"You didn't let your father know."

Grantley laughed.

"Oh, well, a week isn't ten years, nor even five," he reminded Jeremy.
"A man can wait for what he wants. Hang it, even a woman can do that! Look at Mumples!"
Grantley asked explanations, and drew out the story which Mrs. Mumple had told earlier in the evening. Grantley's fancy was caught by it, and he pressed Jeremy for a full and accurate rendering, obtaining a clear view of how Mrs. Mumple herself read the case.
"Quite a romantic picture! The lady and the lover, with the lady outside the castle and the lover inside—just for a change."
Jeremy had been moved by the story, but reluctantly and to his own shame. Now he hesitated whether to laugh or not, nature urging one way, his pose (which he dignified with the title of reason) suggesting the other.
"A different view is possible to the worldly mind," Grantley went on in lazy amusement. "Perhaps the visits bored him. Mumples—if I may presume to call her that—probably cried over him and 'carried on,' as they say. He felt a fool before the warder, depend upon it! And perhaps she didn't look her best in tears—they generally don't. Besides we see what Mumples looks like now, and even ten years ago——! Well, as each three months, or whatever the time may be, rolled round, less of the charm of youth would hang about her. We shouldn't suggest any of this to Mumples, but as philosophers and men of the world, we're bound to contemplate it ourselves, Jeremy."
He drank some brandy and soda and lit a fresh cigar. Jeremy laughed applause. Here, doubtless, was the man of the world's view, the rational and unsentimental view to which he was vowed and committed. Deep in his heart a small voice whispered that it was a shame to turn the light of this disillusioned levity on poor old Mumples' mighty sorrow and trustful love.
"And when we're in love with them they can't do anything wrong; and when we've stopped being in love, they can't do anything right," Grantley sighed humorously. "Oh, yes, there's another interpretation of Mr. Mumple's remarkable conduct! You see, we know he's not by nature a patient man, or he wouldn't have committed the indiscretion that brought him where he is. Don't they have bars, or a grating, or something between them at these painful interviews? Possibly it was just as well for Mumples' sake, now and then!"
Despite the small voice Jeremy laughed more. He braved its accusation of treachery to Mumples. He tried to feel quite easy in his mirth, to enjoy the droll turning upside down of the pathetic little story as pleasantly and coolly as Grantley there on his couch, with his cigar and his brandy and soda. For Grantley's reflective smile was entirely devoid of any self-questioning or of any sense of treachery to anybody or to anything with claims to reverence or loyalty. It was for Jeremy, however, the first time he had been asked to turn his theories on to one he loved and to try how his pose worked where a matter came near his heart. His mirth did not achieve spontaneity. But it was Grantley who said at last, with a yawn:
"It's a shame to make fun out of the poor old soul; but the idea was irresistible, wasn't it, Jeremy?"
And Jeremy laughed again.
Jeremy said good-night and went down the hill, leaving Grantley to read the letters which the evening post had brought him. There had been one from Tom Courtland. Grantley had opened and glanced at that before his guest went away. There were new troubles, it appeared. Lady Harriet had not given her husband a cordial or even a civil welcome; and the letter hinted that Courtland had stood as much as he could bear, and that something, even though it were something desperate, must be done. "A man must find some peace and some pleasure in his life," was the sentence Grantley chose to read out as a sample of the letter; and he had added, "Poor old Tom! I'm afraid he's going to make a fool of himself."
Jeremy had asked no questions as to the probable nature of Courtland's folly (which was not perhaps hard to guess); but the thought of him mingled with the other recollections of the evening, with Mrs. Mumple's story and the turn they had given to it, with Grantley's anecdote about himself, and with the idea of him which Jeremy's acute though raw mind set itself to grope after and to realise. The young man again felt that somehow his theories had begun to be no longer theories in a vacuum of merely speculative thought; they had begun to meet people and to run up against facts. The facts and the people no doubt fitted and justified the theories, but to see how that came about needed some consideration. So far he had got. He had not yet arrived at a modification of the theories, or even at an attitude of readiness to modify them, although that would have been an unimpeachable position from a scientific standpoint.
The sight of Sibylla standing at the gate of their little garden brought his thoughts back to her. He remembered that she had promised to sit up—an irrational proceeding, as her inability to give good ground for it had clearly proved; and it was nearly twelve—a very late hour for Milldean—so well had Grantley's talk beguiled the time. Sibylla herself seemed to feel the need of excuse, for as soon as she caught sight of her brother she cried out to him:
"I simply couldn't go to bed! I've had such a day, Jeremy, and my head's all full of it. And on the top of it came what poor Mumples told us; and—and you can guess how that chimed in with what I must be thinking."
He had come up to her, and she put her hand in his.
"Dear old Jeremy, what friends we've been! We have loved one another, haven't we? Don't stop loving me. You don't say much, and you pretend to be rather scornful—just like a boy; and you try to make out that it's all rather a small and ordinary affair——"
"Isn't it?"
"Oh, I daresay! But to me? Dear, you know what it is to me! I don't want you to say much; I don't mind your pretending. But just now, in the dark, when we're all alone, when nobody can possibly hear—and I swear I won't tell a single soul—kiss me and tell me your heart's with me, because we've been true friends and comrades, haven't we?"
It was dark and nobody was there. Jeremy kissed her and mumbled some awkward words. They were enough.
"Now I'm quite happy. It was just that I wanted to hear it from you too."
Jeremy was glad, but he felt himself compromised. When they went in, his first concern was to banish emotion and relieve the tension. Mrs. Mumple's workbox gave a direction to his impulse. If a young man be inclined, as some are, to assume a cynical and worldly attitude, he will do it most before women, and, of all women, most before those who know him best and have known him from his tender age, since to them above all it is most important to mark the change which has occurred. So Jeremy not only allowed himself to forget that small voice, and, turning back to Mrs. Mumple's story, once more to expose it to an interpretation of the worldly and cynical order, but he went even further. The view which Grantley had suggested to him, which had never crossed his mind till it was put before him by another, the disillusioned view, he represented now not as Grantley's, but as his own. He threw it out as an idea which naturally presented itself to a man of the world, giving the impression that it had been in his mind all along, even while Mrs. Mumple was speaking. And now he asked Sibylla, not perhaps altogether to believe in it, but to think it possible, almost probable, and certainly very diverting.

Sibylla heard him through in silence, her eyes fixed on him in a regard grave at first, becoming, as he went on, almost frightened.

"Do ideas like that come into men's minds?" she asked at the end. She did not suspect that the idea had not been her brother's own in the beginning. "I think it's a horrible idea."

"Oh, you're so high-falutin!" he laughed, glad, perhaps, to have shocked her a little.

She came up to him and touched his arm imploringly.

"Forget it," she urged. "Never think about it again. Oh, remember how much, how terribly she loves him! Don't have such ideas." She drew back a little. "I think—I think it's almost—devilish: I mean, to imagine that, to suspect that, without any reason. Yes—devilish!"

That hit Jeremy; it was more than he wanted.

"Devilish! You call it devilish? Why, it was——" He had been about to lay the idea to its true father-mind; but he did not. He looked at his sister again. "Well, I'm sorry," he grumbled. "It only struck me as rather funny."

Sibylla's wrath vanished.

"It's just because you know nothing about it that you could think such a thing, poor boy!" said she.

It became clearer still that Grantley must not be brought in, because the only explanation which mitigated Jeremy's offence could not help Grantley. Jeremy was loyal here, whatever he may have been to Mrs. Mumple. He kept Grantley out of it. But—devilish! What vehement language for the girl to use!

CHAPTER IV

INITIATION

Mrs. Raymore was giving a little dinner at her house in Buckingham Gate in honour of Grantley Imason and his wife. They had made their honeymoon a short one, and were now in Sloane Street for a month before settling at Milldean for the autumn. The gathering was of Grantley's friends, one of the sets with whom he had spent much of his time in bachelor days. The men were old-time friends; as they had married, the wives had become his acquaintances too—in some cases (as in Mrs. Raymore's) more than mere acquaintances. They had all been interested in him, and consequently were curious about his wife—critical, no doubt, but prepared to be friendly and to take her into the set, if she would come. Mrs. Raymore, as she sat at the head of her table, with Grantley by her and Sibylla on Raymore's right hand at the other end, was thinking that they, in their turn, might reasonably interest the young bride—might set her thinking, and encourage or discourage her according to the conclusions she came to about them. She and Raymore would bear scrutiny well as things went. There was a very steady and affectionate friendship between them; they lived comfortably together, and had brought up their children—a boy and a girl—successfully and without friction. Raymore—a tall man with a reddish face and deliberate of speech—was always patient and reasonable. He had never been very impassioned; there had not been much to lose of what is most easily lost. He might have had a few more intellectual tastes, perhaps, and a keener interest in things outside his business; but she had her own friends, and on the whole there was little to complain of.

Then came the Fanshaws—John and Christine. He was on the Stock Exchange; she, a dainty pretty woman, given up to society and to being very well dressed, but pleasant, kind, and clever in a light sort of way. They liked to entertain a good deal, and got through a lot of money. When Fanshaw was making plenty, and Christine had plenty to spend, things went smoothly enough. In bad times there was trouble, each thinking that retrenchment could best be practised by the other and in regard to the expenses to which the other was addicted: it was, for instance, the stables against the dressmaker then. The happiness of the household depended largely on the state of the markets—a thing which it might interest Mrs. Grantley Imason to hear.

Next came the Selfords—Richard and Janet. He was a rather small frail man, of private means, a dabbler in art. She was artistic too, or would have told you so, and fond of exotic dogs, which she imported from far-off places, and which usually died soon. They were a gushing pair, both towards one another and towards the outside world; almost aggressively affectionate in public. "Trying to humbug everybody," Tom Courtland used to say; but that was too sweeping a view. Their excessive amiability was the result of their frequent quarrels—or rather tiffs, since quarrel is perhaps an over-vigorous word. They were always either concealing the existence of a tiff or making one up, reconciling themselves with a good deal of display. Everybody knew this, thanks in part to their sharp-eyed sharp-tongued daughter Anna, a girl of sixteen, who knew all about the tiffs and could always be got to talk about them.

The last pair were the Courtlands themselves. All the set was rather afraid of Lady Harriet. She was a tall, handsome, fair woman, still young; she patronised them rather, but was generally affable and agreeable when nothing occurred to upset her. Tom Courtland grew more depressed, heavy, and dreary every day. A crisis was expected—but Lady Harriet's small-talk did not suffer. Mrs. Raymore thought that the less Grantley's wife saw or knew of that household the better.

The party was completed by Suzette Bligh, a girl pretty in a faded sort of way, not quite so young as she tried to look, and in Mrs. Raymore's opinion, quite likely not to marry at all; and finally by young Blake, Walter Dudley Blake, a favourite of hers and of many other people's, known as a climber of mountains and a shooter of rare game in his energetic days; suspected of enjoying life somewhat to excess and with riotous revelry in his seasons of leisure; impetuous, chivalrous, impulsive, and notably good-looking. Mrs. Raymore had put him on Sibylla's right—in case her husband should not prove amusing to the honoured guest.

On the whole, she thought, they ought not to frighten Sibylla much. There was one terrible example—the Courtlands; but when it comes to throwing things about, the case is admittedly abnormal. For the rest they seemed, to the student of matrimony, fair average samples of a bulk of fair average merit. Perhaps there might have been an ideal union—just to counter-balance the Courtlands at the other extreme. If such were desirable, let it be hoped that the Imasons themselves would supply it. In regard to one point, she decided, the company was really above the average—and that the most important point. There had been rumours once about Christine Fanshaw—indeed they were still heard sometimes; but scandal had never assailed any other woman there. In these days that was something, thought Mrs. Raymore.

Grantley turned from Christine Fanshaw to his hostess.

"You're very silent. What are you thinking about?" he asked.

"Sibylla's really beautiful, and in a rather unusual way. You might pass her over once; but if you did look once, you'd be sure to look always."

"Another woman's looks have kept your attention all this time?"

"Your wife's," she reminded him with an affectionately friendly glance. "And I was wondering what she thought of us all, what we all look like in those pondering thoughtful questioning eyes of hers."

"Her eyes do ask questions, don't they?" laughed Grantley.

"Many, many, and must have answers, I should think. And don't they expect good answers?"

"Oh, she's not really at all alarming!"

"You can make the eyes say something different, I daresay?"

He laughed again very contentedly. Mrs. Raymore's admiration pleased him, since she was not very easy herself to please. He was glad she approved of Sibylla, though as a rule his own opinion was enough for him.

"Well, they aren't always questioning. That would be fatiguing in a wife—really as bad as continually discussing the Arian heresy, as old Johnson says. But I daresay," he lowered his voice, "Lady Harriet would excite a query or two."

"You've told me nothing about Sibylla. I shall have to find it all out for myself."

"That's the only knowledge worth having; and I'm only learning myself still, you know."

"Really, that's an unusually just frame of mind for a husband. I've high hopes of you, Grantley."

"Good! Because you know me uncommonly well."

She thought a moment.

"No, not so very well," she said. "You're hard to know."

He took that as a compliment; probably most people would, since it seems to hint at something rare and out of the common; inaccessibility has an aristocratic flavour.

"Oh, I suppose we all have our fastnesses," he said with a laugh which politely waived any claim to superiority without expressly abandoning it.

"Doesn't one give up the key of the gates by marrying?"

"My dear Kate, read your Bluebeard again!"

Mrs. Raymore relapsed into the silence that was almost habitual to her, but it passed through her mind that the conversation had soon turned from Sibylla to Grantley himself, or at least had dealt with Sibylla purely in her bearing on Grantley; it had not increased her knowledge of Mrs. Imason as an independent individual.

"Well, with business what it is," said Fanshaw in his loud voice—a voice that had a way of stopping other people's voices—"we must cut it down somewhere."

"Oh, you're as rich as Crœsus, Fanshaw!" objected young Blake.

"I'm losing money every day! Christine and I were discussing it as we drove here."

"I like your idea of discussion, John," remarked Christine in her delicate tones, generally touched with sarcasm. "I couldn't open my lips."

"He closured you, and then threw out your Budget?" asked Grantley.

"He almost stripped my gown from my back, and made an absolute clutch at my diamonds."

"I put forward the reasonable view," Fanshaw insisted rather heatedly. "What I said was, begin with superfluities——"

"Are clothes superfluities?" interjected Christine, watching the gradual flushing of her husband's face with mischievous pleasure.

"Nothing is superfluous that is beautiful," said Selford; he lisped slightly, and spoke with an affected air. "We should retrench in the grosser pleasures—eating and drinking, display, large houses——"

"Peculiar dogs!" suggested Blake, chaffing Mrs. Selford.

"Oh, but they are beautiful!" she cried.

"Horses!" said Christine, with sharp-pointed emphasis. "You should really be guided by Mr. Selford, John."

"Every husband should be guided by another husband. That's axiomatic," said Grantley.

"I'm quite content with my own," smiled Mrs. Selford. "Dick and I always agree."

"They must be fresh from a row," Tom Courtland whispered surlily to Mrs. Raymore.

"About money matters the man's voice must in the nature of things be final," Fanshaw insisted. "It's obvious. He knows about it; he makes it——"

"Quite enough for him to do," Christine interrupted. "At that point we step in—and spend it."

"Division of labour? Quite right, Mrs. Fanshaw," laughed Blake. "And if any of you can't manage your department, I'm ready to help."

"They can manage that department right enough," Fanshaw grumbled. "If we could manage them as well as they manage that——" He took a great gulp of champagne, and grew still redder when he heard Christine's scornful little chuckle.

Raymore turned to Sibylla with a kind fatherly smile.

"I hope we're not frightening you, Mrs. Imason? Not too much of the seamy side?"

Blake chimed in on her other hand:

"I'm here to maintain Mrs. Imason's illusions."

"If we're talking of departments, I think that's mine, Blake, thank you," called Grantley with a laugh.

"I'm sure I've been most considerate." This was Lady Harriet's first contribution to the talk. "I haven't said a word!"

"And you could a tale unfold?" asked Blake.

She made no answer beyond shrugging her fine shoulders and leaning back in her chair as she glanced across at her husband. A moment's silence fell on the table. It seemed that they recognised a difference between troubles and grievances which could be discussed with more or less good-nature, or quarrelled over with more or less acerbity, and those which were in another category. The moment the Courtlands were in question, a constraint arose. Tom Courtland himself broke the silence, but it was to talk about an important cricket-match. Lady Harriet smiled at him composedly, unconscious of the earnest study of Sibylla's eyes, which were fixed on her and were asking (as Mrs. Raymore would have said) many questions.

When the ladies had gone, Fanshaw buttonholed Raymore and exhibited to him his financial position and its exigencies with ruthless elaboration and with a persistently implied accusation of Christine's extravagance. Selford victimised young Blake with the story of a picture which he had just picked up; he declared it was by a famous Dutch master, and watched for the effect on Blake, who showed none, never having heard of the Dutch master. Tom Courtland edged up to Grantley's side; they had not met since Grantley's wedding.

"Well, you look very blooming and happy, and all that," he said.

"First-rate, old boy. How are you?"

Tom lowered his voice and spoke with a cautious air.

"I've done it, Grantley—what I wrote to you. By God, I couldn't stand it any longer! I'd sooner take any risk. Oh, I shall be very careful! I shan't give myself away. But I had to do it."

Grantley gave a shrug.

"Oh, well, I'm sorry," he said. "That sort of thing may turn out so awkward."

"It'd have to be infernally awkward to be worse than what I've gone through. At any rate I get away from it sometimes now, and—and enjoy myself."

"Find getting away easy?"

"No; but as we must have shindies, we may as well have them about that. I told Harriet she made the house intolerable, so I should spend my evenings at my clubs."

"Oh! And—and who is she?"

He looked round warily before he whispered:

"Flora Bolton."

Grantley raised his brows and said one word:

"Expensive!"

Tom nodded with a mixture of ruefulness and pride.

"If you're going to the devil, you may as well go quickly and pleasantly," he said, drumming his fingers on the cloth. "By heaven, if I'd thought of this when I married! I meant to go straight—you know I did?"

Grantley nodded.

"I broke off all that sort of thing. I could have gone straight. She's driven me to it—by Jove, she has."

"Take care, old chap. They'll notice you."

"I don't care if—— Oh, all right, and thanks, Grantley. I don't want to make an exhibition of myself. And I've told nobody but you, of course."

Sibylla, never long in coming to conclusions, had made up her mind about the women before the evening was half over. Lady Harriet was strange and terrible when the known facts of the case were compared with her indolent composure. Mrs. Selford was trivial and tiresome, but a good enough little silly soul. Suzette Bligh was entirely negligible; she had not spoken save to flirt very mildly with Blake. Mrs. Raymore elicited a liking, but a rather timid and distant one; she seemed very clear-sighted and judicial. Christine Fanshaw attracted her most, first by her dainty prettiness, also by the perfection of her clothes (a thing Sibylla much admired), most by her friendly air and the piquant suffusion of sarcastic humour that she had. She seemed to treat even her own grievances in this semi-serious way—one of them certainly, if her husband were one. Such a manner and such a way of regarding things are often most attractive to the people who would find it hardest to acquire the like for themselves; they seem to make the difficulties which have loomed so large look smaller—they extenuate, smooth away, and, by the artifice of not asking too much, cause what is given to appear a more liberal instalment of the possible. They are not, however, generally associated with any high or rigid moral ideas, and were not so associated in the person of pretty Christine Fanshaw. But they are entirely compatible with much worldly wisdom, and breed a tolerance of unimpeachable breadth, if not of exalted origin.

"We'll be friends, won't we?" Christine said to Sibylla, settling herself cosily by her. "I'm rather tired of all these women, except Kate Raymore, and she doesn't much approve of me. But I'm going to like you."

"Will you? I'm so glad."

"And I can be very useful to you. I can even improve your frocks—though this one's very nice; and I can tell you all about husbands. I know a great deal—and I'm representative." She laughed gaily. "John and I are quite representative. I like John really, you know; he's a good man—but he's selfish. And John likes me, but I'm selfish. And I like teasing John, and he takes a positive pleasure sometimes in annoying me."

"And that's representative?" smiled Sibylla.

"Oh, not by itself, but as an element, sandwiched in with the rest—with our really liking one another and getting on all right, you know. And when we quarrel, it's about something, not about nothing, like the Selfords—though I don't know that that is quite so representative, after all." She paused a moment, and resumed less gaily, with a little wrinkle on her brow: "At least, I think John really likes me. Sometimes I'm not sure, though I know I like him; and when I'm least sure I tease him most."

"Is that a good remedy?"

"Remedy? No, it's temper, my dear. You see, there was a time when—when I didn't care whether he liked me or not; when I—when I—well, when I didn't care, as I said. And I think he felt I didn't. And I don't know whether I've ever quite got back."

Ready with sympathy, Sibylla pressed the little richly beringed hand.

"Oh, it's all right. We're very lucky. Look at the Courtlands!"

"The poor Courtlands seem to exist to make other people appreciate their own good luck," said Sibylla, laughing a little.

"I'm sure they ought to make you appreciate yours. Grantley and Walter Blake are two of the most sought-after of men, and you've married one of them, and made quite a conquest of the other to-night. Oh, here come the men!"

Young Blake came straight across to them, and engaged in a verbal fencing-match with Christine. She took him to task for alleged dissipation and over-much gaiety; he defended his character and habits with playful warmth. Sibylla sat by silent; she was still very ignorant of all the life they talked about. She knew that Christine's charges carried innuendoes from the way Blake met them, but she did not know what the innuendoes were. But she was not neglected. If his words were for gay Christine, his eyes were very constantly for the graver face and the more silent lips. He let her see his respectful admiration in the frank way he had; nobody could take offence at it.

"I suppose you must always have somebody to be in love with—to give, oh, your whole heart and soul to, mustn't you?" Christine asked scornfully.

"Yes, it's a necessity of my nature."

"That's what keeps you a bachelor, I suppose?"

He laughed, but, as Sibylla thought, a trifle ruefully, or at least as though he were a little puzzled by Christine's swift thrust.

"Keeps him? He's not old enough to marry yet," she pleaded, and Blake gaily accepted the defence.

Their talk was interrupted by Lady Harriet's rising; her brougham had been announced. Grantley telegraphed his readiness to be off too, and he and Sibylla, after saying good-night, followed the Courtlands downstairs, Raymore accompanying them and giving the men cigars while their wives put their cloaks on. Grantley asked for a cab, which was some little while in coming; Tom Courtland said he wanted a hansom too, and stuck his cigar in his mouth, puffing out a full cloud of smoke. At the moment Lady Harriet came back into the hall, Sibylla following her.

"Do you intend to smoke that cigar in the brougham as we go to my mother's party?" asked Lady Harriet.

"I'm not aware that your mother minds smoke; but as a matter of fact I'm not going to the party at all."

"You're expected—I said you'd come."

"I'm sorry, Harriet, but you misunderstood me."

Tom Courtland stood his ground firmly and answered civilly, though with a surly rough tone in his voice. His wife was still very quiet, yet Raymore and Grantley exchanged apprehensive looks; the lull before the storm is a well-worked figure of speech, but they knew it applied very well to Lady Harriet.

"You're going home, then?"

"Not just now."

"Where are you going?"

"To the club."

"What club?"

"Is my cab there?" Grantley called to the butler.

"Not yet, sir; there'll be one directly."

"What club?" demanded Lady Harriet again.

"What does it matter? I haven't made up my mind. I'm only going to have a rubber."

Then it came—what Sibylla had been told about, what the others had seen before now. They were all forgotten—host and fellow-guests, even the servants, even the cabman, who heard the outburst and leant down from his high seat, trying to see. It was like some physical affliction, an utter loss of self-control; it was a bare step distant from violence. It was the failure of civilisation, the casting-off of decency, a being abandoned to a raw fierce fury.

"Club!" she cried, a deep flush covering her face and all her neck. "Pretty clubs you go to hard on midnight! I know you, I know you too well, you—you liar!"

Sibylla crept behind Grantley, passing her hand through his arm. Tom Courtland stood motionless, very white, a stiff smile on his lips.

"You liar!" she said once again, and without a look at any of them swept down the steps. She moved grandly. She came to the door of her brougham, which the footman held for her. The window was drawn up.

"Have you been driving with the windows shut?"

"Yes, my lady."

"I told you to keep them down when it was fine. Do you want to stifle me, you fool?" She raised the fan she carried; it had stout ivory sticks and a large knob of ivory at the end. She dashed the knob against the window with all her strength; the glass was broken and fell clattering on the pavement as Lady Harriet got in.

The footman shut the door, touched his hat, and joined the coachman on the box.

With his pale face and set smile, with his miserable eyes and bowed shoulders, Tom Courtland went down the steps to his cab. Neither did he speak to any of them.

At last Raymore turned to Sibylla.

"I'm so sorry it happened to-night—when you were here," he said.

"What does it mean?" she gasped.

She looked from Grantley to Raymore and back again, and read the answer in their faces. They knew where Tom Courtland had gone. Grantley patted her hand gently, and said to Raymore:

"Well, who could stand a savage like that?"

It was the recognition of a ruin inevitable and past cure.

CHAPTER V

THE BIRTH OF STRIFE

There are processes undergone which people hardly realise themselves, which another can explain by no record, however minute or laborious. They are in detail as imperceptible, as secret, as elusive as the physical changes which pass upon the face of the body. From day to day there is no difference; but days make years, and years change youth to maturity, maturity to decay. So in matters of the soul the daily trifling sum adds up and up. A thousand tiny hopes nipped, a thousand little expectations frustrated, a thousand foolish fears proved not so foolish. Divide them by the days, and there is nothing to cry about at bedtime, nothing even to pray about, if to pray you are inclined. Yet as a month passes, or two, or three, the atoms seem to join and form a cloud. The sunbeams get through here and there still, but the clear fine radiance is obscured. Presently the cloud thickens, deepens, hardens. It seems now a wall, stout and high; the gates are heavy and forbidding, and they stand where once there was ready and eagerly welcomed entrance and access. Think of what it is to look for a letter sometimes. It comes not on Monday—it's nothing; nor on Tuesday—it's nothing; nor on Wednesday—odd! nor on Thursday—strange! nor on Friday—you can't think! It comes not for a week—you are hurt; for a fortnight—you are indignant. A month passes—and maybe what you prized most in all your life is gone. You have been told the truth in thirty broken sentences.

Sibylla Imason took a reckoning—in no formal manner, not sitting down to it, still less in any flash of inspiration or on the impulse of any startling incident. As she went to and fro on her work and her pleasure, the figures gradually and insensibly set themselves in rows, added and subtracted themselves, and presented her with the quotient. It was against her will that all this happened. She would have had none of it; there was nothing to recommend it; it was not even unusual. But it would come—and what did it come to? Nothing alarming or vulgar or sensational. Grantley's gallantry forbade that, his good manners, his affectionate ways, his real love for her. It was forbidden too by the moments of rapture which she excited and which she shared; they were still untouched—the fairy rides on fairy horses. But is not the virtue of such things to mean more than they are—to be not incidents, but rather culminations—not exceptions, but the very type, the highest expression, of what is always there? Even the raptures she was coming to doubt while she welcomed, to mistrust while she shared. Would she come at once to hate and to strive after them?

In the end it was not the identity her soaring fancy had pictured—not the union her heart cried for, less even than the partnership which naked reason seemed to claim. She had not become his very self, as he was of her very self—nor part of him. She was to him—what? She sought a word, at least an idea, and smiled at one or two which her own bitterness offered to her. A toy? Of course not. A diversion? Much more than that. But still it was something accidental, something that he might not have had and would have done very well without; yet a something greatly valued, tended, caressed—yes, and even loved. A great acquisition perhaps expressed it—a very prized possession—a cherished treasure. Sometimes, after putting it as low as she could in chagrin, she put it as high as she could—by way of testing it. Put it how she would, the ultimate result worked out the same. She made much less difference to Grantley Imason than she had looked to make; she was much less of and in his life, much less of the essence, more of an accretion. She was outside his innermost self—a stranger to his closest fastnesses. Was that the nature of the tie or the nature of the man? She cried out against either conclusion; for either ruined the hopes on which she lived. Among them was one mighty hope. Were not both tie and man still incomplete, even as she, the woman, was in truth yet incomplete, yet short of her great function, undischarged of her high natural office? Was there not that in her now which should make all things complete and perfect? While that hope—nay, that conviction—remained she refused to admit that she was discontent. She waited, trying meanwhile to smother the discontent.

Of course there was another side, and Grantley himself put it to Mrs. Raymore when, in her sisterly affection for him and her motherly interest in Sibylla, she had ventured on two or three questions which, on the smallest analysis, resolved themselves into hints.

"In anything like a doubtful case," he complained humorously (for he was not taking the questions very seriously), "the man never gets fair play. He's not nearly so picturesque. And if he becomes picturesque, if he goes through fits hot and cold, and ups and downs, and all sorts of convulsions, as the woman does and does so effectively, he doesn't get any more sympathy, because it's not the ideal for the man—not our national idea, anyhow. You see the dilemma he's in? If he's not emotional he's not interesting; if he's emotional he's not manly. I'm speaking of a doubtful case all the time. Of course you may have your impeccable Still-Waters-Run-Deep sort of man—the part poor old Tom ought to have played. But then that is a part—a stage part, very seldom real. No; in a doubtful case the man's nowhere. Take it how you will, the woman is bound to win."

"Which means that you don't want to complain or criticise, but if I will put impertinent questions——"

"If you put me on my defence——" he amended, laughing.

"Yes, if I put you on your defence, you'll hint——"

"Through generalities——"

"Yes, through generalities you'll hint, in your graceful way, that Sibylla, of whom you're very fond——"

"Oh, be fair! You know I am."

"Is rather—exacting—fatiguing?"

"That's too strong. Rather, as I say, emotional. She likes living on the heights. I like going up there now and then. In fact I maintain the national ideal."

"Yes, I think you'd do that very well—quite well enough, Grantley."

"There's a sting in the tail of your praise?"

"After all, I'm a woman too."

"We really needn't fuss ourselves, I think. You see, she has the great saving grace—a sense of humour. If I perceive dimly that somehow something hasn't been quite what it ought to have been, that I haven't—haven't played up somehow—you know what I mean?"

"Very well indeed," Mrs. Raymore laughed gently.

"I can put it all right by a good laugh—a bit of mock heroics, perhaps—some good chaff, followed by a good gallop—not at all a bad prescription! After a little of that, she's laughing at herself for having the emotions, and at me for not having them, and at both of us for the whole affair."

"Well, as long as it ends like that there's not much wrong. But take care. Not everything will stand the humorous aspect, you know."

"Most things, thank heaven, or where should we be?"

"Tom Courtland, for instance?"

"Oh, not any longer, I'm afraid."

"It won't do for the big things and the desperate cases; not even for other people's—much less for your own."

"I suppose not. If you want it always, you must be a looker-on; and you'll tell me husbands can't be lookers-on at their own marriages?"

"I tell you! Facts will convince you sooner than I could, Grantley."

He was really very reasonable from his own point of view, both reasonable and patient. Mrs. Raymore conceded that. And he was also quite consistent in his point of view. She remembered a phrase from his letter which had defined what he was seeking—"a completion, not a transformation." He was pursuing that scheme still—a scheme into which the future wife had fitted so easily and perfectly, into which the actual wife fitted with more difficulty. But he was dealing with the difficulty in a very good spirit and a very good temper. If the scheme were possible at all—given Sibylla as she was—he was quite the man to put it through successfully. But she reserved her opinion as to its possibility. The reservation did not imply an approval of Sibylla or any particular inclination to champion her; it marked only a growing understanding of what Sibylla was, a growing doubt as to what she could be persuaded or moulded into becoming. Mrs. Raymore had no prejudices in her favour.

And at any rate he was still her lover, as fully, as ardently as ever. Deep in those fastnesses of his nature were his love for her, and his pride in her and in having her for his own. The two things grew side by side, their roots intertangled. Every glance of admiration she won, every murmur of approval she created, gave him joy and seemed to give him tribute. He eagerly gathered in the envy of the world as food for his own exultation; he laughed in pleasure when Christine Fanshaw told him to look and see how Walter Blake adored Sibylla.

"Of course he does—he's a sensible young fellow," said Grantley gaily. "So am I, Christine, and I adore her too."

"The captive of your bow and spear!" Christine sneered.

"Of my personal attractions, please! Don't say of my money-bags!"

"She's like a very laudatory testimonial?"

"I just wonder how John Fanshaw endures you."

He answered her with jests, never thinking to deny what she said. He did delight in his wife's triumphs. Was there anything unamiable in that? If close union were the thing, was not that close? Her triumphs made his—what could be closer than that? At this time any criticism on him was genuinely unintelligible; he could make nothing of it, and reckoned it as of no account. And Sibylla herself, as he had said, he could always soothe.

"And she's going on quite all right?" Christine continued.

"Splendidly! We've got her quietly fixed down at Milldean, with her favourite old woman to look after her. There she'll stay. I run up to town two or three times a week—do my business——"

"Call on me?"

"I ventured so far—and get back as soon as I can."

"You must be very pleased?"

"Of course I'm pleased," he laughed, "very pleased indeed, Christine."

He was very much pleased, and laughed at himself, as he had laughed at others, for being a little proud too. He had wanted the dynasty carried on. There was every prospect of a start being made in that direction very prosperously. He would have hated to have it otherwise; there would have been a sense of incompleteness then.

"I needn't tell a wise woman like you that there's some trouble about such things," he went on.

"No doubt there is," smiled Christine. "But you can leave most of that to Sibylla and the favourite old woman," she added a moment later, with her eyes on Grantley's contented face, and that touch of acidity in her clear-toned voice.

Between being pleased—even very much pleased indeed—and a little proud over a thing (notwithstanding the trouble there is about it), and looking on it as one of the greatest things that Heaven itself ever did, there is a wide gulf, if not exactly of opinion, yet of feeling and attitude. From the first moment Sibylla had known of it, the coming of the child was the great thing, the overshadowing thing, in life. Nature was in this, and nature at her highest power; more was not needed. Yet there was more, to make the full cup brim over. Her great talent, her strongest innate impulse, was to give—to give herself and all she had; and this talent and impulse her husband had not satisfied. He was immured in his fastness; he seemed to want only what she counted small tributes and minor sacrifices—they had appeared large once, no doubt, but now looked small because they fell short of the largest that were possible. The great satisfaction, the great outlet, lay in the coming of the child. In pouring out her love on the head of the child she would at the same time pour it out at the feet of him whose the child was. Before such splendid lavishness he must at last stand disarmed, he must throw open all his secret treasure-house. His riches of love—of more than lover's love—must come forth too, and mingle in the same golden stream with hers, all separation being swept away. Here was the true realisation, foreshadowed by the fairy ride in the early days of their love; here was the true riding into the gold and letting the gold swallow them up. In this all disappointments should vanish, all nipped hopes come to bloom again. For it her heart cried impatiently, but chid itself for its impatience. Had not Mrs. Mumple waited years in solitude and silence outside the prison gates? Could not she wait a little too?

It need hardly be said that in such a position of affairs as had been reached Mrs. Mumple was much to the fore. Her presence was indispensable, and valued as such, but it had some disadvantages. She shared Sibylla's views and Sibylla's temperament; but naturally she did not possess the charm of youth, of beauty, and of circumstance which served so well to soften or to recommend them. The sort of atmosphere which Mrs. Mumple carried with her was one which should be diffused sparingly and with great caution about a man at once so self-centred and so fastidious as Grantley Imason. Mrs. Mumple was lavishly affectionate; she was also pervasive, and, finally, a trifle inclined to be tearful on entirely inadequate provocation—or, as it appeared to any masculine mind, on none at all, since the tendency assailed her most when everything seemed to be going on remarkably well. Her physical bulk too was a matter which she should have considered; and yet perhaps she could hardly be expected to think of that.

Of course Jeremy Chiddingfold, neither lover nor father, and with his youthful anti-femininism still held and prized, put the case a thousand times too high, exaggerating all one side, utterly ignoring all the other, of what Grantley might be feeling. None the less, there was some basis of truth in his exclamation:

"If they go on like this, Grantley'll be sick to death of the whole thing before it's half over!"

And Jeremy had come to read his brother-in-law pretty well—to know his self-centredness, to know his fastidiousness, to know how easily he might be "put off" (as Jeremy phrased it) by an intrusion too frequent and importunate, or a sentiment extravagant in any degree or the least overstrained. Too high a pressure might well result in a reaction; it would breed the thought that the matter in hand was, after all, decidedly normal.

But altogether normal it was not destined to remain. Minded, as it might seem, to point the situation and to force latent antagonisms of feeling to an open conflict, Mistress Chance took a hand in the game. On arriving at the Fairhaven station from one of his expeditions to town, Grantley found Jeremy awaiting him. Jeremy was pale, but his manner kept its incisiveness, his speech its lucidity. Sibylla had met with an accident. She had still been taking quiet rides on a trusty old horse. To-day, contrary to his advice and in face of Grantley's, she had insisted on riding another—the young horse, as they called it.

"She was in one of her moods," Jeremy explained. "She said she wanted more of a fight than the old horse gave her. She would go. Well, you know that great beast of a dog of Jarman's? It was running loose—I saw it myself; indeed I saw the whole thing. She was trotting along, thinking of nothing at all, I suppose. The dog started a rabbit, and came by her with a bound. The horse started, jumped half his own height—or it looked like it—and she—came off, you know, pitched clean out of her saddle."

"Clear of the——?"

"Yes, thank God—but she came down with an awful—an awful thud. I ran up as quick as I could. She was unconscious. A couple of labourers helped me to take her home, and I got Mumples; and on my way here I stopped at Gardiner's and sent him there, and came on to tell you."

By now they were getting into the dog-cart.

"Do you know at all how bad it is?" asked Grantley.

"Not the least. How should I?"

"Well, we must get home as quick as we can."

Grantley did not speak again the whole way. His mind had been full of plans that morning. His position as a man of land at Milldean was opening new prospects to him. He had agreed to come forward for election as a county alderman; he had been sounded as to contesting the seat for the Division. He had been very full of these notions, and had meant to spend two or three quiet days in reviewing and considering them. This sudden shock was hard to face and realise. It was difficult, too, to conceive of anything being wrong with Sibylla—always so fine an embodiment of physical health and vigour. He felt very helpless and in terrible distress; it turned him sick to think of the "awful thud" that Jeremy described. What would that mean? What was the least it might, the most it could, mean?

"You don't blame me?" Jeremy asked as they came near home.

"You advised her not to ride the beast: what more could you do? You couldn't stop her by force."

He spoke rather bitterly, as though sorrow and fear had not banished anger when he thought of his wife and her wilfulness.

Jeremy turned aside into the garden, begging to have news as soon as there was any. Grantley went into his study, and Mrs. Mumple came to him there. She was pitiably undone and dishevelled. It was impossible not to respect her grief, but no less impossible to get any clear information from her. Lamentations alternated with attempted excuses for Sibylla's obstinacy; she tried to make out that she herself was in some way to blame for having brought on the mood which had in its turn produced the obstinacy. Grantley, striving after outward calm, raged in his heart against the fond foolish old woman.

"I want to know what's happened, not whose fault it'll be held to be at the Day of Judgment, Mrs. Mumple. Since you're incapable of telling me anything, have the goodness to send Dr. Gardiner to me as soon as he can leave Sibylla."

Very soon, yet only just in time to stop Grantley from going upstairs himself, Gardiner came. He was an elderly quiet-going country practitioner; he lived in one of the red villas at the junction with the main road, and plied a not very lucrative practice among the farmhouses and cottages. His knowledge was neither profound nor recent; he had not kept up his reading, and his practical opportunities had been very few. He seemed, when he came, a good deal upset and decidedly nervous, as though he were faced with a sudden responsibility by no means to his liking. He kept wiping his brow with a threadbare red silk handkerchief and pulling his straggling grey whiskers while he talked. In a second Grantley had decided that no confidence could be placed in him. Still he must be able to tell what was the matter.

"Quickly and plainly, please, Dr. Gardiner," he requested, noting with impatience that Mrs. Mumple had come back and stood there listening; but she would cry and think him a monster if he sent her away.

"She's conscious now," the doctor reported, "but she's very prostrate—suffering from severe shock. I think you shouldn't see her for a little while."

"What's the injury, Dr. Gardiner?"

"The shock is severe."

"Will it kill her?"

"No, no! The shock kill her? Oh, no, no! She has a splendid constitution. Kill her? Oh, no, no!"

"And is that all?"

"No, not quite all, Mr. Imason. There is—er—in fact, a lesion, a local injury, a fracture, due to the force of the impact on the ground."

"Is that serious? Pray be quiet, Mrs. Mumple. You really must restrain your feelings."

"Serious? Oh, undoubtedly, undoubtedly! I—I can't say it isn't serious. I should be doing wrong——"

"In one word, is it fatal or likely to be fatal?"

Grantley was nearly at the end of his forced patience. He had looked for a man—he had, it seemed, found another old woman; so he angrily thought within himself as old Gardiner stumbled over his words and worried his whiskers.

"If I were to explain the case in detail——"

"Presently, doctor, presently. Just now I want the result—the position of affairs, you know."

"For the moment, Mr. Imason, there is no danger to Mrs. Imason—I think I may say that. But the injury creates a condition of things which might, and in my judgment would, prove dangerous to her as time went on. I speak in view of her present condition."

"I see. Could that be obviated?"

Gardiner's nervousness increased.

"By an operation directed to remove the cause which would produce danger. It would be a serious, perhaps a dangerous, operation——"

"Is that the only way?"

"In my judgment the only way consistent with——"

A loud sob from Mrs. Mumple interrupted him. Grantley swore under his breath.

"Go on," he said harshly.

"Consistent with the birth of the child, Mr. Imason."

"Ah!" At last he had got to the light, and the nervous old man had managed to deliver himself of his message. "I understand you now. Setting the birth of the child on one side, the matter would be simpler?"

"Oh, yes, much simpler—not, of course, without its——"

"And more free from danger?"

"Yes, though——"

"Practically free from danger to my wife?"

"Yes; I think I can say practically free in the case of so good a subject as Mrs. Imason."

Grantley thought for a minute.

"You probably wouldn't object to my having another opinion?" he asked.

Relief was obvious on old Gardiner's face.

"I should welcome it," he said. "The responsibility in such a case is so great that——"

"Tell me the best man, and I'll wire for him at once."

Even on this point Gardiner hesitated, till Grantley named a man known to everybody; him Gardiner at once accepted.

"Very well; and I'll see my wife as soon as you think it desirable." He paused a moment, and then went on: "If I understand the case right, I haven't a moment's hesitation in my mind. But I should like to ask you one question: am I right in supposing that your practice is to prefer the mother's life to the child's?"

"That's the British medical practice, Mr. Imason, where the alternative is as you put it. But there are, of course, degrees of danger, and these would influence——"

"You've told me the danger might be serious. That's enough. Dr. Gardiner, pending the arrival of your colleague, the only thing—the only thing—you have to think of is my wife. Those are my definite wishes, please. You'll remain here, of course? Thank you. We'll have another talk later. I want to speak to Jeremy now."

He turned towards the window, meaning to join Jeremy in the garden and report to him. Mrs. Mumple came forward, waving her hands helplessly and weeping profusely.

"Oh, Mr. Imason, imagine the poor, poor little child!" she stammered. "I can't bear to think of it."

Grantley's impatience broke out in savage bluntness.

"Against her I don't care that for the child!" he said, snapping his fingers as he went out.

CHAPTER VI

NOT PEACE BUT A SWORD

No doubt the bodily shock, the laceration of her nerves, and the condition she was in had something to do with the way Sibylla looked at the matter and with the attitude which she took up. These accidental circumstances gave added force to what was the natural outcome of her disposition. A further current of feeling, sweeping her in the same direction, lay in the blame which she eagerly fastened on herself. Her wilfulness and heedlessness cried out to her for an atonement; she was eager to make an appeasing sacrifice and caught at the opportunity, embracing readily the worst view of the case, drawing from that view an unhesitating conclusion as to what her duty was. Thus deduced, the duty became a feverish desire, and her only fear was that she might be baulked of its realisation. She had risked her child's life; let her risk her life for her child. That idea was by itself, and by its innate propriety, enough to inspire her mind and to decide her will. It was but to accumulate reasons beyond need when she reminded herself that even before the accident all her weal had hung on the child, every chance that remained of overcoming certain failure, of achieving still the splendid success of which she had dreamed, in her life and marriage. The specialist was to arrive the next morning; she was reluctant to wait even for that. Old Gardiner was for her an all-wise all-sufficient oracle of the facts, because he had declared them to be such as fitted into the demands of her heart and of her mood. Left to herself, she would have constrained his fears, overborne his doubts, and forced him to her will; he would have stammered all in vain about what was the British medical practice. As it was, open-eyed, refusing to seek sleep, strung up by excitement, all through the evening she battled against her husband for her way.

If she had no hesitation in one view, Grantley never wavered from the other. The plain unreasonableness of not awaiting the specialist's verdict was not hard to enforce. Sibylla, professing to yield, yet still assumed what the verdict should be, and pressed for a promise. At first he evaded her urgency by every device of soothing counsels, of entreaties that she would rest, of affectionate reproofs. She would not allow evasion. Then when his refusal came, it came tenderly, inspired by his love for her, based on an appeal to that. It was on this that he had relied. He was puzzled that it failed of the full effect he had looked for; and, beyond the puzzle, gradually a sense of bitter hurt and soreness grew up in his mind. He did not know of the secret connection in her thoughts between the child and an ideal perfecting of the love between her and him; she was at once too centred on her own desire to make him see, and too persuaded that such hopes must be secret if they were to remain hopes at all. He saw only that when he persuaded, cajoled, flattered, and caressed as a lover he failed. His power seemed gone. Her appeal was to him in another character, and that very fact seemed to put him on a lower plane. He had not doubted, for a moment, what came first to him—it was her life, her well-being, his love of her. As she persisted in her battle, the feeling grew that she made an inadequate return, and showed an appreciation short of what was his due. Gradually his manner hardened, his decision was expressed more firmly; he stiffened into a direct antagonism, and interposed his will and his authority to effect what his love and his entreaties had failed to do. He never lacked courtesy; he could not, under such circumstances as these, desire to fail in gentleness. But it was his will against hers now, and what his will was he conveyed clearly.

A trained nurse had arrived from Fairhaven; but Sibylla vehemently preferred the presence of Mrs. Mumple, and it was Mrs. Mumple whom Grantley left with her when he came down to his study about midnight. He had not dined, and a cold supper was laid out on the table. Jeremy was there, trying to read, eyeing the supper ravenously, yet ashamed of being hungry. He fell on the beef with avidity when Grantley observed that anyhow starving themselves could serve no useful purpose. Grantley was worried, but not anxious; he had confidence in the specialist, and even in Gardiner's view there was no danger if the right course were followed. To the disappointment which that course involved he had schooled himself, accepting it almost gladly as by so far the lesser evil.

"If you were to talk to Sibylla now," he said, "I think you'd be reminded of those old days you once told me about. Fate has thumped her pretty severely for anything she did, but she's mortally anxious to be thumped more, and very angry with me because I won't allow it. Upon my word, I believe she'd be disappointed if Tarlton told us that the thing wasn't so bad after all, and that everything would go right without anything being done."

"I daresay she would; but there's no chance of that?"

"Well, I'm afraid not. One must believe one's medical man, I suppose, even if he's old Gardiner—and he seems quite sure of it." Grantley drank and sighed. "It's uncommonly perverse, when everything was so prosperous before."

The day had left its traces on Jeremy. Though he had not told Grantley so, yet when he saw Sibylla thrown he had made no doubt she was killed—and she was the one person in the world whom he deeply loved. That fear was off him now, but the memory of it softened him towards her—even towards her foolishness, which he had been wont to divide very distinctly from her, and to consider himself free to deal with faithfully.

"At best it'll be a most awful disappointment to her."

"Yes, it must be that—and to me too," said Grantley.

"She was just living in and for the thing, you know."

Grantley made no answer this time; a shade of annoyance passed over his face.

"She never could give herself to more than one thing at a time—with her that one thing was always the whole hog, and there was nothing else. That's just how it's been now."

Jeremy's words showed true sympathy, and, moreover, a new absence of shame in expressing it; but Grantley did not accord them much apparent welcome. They came too near to confirming his suspicions; they harmonised too well with the soreness which remained from his impotent entreaties and unpersuasive caresses. Again without answering, he got up and lit his cigar.

"Oh, by the way," Jeremy went on, "while you were with Sibylla that girl from the rectory came up—you know, Dora Hutting—to ask after Sibylla and say they were all awfully sorry and anxious, and all that, you know."

"Very kind of them. I hope you told her so, and said what you could?"

"Yes, that's all right. The girl seems awfully fond of Sibylla, Grantley. By Jove, when we got talking about her, she—she began to cry!"

Grantley turned round, smiling at the unaccustomed note of pathos struck by Jeremy's tone.

"Rather decent of her, wasn't it?" asked Jeremy.

"Very nice. Did you console her?"

"Oh, I didn't see what the devil I could say! Besides I didn't feel very comfortable—it was rather awkward."

"I believe the girl's afraid of me—she always seems to come here when I'm away. Is she a pleasant girl, Jeremy?"

"Oh, she—she seemed all right; and I—I liked the way she felt about Sibylla."

"So do I, and I'll thank her for it. Is she getting at all prettier?"

"Well, I shouldn't call her bad-looking, don't you know!"

"She used to be a bit spotty," yawned Grantley.

"I don't think she's spotty now."

"Well, thank heaven for that anyhow!" said Grantley piously. "I hate spots above anything, Jeremy."

"She hasn't got any, I tell you," said Jeremy, distinctly annoyed.

Grantley smiled sleepily, threw himself on to his favourite couch, laid down his cigar, and closed his eyes. After the strain he was weary, and soon his regular breathing showed that he slept. Jeremy had got his pipe alight and sat smoking, from time to time regarding his brother-in-law's handsome features with an inquiring gaze. There was a new stir of feeling in Jeremy. A boy of strong intellectual bent, he had ripened slowly on the emotional side, and there had been nothing in the circumstances or chances of his life to quicken the process thus naturally very gradual. To-day something had come. He had been violently snatched from his quiet and his isolation, confronted with a crisis that commanded feeling, probed to the heart of his being by love and fear. Under this call from life nascent feelings grew to birth and suppressed impulses struggled for liberty and for power. He was not now resisting them nor turning from them. He was watching, waiting, puzzling about them, hiding them still from others, but no longer denying them to himself. He was wondering and astir. The manhood which had come upon him was a strange thing; the life that called him seemed now full of new and strange things. Through his fear and love for Sibylla he was entering on new realms of experience and of feeling. He sat smoking hard and marvelling that Grantley slept.

Connected with this upheaval of mental conceptions which had hitherto maintained an aspect so boldly fundamental, and claimed to be the veritable rock of thought whereon Jeremy built his church, was the curious circumstance that he suddenly found himself rather sensitive about Grantley's careless criticism of Miss Dora Hutting's appearance. He had not denied the fact alleged about it, though he had the continuance of it. But he resented its mention even as he questioned the propriety of Grantley's sleeping. The reference assorted ill with his appreciation of Dora's brimming eyes and over-brimming sympathies. That he could not truthfully have denied the fact increased his annoyance. It seemed mean to remember the spots that had been on the face to which those brimming eyes belonged—as mean as it would have been in himself to recall the bygone grievances and the old—the suddenly old-grown—squabbles which he had had with the long-legged rectory girl. That old epithet too! A sudden sense of profanity shot across him as it came into his mind; he stood incomprehensively accused of irreverence in his own eyes.

Yet the spots had existed; and Sibylla had been wrong—had been wrong, and was now, it appeared, unreasonable. Moreover, beyond question, Mumples was idiotic. Reason was alarmed in him, since it was threatened. He told himself that Grantley was very sensible to sleep. But himself he could not think of sleep, and his ears were hungry for every sound from the floor above.

The stairs creaked—there was a sniff. Mrs. Mumple was at the door. Jeremy made an instinctive gesture for silence because Grantley slept. He watched Mrs. Mumple as she turned her eyes on the peacefully reposing form. The eyes turned sharp to him, and Mrs. Mumple raised her fat hands just a little and let them fall softly.

"He's asleep?" she whispered.

"You see he is. Best thing for him to do, too." His answering whisper was gruff.

"She's not sleeping," said Mrs. Mumple; "and she's asking for him again."

"Then we'd better wake him up." He spoke irritably as he rose and touched Grantley's shoulder. "He must be tired out, don't you see?"

Mrs. Mumple made no answer. She raised and dropped her hands again.

Grantley awoke lightly and easily, almost unconscious that he had slept.

"What were we talking about? Oh, yes, Dora Hutting! Why, I believe I've been asleep!"

"You've slept nearly an hour," said Jeremy, going back to his chair.

Grantley's eyes fell on Mrs. Mumple; a slight air of impatience marked his manner as he asked:
"Is anything wrong, Mrs. Mumple?"
"She's asking for you again, Mr. Imason."
"Dear me, Gardiner said she should be kept quiet!"
"The doctor's lying down. But she'll not rest without seeing you; she's fretting so."
"Have you been letting her talk about it and excite herself? Have you been talking to her yourself?"
"How can we help talking about it?" Mrs. Mumple moaned.
"It's infernally silly—infernally!" he exclaimed in exasperation. "Well, I must go to her, I suppose." He turned to Jeremy. "It'll be better if you'll keep Mrs. Mumple with you. We'll get the nurse to go to Sibylla."
"I can't leave her as she is," said Mrs. Mumple, threatening a fresh outburst of tears.
Grantley walked out of the room, muttering savagely.
The strain of irritation, largely induced by Mrs. Mumple's lachrymosely reproachful glances and faithful doglike persistency, robbed him of the tenderness by which alone he might possibly have won his wife's willing obedience and perhaps convinced her reason through her love. He used his affection now, not in appeal, but as an argumentative point. He found in her a hard opposition; she seemed to look at him with a sort of dislike, a mingling of fear and wonder. Thus she listened in silence to his cold marshalling of the evidences of his love and his deliberate enforcing of the claims it gave him. Seeing that he made no impression, he grew more impatient and more imperious, ending with a plain intimation that he would discuss the question no further.
"You'll make me the murderess of my child," she said.
The gross irrational exaggeration drove him to worse bitterness.
"I've no intention of running even the smallest risk of being party to the murder of my wife," he retorted.
Lying among her pillows, very pale and weary, she pronounced the accusation which had so long brooded in her mind.
"It's not because you love me so much; you do love me in a way: I please you, you're proud of me, you like me to be there, you like to make love to me, you like taking all I have to give you, and God knows I liked to give it—but you haven't given the same thing back to me, Grantley. I don't know whether you've got it to give to anybody, but at any rate you haven't given it to me. I haven't become part of you, as I was ready to become—as I've already become of my little unborn child. Your life wouldn't be made really different if I went away. In the end you've been apart from me. I thought the coming of the child must make all that different; but it hasn't: you've been about the child just as you've been about me."
"Oh, where on earth do you get such notions?" he exclaimed.
"Just the same as about me. You wanted me and you wanted a child too. But you wanted both with—well, with the least disturbance of your old self and your old thoughts: with the least trouble—it almost comes to that really. I don't know how to put it, except like that. You enjoyed the pleasant parts very much, but you take as little as you can of the troublesome ones. I suppose a lot of people are—are like that. Only it's a—a little unfortunate that you should have happened on me, because I—I can't understand being like that. To me it seems somehow rather cruel. So, knowing you're like that, I can't believe you when you tell me that you think of nothing but your love for me. I daresay you think it's true—I know you wouldn't say it if you didn't think it true; and in a way it's true. But the real, real truth is——" She paused, and for the first time turned her eyes on him. "The real truth is not that you love me too much to do what I ask."
"What else can it be?" he cried desperately, utterly puzzled and upset by her accusation.
"What else can it be? Ah, yes, what else?" Her voice grew rather more vehement. "I can answer that. What have I been doing these five months but learning the answer to that? I'll tell you. It's not that you love me so much, it's that you don't care about the child."
The words brought a suspicion into his mind.
"That old fool Mrs. Mumple has been talking to you? She's been repeating something I said? Well, I expressed it carelessly, awkwardly, but——"
"What does it matter what Mumples has repeated? I knew it all before."
"Meddlesome old idiot!" he grumbled fiercely.
To him there was no reason in it all. The accusation angered him fiercely and amazed him even more; he saw no shadow of justice in it. He put it all down to Sibylla's exaggerated way of talking and thinking. He was conscious of no shortcomings; the accusation infuriated the more for its entire failure to convince. "When two women put their heads together and begin to talk nonsense, there's no end to it; bring a baby, born or unborn, into the case, and the last chance of any limit to the nonsense is gone." He did not tell her that (though it expressed what he felt) in a general form; he fell back on the circumstances of the minute.
"My dear Sibylla, you're not fit to discuss things rationally at present. We'll say no more now; we shall only be still more unjust to one another if we do. Only I must be obeyed."
"Yes, you shall be obeyed," she said. "But since it's like that, I think that, whatever happens now, I—I won't have any more children, Grantley."
"What?"
He was startled out of the cold composure which he had achieved in his previous speech.
She repeated her words in a low tired voice, but firmly and coolly.
"I think I won't have any more children, you know."
"Do you know what you're saying?"
"Oh, surely, yes!" she answered, with a faint smile.
Grantley walked up and down the room twice, and then came and stood by her bed, fixing his eyes on her face in a long sombre contemplation. The faint smile persisted on her lips as she looked up at him. But he turned away without speaking, with a weary shrug of his shoulders.
"I'll send the nurse to you," he said as he went towards the door.
"Send Mumples, please, Grantley."
Mrs. Mumple had done all the harm she could. "All right," he replied. "Try to sleep. Good-night."

He shut the door behind him before her answer came.

On the stairs he met Mrs. Mumple. The fat woman shrank out of his path, but he bade her good-night not unkindly, although absently; she needed no bidding to send her to Sibylla's room. He found Jeremy still in the study, still wide awake.

"Oh, go home to bed, old fellow!" he exclaimed irritably, but affectionately too. "What good can you do sitting up here all night?"

"Yes, I suppose I may as well go—it's half-past two. I'll go out by the garden." He opened the window which led on to the lawn. The fresh night air came in. "That's good!" sniffed Jeremy.

Grantley stepped into the garden with him, and lit a cigarette.

"But is it all right, Grantley? Is Sibylla reasonable now?"

"All right? Reasonable?" Grantley's innermost thoughts had been far away.

"I mean, will she agree to what you wish—what we wish?"

"Yes, it's all right. She's reasonable now."

His face was still just in the light of the lamp which stood on a table in the window. Jeremy saw the paleness of his cheeks and the hard set of his eyes. There was no sign of relief in him or of anxiety assuaged.

"Well, thank heaven for that much, anyhow!" Jeremy sighed.

"Yes, for that much anyhow," Grantley agreed, pressing his arm in a friendly way. "And now, old boy, good-night."

Jeremy left him there in the garden smoking his cigarette, standing motionless. His face was in the dark now, but Jeremy knew the same look was in the eyes still. It was hard for the young man, even with the new impulses and the new sympathies that were alive and astir within him, to follow, or even to conjecture, what had been happening that night. Yet as he went down the hill it was plain even to him, plain enough to raise a sharp pang in him, that somehow the little child, unborn or whether it should yet be born, had brought not union, but estrangement to the house; not peace but a sword.

CHAPTER VII

A VINDICATION OF CONSCIENCE

It was a dull chilly afternoon in March. Christine Fanshaw huddled her slight little figure—she looked as if the cold would cut right through her—over a blazing fire in her boudoir. She held a screen between the flames and her face, and turned her eyes on Anna Selford, who was paying her a call. Anna was a plump dark girl, by no means pretty, but with a shrewd look about her and an air of self-confidence rather too assured for her years; she was dressed in a would-be artistic fashion, not well suited to her natural style.

"Awfully sad, isn't it?" she was saying. "But mamma says Mrs. Raymore is splendid about it. Mr. Raymore was quite upset, and was no good at all at first. It was Mrs. Raymore who went and got Charley away from the woman, and hushed up all the row about the money—oh, he had taken some from the office: he was in a solicitor's office, you know—and arranged for him to be sent out to Buenos Ayres—did the whole thing in fact. She's quite heart-broken about it, mamma says, but quite firm and brave too. How awful to have your son turn out like that! He was only nineteen, and Mrs. Raymore simply worshipped him."

"He used to be a very pretty little boy. A little boy! And now!" Christine plucked idly at the fringes of her hand-screen.

"And mamma says the woman was thirty, and not very good-looking either!"

"What a lot you know, Anna! You're hardly seventeen, are you? And Suzette Bligh's twenty-seven! But she's a baby compared to you."

"Oh, mamma always tells me things—or else I hear her and papa talking about them. When I'm washing the dogs, they forget I'm there, especially if they're squabbling at all. And I keep my ears open."

"Yes, I think you do."

"But generally mamma tells me. She always must talk to somebody, you see. When I was little she used to tell me things, and then forget it and box my ears for knowing them!"

Anna spoke without rancour; rather with a sort of quiet amusement, as though she had given much study to her mother's peculiarities and found permanent diversion in them.

"Poor Kate Raymore! So they're in trouble too!"

"Charley was awfully sorry; and they hope he'll come back some day, if he behaves well out there."

"Poor Kate Raymore! Well, there's trouble everywhere, isn't there, Anna?" She shivered and drew yet a little nearer the fire. "How are things at home with you?"

"Just as usual; nothing ever happens with us."

"It might be much worse than that."

"I suppose it might. It's only just rather dull; and I suppose I shall have to endure it for a long while. You see, I'm not very likely to get married, Mrs. Fanshaw. No men ever come to our house—they can't stand it. Besides I'm not pretty."

"Oh, come and meet men here; and never mind not being pretty; I could dress you to look quite smart. That's it! You should go in for smartness, not prettiness. I really believe it pays better nowadays. Get Janet—get your mother to give you an allowance, and we'll put our heads together over it."

"That's awfully kind of you, Mrs. Fanshaw."

"Oh, I like dressing people; and I do think girls ought to have their chances. But in those things she makes you wear—oh, my dear Anna!"

"Yes, I know. I'll ask her. And——"

Anna hesitated, then rose, and came over to Christine. Suddenly she kissed her.

"It's nothing, my dear," said Christine, amused but annoyed; she was very ready to help Anna, but did not care in the least for being kissed by her.

Anna sat down again, and there ensued a long pause.

"And as for not marrying," Christine resumed, "it's six of one and half a dozen of the other, I think. Oh, I should have hated to be an old maid; but still one would have avoided so much worry. Look at these poor Raymores! They've always got on so well too, up to now!"

She laid down her screen and pulled up her dress, to let the warmth get to her ankles. Anna looked at her dainty face lit up by the glow.

"I wish I was like you, Mrs. Fanshaw!"

Christine did not refuse the compliment; she only denied the value of the possession which won it for her.

"Much good it's done me, my dear!" she sighed. "But people who've not got looks never will believe how little good they are. Oh, I didn't mean to be rude, Anna! I believe in you, you know. I can do something with you. Only——" She stopped, frowning a little and looking vaguely unhappy. "Well," she resumed, "if it turns out that I can't take you under my wing, we must get hold of Sibylla. She's always ready to do things for people—and they've got lots of money, anyhow."

Anna's curiosity was turned in the direction of Sibylla.

"What was the truth about Mrs. Imason, Mrs. Fanshaw?"

"I made sure you'd know that too!" smiled Christine. "And if you don't, I suppose I oughtn't to tell you."

"I know she—she had an accident."

"Oh, well, everybody knows. Yes, she had, and they thought it was worse than it was. The country doctor down at Milldean made a mistake—took too serious a view, you know. And—and there was a lot of bother. But the London man said it would be all right, and so it turned out. The baby came all right, and it's a splendid boy."

"It all ended all right, then?"

Christine looked a little doubtful.

"The boy's all right, and Sibylla's quite well," she answered.

"But mamma said Mrs. Raymore hinted——"

"Well, Sibylla wouldn't believe the London man, you see. She thought that he—that he'd been persuaded to say she needn't have the operation she wanted to have, and that they meant to—— Well, really, Anna, I can't go into details. It's quite medical, my dear, and I can't express myself discreetly. Anyhow Sibylla made a grievance of it, you know, and relations were a little strained, I think."

"Oh, well, I suppose that's over now, since everything's gone right, Mrs. Fanshaw?"

"It ought to be," said Christine, shy of asserting the positive fact. "But very often fusses about nothing do just as much harm as fusses about something big. It's the way one looks at them."

"Yes, I ought to know that, living in our house," remarked Anna Selford.

"You do give your parents away so!" Christine complained, with a smile in which pity was mingled.

The pity, however, was not for the betrayed, but for the traitor. Anna's premature knowingness and the suggestion of hardness it carried with it were the result of a reaction against the atmosphere of her home, against the half-real gush and the spasmodic emotionality of the family circle. In this revolt truth asserted itself, but sweetness suffered, and freshness lost its bloom. Christine was sorry when that sort of thing happened to young girls. But there it was. Anna was not the *ingénue*, and it was no good treating her as if she were.

"I'm really half glad you don't live in this house. I'm sure John and I couldn't bear the scrutiny—not just now, anyhow." She answered Anna's questioning eyes by going on: "Oh, it's terrible, my dear. We've no money—now, really, don't repeat that! And John's full of business worries. It's positively so bad that I have to try to be amiable about it!"

"I'm so sorry, and I really won't talk about it, Mrs. Fanshaw."

"No, don't, my dear—not till we're in the bankruptcy court. Then everybody'll know. And I daresay we shall have some money again; at least bankrupts seem to have plenty generally."

"Then why don't you?"

"Anna! John would cut his throat first. Oh, I really believe he would! You've no idea what a man like him thinks of his business and of his firm's credit. It's like—well, it's like what we women ought to think (again Christine avoided asserting the actual fact) about our reputations, you know. So you may imagine the state of things. The best pair is being sold at Tattersall's this very day. That's why I'm indoors—cabs are so cold and the other pair will have to go out at night."

Shiveringly she nestled to the fire again.

"I'm so awfully sorry, Mrs. Fanshaw! It'll all come right, won't it?"

"It generally does; but I don't know. And John says I've always been so extravagant—and I suppose I have. Well, I thought it was just that John was stingy. He had a splendid business, you know." She paused and smiled at Anna. "So now you know all of everybody's troubles," she ended.

Christine was not in the habit of giving praise beyond measure or without reservation either to herself or to other people, and she had done no more than justice to her present effort to be amiable. Money was the old cause of quarrel between her husband and herself; the alternation of fat and lean years had kept it always alive and intermittently active. But hitherto, while the fat seasons had meant affluence, the lean had never fallen short of plenty or of solvency. It had been a question of more or less lavish expenditure; that was all. Christine was afraid there was more now. Her husband was worried as he had never been before; he had dropped hints of speculations gone wrong and of heavy commitments; and Christine, a constant glancer at City articles and an occasional dabbler in stocks, had read that there was a crisis in the market in which he mainly dealt. Things were black; she knew it almost as well as he. Both showed courage, and the seriousness of the matter forbade mere bickering. Nor was either invulnerable enough to open the battle. Her extravagance exposed her to attack; he was conscious of hazardous speculations which had wantonly undermined the standing, and now threatened the credit, of a firm once strong and of excellent repute. Each needed at once to give and to receive charity. Thus from the impending trouble they had become better friends, and their underlying comradeship had more openly asserted itself. This amount of good there was in it, Christine thought to herself; and John, in his blunt fashion, had actually said as much to her.

"We're in the same boat, and we must both pull at our oars, old girl," he said, and Christine was glad he should say it, although she hated being called "old girl." John had a tendency towards plebeian endearments, she thought.

So the best pair went to Tattersall's, and some of the diamonds to a corresponding establishment in the jewellery line; and various other things were done or attempted with the view of letting free a few thousand pounds and of diminishing expenditure in the future. But John Fanshaw's brow grew no clearer. About these sacrifices there hung the air of doing what was right and proper—what, given the worst happening, would commend itself to the feelings of the creditors and the Official Receiver—rather than of achieving anything of real service. Christine guessed that the speculations must have been on a very large scale and the commitments very heavy. Could it be that ruin—real ruin—was in front of them? She could hardly realise that—either its coming or what life would be after it had come. And in her heart—here too she had said no more than truth—she did doubt whether John would stay in the world to see. Well, what could she do? She had three hundred a year of her own tied up, and (since they had no children) to go back to her people on her death. If the ruin came, she could find crusts for herself and John—if John were there. These were the thoughts which had kept intruding into her mind as she talked to Anna Selford and shivered now and then over the blazing fire. Yet she could face them better than John, thanks to a touch of fatalism in her nature. She would think of no violent step to avoid what she feared. Hating it, she would sit shivering by the fire, and wait for it all the same. She knew this of herself, and therefore was even more sorry for John than on her own account. This state of mind made the amiability easier. It also awoke her conscience from a long sleep with regard to the way in which she had treated John in the past. Against this, however, she struggled not only fiercely, but with a conviction of justice. Here conscience was overdoing its part, and passing from scrupulousness to morbidity. The thing in question, the thing conscience had awoken about, belonged to the far past; it had been finished off and written off, enjoyed and deplored, brooded over and violently banished from thought, ever so long ago. Hardly anybody knew about it; it was utterly over. None the less, the obstinate irrational digs which conscience—awake again—gave her about it increased as John's face grew gloomier.

Late in the afternoon John Fanshaw came to his wife's room for a cup of tea.

"The pair went for only two hundred and forty-five," he said; "I gave four hundred for them six months ago. Ah, well, a forced sale, you know!"

"It doesn't make much difference, does it?" she asked.

"No," he said, absently stirring his tea. "Not much, Christine."

She sat very quiet by the fire watching him; her screen was in her hand again.

"It's no use, we must face it," he broke out suddenly. "Everything's gone against me again this week. I had a moral certainty; but—well, that isn't a certainty. And——"

He took a great gulp of tea.

A faint spot of colour came on Christine's cheek.

"What does it mean?" she asked.

"I've been to see Grantley Imason to-day. He behaved uncommonly well. The bank can't do anything more for me, but as a private friend——"

"Had you to ask him for money, John?"

"Well, friends often lend one another money, don't they? I don't see anything awful in that. I daren't go to the money-lenders—I'm afraid they'll sell the secret."

"I daresay there's nothing wrong in it. I don't know about such things. Go on."

"He met me very straight; and I met him straight too. I told him the whole position. I said, 'The business is a good one, but I've got into a hole. Once I get out of that, the business is there. On steady lines (I wish to God I'd kept on them!) it's worth from eight to ten thousand a year. I'll pay you back three thousand a year, and five per cent. on all capital still owing.' I think he liked the way I put it, Christine. He asked if he could take my word for it, and I said he could; and he said that on the faith of that he'd let me have fifteen thousand. I call that handsome."

"Grantley always likes to do the handsome thing." She looked at him before she put her question. "And—and is that enough?"

He was ashamed, it was easy to see that—ashamed to show her how deep he was in the bog, how reckless he had been. He finished his tea, and pottered about, cutting and lighting a cigar, before he answered.

"I suppose it's not enough?" said Christine.

"It's no use unless I get some more. I don't know where else to turn, and I must raise thirty thousand in a fortnight—by next settling day—or it's all up. I shall be hammered, Christine."

"If we sold up absolutely everything——?"

"For God's sake no! That would ruin our credit; and then it wouldn't be thirty thousand we should want, but—oh, I don't know! Perhaps a hundred! We've sold enough already; there's nothing more we can do on the quiet."

He sat down opposite to her, and stared gloomily at the fire. Christine rather wondered that he did not turn to abuse of himself for having got into the bog, but she supposed that the speculative temper, which acknowledges only bad luck and never bad judgment, saved him from that. He looked at her covertly once or twice; she saw, but pretended not to, and waited to hear what was in his mind: something, clearly, was there.

"No, I don't know where to turn—and I shall be hammered. After thirty years! and my father forty years before me! I never though of its coming to this." After a long pause he added: "I want another fifteen thousand, and I don't know where to turn." He smoked hard for a minute, then flung his cigar peevishly into the fire.

"I do wish I could help you, John!" she sighed.

"I'm afraid you can't, old lady." Again he hesitated. "Unless——" He broke off again.

Christine had some difficulty in keeping her nerves under control. When he spoke again it was abruptly, as though with a wrench.

"I say, do you ever see Caylesham now?"

A very slight, almost imperceptible, start ran over her.

"Lord Caylesham! Oh, I meet him about sometimes. He's at the Raymores' now and then—and at other places of course."

"He never comes here now, does he?"

"Very seldom: to a party now and then." She answered without apparent embarrassment, but her eyes were very sharply on the watch; she was on guard against the next blow.

"He was a good chap, and very fond of us. Lord, we had some fine old times with Caylesham!" He rose now and stood with his back to the fire. "He must be devilish rich since he came into the property."

He looked at her inquiringly. She said nothing.

"He's a good chap too. I don't think he'd let a friend go to the wall. What do you think? He was as much your friend as mine, you know."

"You'd ask him, John? Oh, I shouldn't do that!"

"Why not? He's got plenty."
"We see so little of him now; and it's such a lot to ask."
"It's not such a lot to him; and it's only accidental that we haven't met lately." He looked at her angrily. "You don't realise what the devil of a mess we're in. We've no choice, I tell you, but to get it from somewhere; and there's nobody else I know to ask. Why, he'll get his money back again, Christine."
Her screen was before her face now, so that he saw no more than her brow.
"I want you to go and ask him, Christine. That's what you can do for me. You said you wanted to help. Well, go and ask Caylesham to lend me the money."
"I can't do that, John."
"Why not? Why can't you?"
"I should hate your asking him, and I simply couldn't ask him myself."
"Why do you hate my asking him? You said nothing against my asking Grantley, and we haven't known him any better."
She had no answer to that ready. The thrust was awkward.
"Anyhow I couldn't ask him—I really couldn't. Don't press me to do that. If you must ask him, do it yourself. Why should I do it?"
"Why, because he's more likely to give it to you."
"But that's—that's so unfair. To send a woman because it's harder to refuse her! Oh, that isn't fair, John!"
"Fair! Good heavens, can't you understand how we're situated? It's ruin if we don't get it—and I'm damned if I'll live to see it! There!"
She saw his passion; his words confirmed her secret fear. She saw, too, how in the stress of danger he would not stand on scruples or be baulked by questions of taste or of social propriety. He saw possible salvation, and jumped at any path to it; and the responsibility of refusing to tread the path he put on her, with all it might mean.
"If I went and he said 'No,' you couldn't go afterwards. But you can go first, and you must go."
Christine raised her head and shook it.
"I can't go," she said.
"Why not? You're infernally odd about it! Why can't you go? Is it anything about Caylesham in particular?"
"No, no, nothing—nothing like that; but I—I hate to go."
"You must do it for me. I don't understand why you hate it so much as all that."
He was regarding her with an air at once angry and inquisitive. She dared hide her face no longer. She had to look at him calmly and steadily—with distress perhaps, but at all costs without fear or confusion.
"My good name depends on it, and all we have in the world; and—by God, yes!—my life too, if you like!" he exclaimed in rising passion. "You shall go! No, no! I don't mean that—I don't want to be rough! But, for heaven's sake—if you've ever cared about me, old woman—for heaven's sake, go!"
She hesitated still, and at this his passing touch of tenderness vanished; but it had moved her, and it worked with the fear that was on her.
"If you've a special reason, tell it me," he urged impatiently: "a special reason against asking Caylesham; somebody we must ask."
"I have no special reason against asking Lord Caylesham," she answered steadily.
"Then you'll go?"
A last struggle kept her silent a moment. Then she answered in a low voice:
"Yes, I'll go."
"There's a brave little woman!" he cried delightedly, and bent down as if he would kiss her; but she had slipped her screen up nearly to her eyes again, and seemed so unconscious of his purpose that he abandoned it. His spirits rose in a moment, as his sanguine mind, catching hold of the bare chance, twisted it into a good chance—almost into a certainty.
"Gad, I believe he'll give it you! You'll put it in such a fetching way. Oh, his money's safe enough, of course! But—well, you'll make him see that better than I could. He liked you so much, you know. By Jove, I'm sure he'll do it for you, you know!"
Christine's pain-stricken eyes alone were visible above the screen. Underneath it her lips were bent in an involuntary smile of most mocking bitterness. Conscience had not been at her without a purpose. At her husband's bidding she must go and ask Caylesham for money. She bowed to conscience now.

CHAPTER VIII
IDEALS AND ASPIRATIONS

A sudden rigidity seemed to affect Mrs. Raymore from the waist upwards. Her back grew stiff, her head rose very straight from the neck, her eyes looked fixedly in front of her, her lips were tight shut. These symptoms were due to the fact that she saw Tom Courtland approaching, in company with a woman who was certainly not Lady Harriet. Thanks to the gossip about among Tom's friends, Kate Raymore guessed who she was; the woman's gorgeous attire, her flamboyant manner, the air of good-natured rowdyism which she carried with her, all confirmed the guess. Yet Tom was walking with her in the broad light of day—not in the street, it is true; it was in a rather retired part of the Park. Still, people came there and drove by there, and to many his companion was known by sight and by repute. His conduct betrayed increasing recklessness. There was nothing to do but to pass him by without notice; he himself would wish nothing else and would expect nothing else. Still Mrs. Raymore was sorry to have to do it; for Tom had been kind and helpful in obtaining that position in a railway company's office in Buenos Ayres which had covered the disastrous retreat of her well-beloved son.

This lamentable affair had been hushed up so far as the outer world was concerned; but their friends knew the truth. In the first terrible days, when there had been imminent risk of a criminal prosecution, Raymore had rather lost his head and had gone round to Grantley Imason, to Tom Courtland, to John Fanshaw, making lament and imploring advice. So they all knew—they and their wives; and the poor boy's sister Eva had been told, perforce. There the public shame stopped, but the private shame was very bitter to the Raymores. Raymore was driven to accuse himself of all kinds of faults in his bringing-up of the boy—of having been too indulgent here or too strict there—most of all, of having been so engrossed in business as not to see enough of the boy or to keep proper watch on his disposition and companions, and the way he spent his time. Kate Raymore, who even now could not get it out of her head that her boy was a paragon, was possessed by a more primitive feeling. To her the thing was a nemesis. She had been too content, too sure all was well with their household, too uplifted in her kindly but rather scornful judgment of the difficulties and follies which the Courtland family, and the Fanshaw family, and other families of her acquaintance had brought before her eyes. She had fallen too much into the pose of the judge, the critic, and the censor. Well, she had trouble enough of her own now; and that, to say nothing of Tom's kindness about Buenos Ayres, made her sorrier to have to cut him in the Park.

She was a religious woman, of a type now often considered old-fashioned. The nemesis which she instinctively acknowledged she accepted as a just and direct chastisement of Heaven. Her husband was impatient with this view, but he had more sympathy with the merciful alleviation of her sorrow which Heaven had sent. In the hour of affliction her son's heart, which had wandered from her in the waywardness of his heady youth, had come back to her. They could share holy memories of hours spent before Charley went, after forgiveness had been offered and received, and they were all drawn very close together. With these memories in their hearts they could endure, and with a confident hope look forward to, their son's future. Meanwhile they who remained were nearer in heart too. Eva, who had been inclined to flightiness, was frightened and sobered into a greater tenderness and a more willing obedience; and Edgar Raymore himself, when once he had pulled himself together, had behaved so well and been such a help to his wife in the trial that their old relations of mellow friendship took on a more intimate and affectionate character.

It was Sibylla Imason whom Mrs. Raymore chose to pour out these feelings to. Who could better share them than the young wife still in the first pride and glory of her motherhood?

"Children bring you together and keep you together, whether in trouble or in joy. That's one reason why everybody ought to have children," Kate Raymore said with a rather tremulous smile. "If there are none, there's such a danger of the whole thing getting old and cold, and—and worn-out, you know."

Sibylla was in wonderful health now, and at the best of her looks. Her manner too had grown more composed and less impulsive, although she kept her old graciousness. To Kate Raymore she seemed very fair and good to gaze on. She listened with a thoughtful gravity and the wonted hint of questioning or seeking in her eyes. There was a hint of pain in them also, and of this Mrs. Raymore presently became aware.

"That's how it ought to be," said Sibylla. "But—well, the Courtlands have children too."

The remark struck Kate Raymore as rather odd, coming from Sibylla, and associated with the hint of pain in Sibylla's eyes; but she was just now engrossed in her own feelings. She went on describing family life on the true lines—she wouldn't have it that they were unreal or merely ideal—and was quite content that Sibylla should listen.

Sibylla did listen; it was easier to do that than to talk on the subject herself. But she listened without much interest. It was old ground to her, broken by imagination, if not by experience—very familiar to her thoughts some months before. She had lived with—nay, seemed to live on—such ideas in the early days of her marriage, before the accident and all that had come from it. The things Kate Raymore said were no doubt true sometimes; but they were not true for her. That was the upshot of the matter. They were not true for Grantley Imason's wife, nor for the mother of his child. Her reason, dominated by emotion and almost as impulsive as its ruler, had brought her to that conclusion before ever her child was born. It dated from the night when she battled with Grantley, and she had never wavered in it since. She had abandoned hope of the ideal.

What of that? Do not most people have to abandon the ideal? Many of them do it readily enough, even with a secret sense of relief, since there is always something of a strain about an ideal: it is, in famous phrase, so categorically imperative. But Sibylla was a stickler for ideals; they were what she dealt in, what she proposed to barter and to bargain with; she had no place in her stock for humbler wares. Ideals or nothing! And, in the ideal, wifehood and motherhood were so indissolubly united that the failure of one soured her joy in the other. She loved the little child, but loved him with bitterness. He had become the symbol of her lost ideal.

But she did not say this to Kate Raymore, for with the loss of the ideal comes a certain shame of it. We see it then as we did not before, as we know now that others—so many others—see it; and we veil the broken image. The heart, once its throne, becomes its hiding-place.

All this was not for Kate Raymore. She must be left to wonder that Sibylla said so little about the baby—left to be amazed at an apparent coldness in the young mother—left to miss gracious extravagances of maternal joy and pride. For if Sibylla could not be open, neither would she play the hypocrite by parading a light-hearted enjoyment and exultation in the child. How should she display the boy and her proud pleasure in him to the world outside, when her pleasure was not shared at home, and her pride made her love covert there?

Christine Fanshaw, sharply guessing, had cried once:

"But surely Grantley's manner is irreproachable?"

Even now Sibylla's humour rose at the challenge.

"Yes, irreproachable. Of course it would be. All through, his solicitude for both of us was—beautiful! Even Mumples was shaken!"

"Shaken? Why, I thought——"

"Shaken in her bad opinion, I mean, Christine dear. Yes, if ever a man did his duty, did and said all the proper things, Grantley did. And he wasn't the least angry with me; he was only annoyed with Adam and Eve, you know. Of course he was awfully busy just then: County Council elections and what not. But you'd never have guessed it. He never seemed hurried, and he was always very—very solicitous."

"And now, Sibylla?"

"Just the same—and quite pleased. Only I think he wishes babies were like kittens—more animated and growing up quicker, you know. We happen to have a kitten, and I think he's more at his ease with that."

"Nonsense! Men are men, you know."

"Most of them seem to be," admitted Sibylla.

"It would be becoming," Christine observed, "if you recollected that you'd been in the wrong all through. You believed in the wrong doctor, you wanted the wrong thing, you were quite unreasonable. Hadn't you better remember that?"

"I do remember it. And if you want another admission—well, Grantley never reminds me of it by a look or a word."

"He's very much of a gentleman, Sibylla."

"He's never the least ungentlemanlike, Christine."

Christine enjoyed a distinction; she laughed gently.

"And you're a very lucky woman," she went on.

"Don't I say so in my prayers?"
"In a very dangerous state of mind."
Christine's eyes were set on her friend. Sibylla met them full and square. Her mirth, real or affected, vanished. She looked hard at Christine, and made no answer for a moment.
"Yes, I suppose I know what you mean by that," she said at last.
"It's so much easier to despair of your husband than of anybody else in the world—except your wife."
"I try to consider him a type."
"Well, don't find an exception. Oh, I'm not talking at random. I know!" She paused a moment and then went on: "There's a question I should like to ask you, but I suppose it's a question nobody ought to ask; it's too impertinent, even for me, I'm afraid."
Sibylla looked at her, and a faint touch of colour rose on her cheeks. There was a little defiance about her manner, as though she were accused, and stood on her defence rather uneasily. She understood what question it was that even Christine could not ask.
"Grantley and I are—perfectly good friends," she said.
Christine's next question was drawled out in a lazy murmur, and was never completed, apparently from mere indolence.
"It's you who——?"
Sibylla nodded in an abrupt decisive fashion.
"And who do you see most of?" asked Christine.
The colour deepened a little on Sibylla's face.
"That doesn't follow. Don't talk like that."
"I've gone a great deal too far?"
"I really think you have, rather, and without an atom of reason."
"Oh, entirely! I apologise. That sort of thing happens to be—to be in my thoughts."
Sibylla, in some anger, had risen to go. The last words arrested her movement, and she stood in the middle of the room, looking down on Christine's little figure, nestling in a big armchair.
"Your thoughts? That sort of thing in your thoughts?"
"Oh, entirely in retrospect, my dear; and it generally comes of not being appreciated, and of wanting an outlet for—for—well, for something or other, you know."
"Are you going to speak plainly, Christine?"
"Not for worlds, my dear! Are you going to drop my acquaintance?"
"Why is it in your thoughts? You say it's—it's all in the past?"
"Really I'm beginning to doubt if there's such a thing as the past; and if there isn't, it makes everything so much worse! I thought it was all done with—done with long ago; and now it isn't. It's just all—all over my life, as it used to be. And I—I'm afraid again. And I'm lying again. It means so many lies, you know." She looked up at Sibylla with a plaintiveness coloured by malice. "So if I've been impertinent, just put it down to what I happen to be thinking about, my dear."
Sibylla stood very quiet, saying nothing. Christine went on after a minute:
"Can't you manage to be wrapped up in the baby, my dear?"
"No, I can't." The answer was hard and unhesitating. "You've told me something people don't generally tell. I'll tell you something that I didn't think I ever should tell. I love my baby—and sometimes I hate to have to see him." Her eyes were on Christine's face, and there was distress—hopeless distress—in them. "Now I should think you'd drop my acquaintance," she ended with a laugh.
"Oh, I've never had a baby—I'm not shocked to death. But—but why, Sibylla?"
"Surely you can guess why! It's horrible, but it's not unintelligible, surely?"
"No, I suppose it's not," Christine sighed.
Christine's legs had been curled up on her chair; she let them down to the ground and rose to her feet.
"That's all from both of us for to-day?" she asked, with a wry smile.
"All for to-day, I think," answered Sibylla, buttoning her glove.
"I meant to be—friendly."
"You have been. I never guessed anything—anything of what you've said—about you."
"Nobody hinted it? Not even Harriet Courtland? She knew."
"I never see her. How did she know?"
"She was my great friend then. Rather funny, isn't it? I'm told Tom's getting quite regardless of appearances."
"Oh, I can't bear to talk about that!"
"No? Well, you can think of it now and then, can't you? It's rather wholesome to reflect how other people look when they're doing the things that you want——"
"Christine! Good-bye!"
"Oh, good-bye, my dear! And take care of yourself. Oh, I only mean the wind's cold."
But her look denied the harmless meaning she claimed for her parting words.
Grantley's attitude admits of simpler definition than his wife's. He attributed to her an abnormally prolonged and obstinate fit of sulks. People who have been in the wrong are generally sulky; that went a long way to account for it. Add thereto Sibylla's extreme expectations of a world and of an institution both of which deal mostly with compromises and arrangements short of the ideal, and the case seemed to him clear enough and not altogether unnatural, however vexatious it might be. He flew to no tragical or final conclusion. He did not despair; but neither did he struggle. He made no advances; his pride was too wounded, and his reason too affronted for that. On the other hand he offered no provocation. The irreproachability of his manner continued; the inaccessibility of his feelings increased. He devoted his mind to his work, public and commercial; and he waited for Sibylla to come to her senses. Given his theory of the case, he deserved credit for much courtesy, much patience, and entire consistency of purpose. And he, unlike Sibylla, neither talked to intimate friends nor invited questions from them. Both pride and wisdom forbade. Finally, while he acknowledged great discomfort (including a disagreeable element

of the ludicrous), the idea of danger never crossed his mind; he would have laughed at Christine Fanshaw's warning, had it been addressed to him.

Whatever Sibylla's faults, levity was not among them, and danger in Christine's sense—danger of a break-up of the household, as distinguished from a continuance of it, however unsatisfactory that continuance might be—there would probably have been none, had not Walter Blake, after a lively, but not very profitable, youth, wanted to reform his life. He might have wanted to be wicked without creating any peril at all for the Imason household. But he wanted to be good, and he wanted Sibylla to make him good. This idea had occurred to him quite early in their acquaintance. He too had a faculty—even a facility—for idealising. He idealised Sibylla into the image of goodness and purity, which would turn him from sin and folly by making virtue and wisdom not better (which of course they were already), but more attractive and more pleasurable. If they were made more attractive and more pleasurable, he would be eager to embrace them. Besides he had had a good deal of the alternatives, without ever being really content with them. By this time he was firmly convinced that he must be good, and that Sibylla, and Sibylla alone, could make him good. He did not at all think out what the process was to be, nor whither it might lead. He had never planned much, nor looked where things led to. Until they led to something alarming, he did not consider the question much. How she was to reform him he seemed to leave to Sibylla, but his demand that she should do it grew more and more explicit.

This was to attack Sibylla on her weak spot, to aim an arrow true at the joint in her harness. For (one is tempted to say, unfortunately) she knew the only way in which people could be reformed and made good, and caused to feel that wisdom and virtue were not only better (which of course they felt already), but also more pleasurable than folly and sin. (People who want to be reformed are sometimes, it must be admitted, a little exacting.) That could be done only by sympathy and understanding. And if they are thorough, sympathy and understanding compose, or depend on, or issue in love—in the best kind of love, where friend gives himself unreservedly to friend, entering into every feeling, and being privy to every thought. This close and intimate connection must be established before one mind can, lever-like, raise another, and the process of reformation be begun. So much is old ground, often trodden and with no pretence of novelty about it. But much of the power of a proposition may depend not on its soundness, but on the ardour with which it is seized upon, and the conviction with which it is held—which things, again, depend on the character and temper of the believer. Sibylla's character and temper made the proposition extraordinarily convincing. Her circumstances, as she conceived them, were equally provocative in the same direction. What was wrong with her? In the end that she was not wanted, or not wanted enough, that she had more to give than had been asked of her, and no outlet (as Christine had put it) sufficient to relieve the press of her emotions. It was almost inevitable that she should respond to Blake's appeal. He was an outlet. He was somebody who wanted her very much, whom she could help, with whom she could expand, to whom she could give what she had to give in such abundant measure.

Thus far the first stage. The next was not reached. There was plenty of time yet. Sibylla loved the child. Blake had set up his idol, but he had not yet declared that he was the only devotee who knew how properly to honour and to worship it.

He sat watching Sibylla as she played with her baby-boy. He took a hand in the game now and then, since, for a bachelor, he was at his ease with babies; but most of the time he watched. But he watched sympathetically; Sibylla did not fear to show her love before his eyes. The baby was very young for games—for any that a man could play. But Sibylla knew some that he liked; he gave evidence of a strangely dawning pleasure distinct from physical contentment—of wonder, of amusement, of an appreciation of fun, of delight in the mock assaults and the queer noises which his mother directed at him. Sometimes he made nice, queer, gurgling noises himself, full of luxurious content, like a cat's purring, and laden with a surprise, as though all this was very new. She had infinite patience in seeking these signs of approval; half a dozen attempts would miscarry before she succeeded in tickling the infant groping senses. When she hit the mark, she had infinite delight. She would give a cry of joy and turn round to Blake for approval and applause; it was a very difficult thing, but she had kept confidence in her instinct, and she had won the day! Spurred to fresh effort, she returned to her loved work. A gurgle from the little parted lips, a movement of the wide-open little eyes—eyes of that marvellous transient blue—marked a new triumph.

"Isn't he wonderful?" she called to Blake over her shoulder.

"Oh, yes, rather!" he laughed, and added, after a short moment: "And so are you."

Sibylla was not looking for compliments. She laughed gaily and went back to her work.

"But can't he talk, Mrs. Imason?"

"How silly you are! But he's just wonderful for his age as he is."

"Oh, they all are!"

He was so obviously feigning scorn that Sibylla only shook her head at him in merry glee.

Was not this the real, the great thing? Blake's mind, disengaging from the past memories of what had once been its delights, and turning now in distaste from them, declared that it was. Nature had the secret of the keenest pleasure—it was to be found along nature's way. There pleasure was true to a purpose, achieving a great end, concentrated in that, not dissipated in passing and unfruitful joys. Blake was sure that he was right now, sure that he wanted to be reformed, more sure than ever that wisdom and virtue were more pleasurable (as well as being better) than their opposites. A man of ready sensibility and quick feeling, he was open to the suggestion and alive to the beauty of what he saw. It seemed to him holy—and the feelings it evoked in him seemed almost holy too. "Motherhood!" he said to himself, not knowing, at least not acknowledging, that his true meaning was this woman as mother, motherhood incarnate in her. Yet that it was. If his aspirations were awake, his blood too was stirred. But the moment for that to come to light was not yet. The good seemed still unalloyed, his high-soaring aspirations were guiltless of self-knowledge.

Sibylla played with the child till she could play no more—till she feared to tire him, she would have said—in truth till the tenderness which had found a mask in the sport would conceal its face no more, and in a spasm of love she caught the little creature to her, pressing her face to his.

"Poor little darling!" Blake heard her say in a whisper full of pity as well as of love.

Whence came the pity? The mother's natural fear that her sheltering may not avail against all the world? Most likely it was only that. But the pity was poignant, and he wondered vaguely.

They were thus, she and the child locked together, the young man dimly picturing the truth as he watched, when Grantley Imason came in. A start ran through Sibylla; she caught a last kiss from the little face, and then laid her baby down. Swiftly she turned round to her husband. Blake had risen, watching still—nay, more eagerly. For all he could do, his eyes sought her face and rested there, trying to trace what feeling found expression as she turned to her husband from her child.

"Glad to see you, Blake. Ah, you've got the little chap there!"

He chucked the child under its chin, as he went by, gently and affectionately, and came with outstretched hand to his friend—for he liked sunny impetuous young Blake, though he thought very lightly of him. As they shook hands, Blake's eyes travelled past him, and dwelt again on Sibylla. She stood by her child, and her regard was on her husband. Then, for a moment, she met Blake's inquiring gaze. The slightest smile came on her lips, just a touch of colour in her cheeks.

"Yes, but it's time for him to go upstairs," she said.

Grantley had passed on to the table, and was pouring himself out a cup of tea. Sibylla walked across the room and rang the bell for the baby's nurse. Blake took up his hat.

The spell was broken. What had it been and why was it dispelled? Blake did not know, but turgid feelings mingled with his aspirations now, and he looked at Grantley Imason with a new covert hostility.

CHAPTER IX

A SUCCESSFUL MISSION

Efforts were on foot to avert the scandal and public disaster which so imminently threatened the Courtlands. Grantley Imason, who had a real friendship for Tom, interested himself in them. Not merely the home was in danger, but Tom's position and career, also Tom's solvency. He had always lived up to his income; now, without doubt, he was spending sums far beyond it; and, as has been seen, the precautions which he had declared he would use were falling into neglect as the sense of hopelessness grew upon his mind. From such neglect to blank effrontery and defiance looked as though it would be but a short step. And he refused obstinately to make any advances to his wife; he would not hear of suing for peace.

"My dear fellow, think of the children!" Grantley urged.

Poor Tom often thought of the children, and often tried not to. He knew very well where he was going and what his going there must mean to them. Yet he held on his way, obstinately assuring himself that the fault for which they must suffer was not his.

"I do think of them, but—— It was past bearing, Grantley."

"I think you must have given her a real fright by now. Perhaps she'll be more amenable."

"Harriet amenable! Good Lord!"

"Look here, if she can be got to express regret and hold out the olive branch, you know, will you drop all this, and give the thing one more trial?"

It was a favourable moment for the request, since Tom happened to be cross with his pleasures too—they were so very expensive. He allowed himself to be persuaded to say yes.

But who was to beard Lady Harriet in her den? There was no eagerness to undertake the task; yet everybody agreed that a personal interview was the only chance. Grantley fairly "funked it," and honestly said so. Raymore's nerves were still so upset that his excuses were accepted—it was morally certain that Harriet, if she became angry, would taunt him about his boy. Selford? That was absurd. And it was not a woman's work. The lot fell on John Fanshaw—John, with his business prestige and high reputation for common sense. And Lady Harriet liked him best of them all. The choice was felt to be excellent by everyone—except John himself.

"Haven't I enough worries of my own?" he demanded. "Why the devil am I to take on Tom Courtland's too?"

"Oh, do try! It can't hurt you if she does fly into a passion, John."

He grumbled a great deal more; and Christine, in an unusually chastened mood, performed the wifely function of meeting his grumbles with mingled consolation and praise.

"Well, I'll go on Sunday," he said at last, and added, with a look across the table: "Perhaps some of my own troubles will be off my mind by then."

Christine flushed a little.

"Oh, I hope so," she said rather forlornly.

"I do hope so!" he declared emphatically. "I build great hopes on it. It is to-day you're going, isn't it?"

"Yes, to-day. After lunch I said I'd come."

"Did he write back cordially?"

"Well, what could the poor man do, John?"

"Ha, ha! Well, I suppose a fellow generally does answer cordially when a pretty woman proposes to call on him. Ha, ha!" John's hopes made him merry and jovial. "I say, I shall get back as early as I can from the City, and try to be here in time to welcome you. And if it's gone all right, why——"

"Don't let yourself be too sure."

"No, I won't. Oh, no, I won't do that!"

But it was not hard to see how entirely he built all his trust on this last remaining chance. He rose from the breakfast-table.

"All right. To-day's Thursday. I'll go to Lady Harriet on Sunday. Not much harm can happen in three days. Good-bye, old girl, and—and good luck!"

Christine suffered his kiss—a ceremony not usual to their daily parting in the morning. When he had gone, she sat on a long while behind the tea-things at the breakfast-table, deep in thought, trying to picture the work of the day which lay before her. It was extraordinarily hateful to her, and she had hardly been able to endure John's jocularity and his talk about pretty women coming to call.

Because there had once been some talk, she had told Caylesham that she would bring a friend with her, naming Anna Selford. Anna would go in with her, and wait in another room while they had their meeting. Caylesham thought this rather superfluous, but had no objection to make. He could not form any idea why she was coming, until it occurred to him that perhaps he had a few letters of hers somewhere, and that women were apt to get frights about letters, picturing sudden deaths, and not remembering that a wise man chooses a discreet executor. With this notion in his head he hunted about, and did find two or three letters. But they were quite harmless; in order to see this he read them through, and then laid them down with a smile. After a few moments of reflection he put them into an envelope, sealed them up, and placed them on a table by him, ready for Christine. He was a man of forty-five, and he looked it. But he was tall, thin, well set-up, and always exceedingly well turned-out. Beyond his rank and his riches, his only fame lay in sporting circles. He and John Fanshaw had first made acquaintance over horses, and he still went in for racing on a considerable scale. He was unmarried, and likely to remain so. There was a nephew to inherit: and he had pleased himself so much that he found it hard to please himself any more now. And he had, unlike Walter Blake, no aspirations. He had a code of morals, and a very strict one, so far as it went; but it was not co-extensive with more generally recognised codes.

Directly Christine came in, he noticed how pretty and dainty and young she looked; she, at least, pleased him still. He greeted her with great cordiality and with no embarrassment, and made her sit down in a chair by the fire. She was a little pale, but he did not observe that; what he noted—and noted with a touch of amusement—was that she met his eyes as seldom as possible.

"I really couldn't think to what I owed this pleasure——" he began.

But she interrupted him.

"You couldn't possibly have guessed. I've got to tell you that."

"It's not these?"

He held up the letters in their envelope.

"What are they?"

"Only two or three notes of yours—all I've got, I think."

"Notes of mine? Oh, put them in the fire! It wasn't that."

"I suppose we may as well put them in the fire," he agreed.

As the fire burnt up the letters, Christine looked at the fire and said:

"John has sent me here."

"John sent you here?"

He was surprised, and again perhaps a trifle amused.

"You don't suppose I should have come of my own accord? I hate coming."

"Oh, don't say that! We're always friends, always friends. But suppose you do insist on 'hating' to come—well, why have you come?"

She looked at him now.

"I couldn't help it. I refused at first, but I—I had no reason to give if I'd gone on refusing. He'd have—suspected."

"Ah!" The explanation drew an understanding nod from him.

"So I came. He's sent me to borrow money from you."

"To borrow money? What, is John——?"

"Yes, he's in great difficulties. He wants a lot of money at once."

"But why didn't he come himself? It's rather odd to——"

"I suppose he hated it too. He has done it once. I mean, he's been to Grantley Imason. And—and he thought—you'd be more likely to do it if I asked."

"Did he? Does that mean——?"

"No, no, not in the least. He only thought you were—that you liked pretty women." She held out a piece of paper. "He's put it all down there. I think I'd better give it to you. It says what he wants, and when he must have it, and how he'll pay it back. I promised to tell you all that, but you'd better read it for yourself."

He took the paper from her and studied it. She looked round the room, which she had known very well. It was quite unchanged. Then she watched him while he read. He had grown older, but he had not lost his attractiveness. For a moment or two she forgot the present state of things.

"Fifteen thousand! It's a bit of money!" This remark recalled Christine's thoughts. "Has Imason lent him that?"

"Yes, on the same terms that he suggests there."

"Well, Imason's a good fellow, but he's a banker, and—well, I should think he expects to get it back. I say, John's been having a bit of a plunge, eh? Consequently he's in deep water now? Is he very much cut up?"

"Terribly! It means ruin, and the loss of his reputation, and—oh, I don't know what besides!"

"Poor old John! He's a good chap, isn't he?"

She made no answer to that, and he muttered:

"Fifteen thousand!"

"Frank," she said, "I've done what I had to do, what I promised to. I've shown you the paper; I've told you how much this money means to us; I've told you it means avoiding ruin and bankruptcy and all that disgrace. That's what John made me promise to tell you, and its all I have to tell you from him. I've done what I said I would on his behalf."

"Yes, yes, that's all right. Don't distress yourself, Christine. I just want to have another look at this paper, and to think it over a little. It is a goodish bit of money, you know. But then old John's always been a good friend of mine, and if times weren't so uncommon bad——"

He wrinkled his brow over the paper again.

"And now I have to speak on my own account. Frank, you must find some good, some plausible, reason for refusing. You mustn't lend John the money."

"Hallo?"

He looked up from the paper in great surprise.

"You see, John doesn't know the truth," she answered.

He rose and stood by the fire, looking down on her thoughtfully.

"No, of course he doesn't, or—or you wouldn't be here," he said after a pause.

Then he fell into thought again.

"And if he did know, he'd never ask you for the money," she said.

Caylesham made a wry little grimace. That might be true of John, but he would hesitate to say the same about every fellow. Christine, however, did not see the grimace.

"And you don't want me to lend it—not though it means all this to John?"

"I don't want you to lend it, whatever it means. Pray don't lend it, Frank!"

"Is that—— Well, I don't quite know how to put it. I mean, is that on John's account or on your own?"

"I can't give you reasons; I can't put them in words. It's just terribly hateful to me."

He was puzzled by the point of view, and still more by finding it in her. Perhaps the last six years had made a difference in her way of looking at things; they had made none in his.

"And if I do as you wish, what are you going to say to John? Are you going to say to him that in the end you told me not to lend the money?"

"Of course not. I shall say that you said you couldn't; you'll have to give me the reasons."

He looked discontented.

"It'll look rather shabby," he suggested.

"Oh, no! It's a large sum. It would be quite likely that it wouldn't be convenient to you."

"Is he expecting to get it?"

"I don't think that has anything to do with it. I suppose—well, drowning men catch at straws."

She smiled dolefully.

The phrase was unlucky for her purpose. It stirred Caylesham's pity.

"Poor old John!" he murmured again. "What'll he do if he doesn't get it?"

"I don't know—I told you I didn't know."

He was puzzled still. He could not get down to the root of her objection; and she could not, or would not, put it plainly to him. She could not express the aspect of the affair that was, as she said, so terribly hateful to her. But it was there. All she had given she had given long ago—given freely long ago. Now was she not asking a price for it—and a price which her husband was to share? Only on that ground really was she there. For now the man loved her no more; there was no glamour and no screen. After all these years she came back and asked a price—a price John was to share.

But the case did not strike Caylesham at all like this. John suspected nothing, or John would not have sent his wife there. John had been a very good friend, he would like to do John a good turn. In his case the very circumstances which so revolted Christine made him more inclined to do John a good turn. Although he could not pretend that the affair had ever made him uncomfortable, still its existence in the past helped John's cause with him now.

"You're not a very trustworthy ambassador," he said, smiling. "I don't think you're playing fair with John, you know."

"Why, do you—you—expect me to?" she asked bitterly.

He shrugged his shoulders in a discreet evasion, seeing the threatened opening of a discussion of a sort always painful and useless.

"John will take failure and all that devilish hard."

He took up the paper again and looked at it. He knew the business was a very good one; after such a warning as this a man would surely go steady; and Grantley Imason had lent money. He built a good deal on that. And—yes—in the end he was ready to run a risk, being a good-natured man and fond of John, and feeling that it would be a very becoming thing in him to do a service to John.

"Look here, I shall attend to your official message. I shan't take any notice of these private communications," he said lightly, but kindly, almost affectionately. "And you mustn't feel that sort of way about it. Why, I've got a right to help you, anyhow; and I can't see why I mustn't help John."

He went to the table and wrote. He came back to her, holding a cheque in his hand.

"Here it is," he said. "John will send me a letter embodying the business side. I've post-dated the cheque four days, because I must see my bankers about it. Oh, it's not inconvenient; only needs a few days' notice—and it'll be in time for what John wants. Here, take it, Christine."

He pressed the cheque into her hands, and with a playful show of force shut her fingers upon it.

"I know this has been a—a——" He looked round the room, seeming to seek an apt form of expression. "This has been an uncomfortable job for you, but you really mustn't look at it like that, you know."

"If you give it me, I must take it. I daren't accept the responsibility of refusing it."

He was quite eager to comfort her.

"You're doing quite right. You were perfectly square with me; now you're being perfectly square with John."

Perfectly square with John! Christine's lips curved in a smile of scorn. But—well, sometimes one loses the right or the power to be perfectly square.

"And I'm downright glad to help—downright glad you came to me."

"I only came because I couldn't help it."

"Then I'm downright glad you couldn't help it."

She had loved this unalterable good-temper of his, and admired the tactful way he had of humouring women. If they wouldn't have it in one way, he had always been quite ready to offer it to them in the other, so long as they took it in the end; and this they generally did. She rose to her feet, holding the cheque in her hand.

"Your purse, perhaps?" he suggested, laughing. "You see, it might puzzle your young friend. And give old John my remembrances—and good luck to him. Are you going now?"

"Yes, Frank, I'm going now."

"Good-bye, Christine. I often think of you, you know. I often remember—— Ah, I see I mustn't often remember! Well, you're right, I suppose. But I'm always your friend. Don't be in any trouble without letting me know."

"I shall never come to you again."

He grew a little impatient at that, but still he was quite good-natured about it.

"What's the use of brooding?" he asked. "I mean, if you're running straight now, it's no good being remorseful and that sort of thing; it just wears you out. It would make you look old, if anything could. But I don't believe anything could, you know."

She gave him her hand. Her lips trembled, but she smiled at him now.

"Good-bye, Frank. If I have any hard thoughts, they won't be about you. You can always"—she hesitated a minute—"always disarm criticism, can't you?"

Caylesham stooped and kissed her hand lightly.

"Don't fret, my dear," he said. "You're better than most by a long way. Now take your cheque off to poor old John, and both of you be as jolly as you can." He pressed her hand cordially and led her to the door. "I'm glad we've settled things all right. Good-bye."

She shook her head at him, but still she could not help smiling as she said her last good-bye. With the turning of her face the smile disappeared.

Caylesham's smile lasted longer. He stood on his hearthrug, smiling as he remembered; and an idea which forced its way into his head did not drive away the smile. He wondered whether, by any chance, old John had any vague sort of—well, hardly suspicion—but some vague sort of an inkling. He would not have hinted that to Christine, since evidently she did not believe it, and it might have upset her. But really, in the end, was it not more odd to send Christine if he had no inkling at all than if he had just some sort of an idea that there was a reason why her request might be very much more potent than his own? He was inclined to think that John suspected just a flirtation. The notion made him considerably amused at John, but not at all angry with him. It was not a thing he would have done himself, perhaps. Still you can never tell what you will do when you are in a really tight corner. His racing experiences had presented him with a good many cases which supported this conclusion.

Christine felt very tired, but she was not going to give way to that; Anna Selford was too sharp-witted. She chatted gaily as they drove home, mainly about the subject which grieved them both so much—Mrs. Selford's taste in frocks. Matters were in an even more dire way now; Anna could get no frocks! Between pictures and dogs, she declared, her wardrobe stood no chance. Christine was genuinely unable to comprehend such a confusion of relative importance.

"I detest fads," she said severely.

"It doesn't give me a fair chance," lamented Anna, "because I should pay for dressing, shouldn't I, Mrs. Fanshaw?"

Christine reiterated her belief to that effect. It was a melancholy comfort to poor Anna.

"Suppose I'd been going to see Lord Caylesham, dressed like this!"

"My dear, he's old enough to be your father."

"That doesn't matter. He's so smart and good-looking. I see him riding sometimes with Mr. Imason, and he's just the sort of man I admire. I know I should fall in love with him."

Christine laughed, but turned her face a little away.

"I won't help you there; our alliance is only on the subject of frocks."

But how well she knew what Anna meant and felt! And now she was a trifle uneasy. Had any of that talk filtered through leaky Selford conversations to Anna's eagerly listening ears?

"Mamma once told me he'd been very, very wild."

"Stuff! They always say that about a man if he's a bachelor. Sheer feminine spite, in my belief, Anna!"

"What did you go to see him about? Oh, is it a secret?"

Christine was really rather glad to hear the question. It showed that nothing very much of the talk had filtered. And she had her story ready.

"Oh, about a horse. You know we've had to sell our bays, and he's got one that we thought we could buy cheap. John was so busy that I went. But, alas, it's beyond us, after all."

"Yes, you told me you'd sold a pair." Anna nodded significantly.

Christine smiled. She was reflecting how many crises of life demand a departure from veracity, and what art resides in the choice of a lie. She had chosen one which, implying that Anna was in her confidence, pleased and quieted that young woman, and sent her off home without any suspicions as to the visit or its connection with the financial crisis otherwise than through the horses.

She did not ask Anna in to tea, because John would be there, home early from the City, waiting. Now that the thing was done, she was minded to make as light of it as possible. Since she had been compelled to go, let John forget under what pressure and how unwillingly she had gone. Thus the faintest breath of suspicion would be less likely to rest on her secret. She trusted to her self-control; she would chaff him a little before she told him of the success of her mission.

But the first sight of his face drove the idea out of her head. It might be safer for her; it would actually be not safe for him. She was convinced of this when she saw the strain in his eyes and how his whole figure seemed in a tension of excitement. She closed the door carefully behind her.

"Well," he cried, "what news? By God, I've been able to do no work! I haven't been able to think of anything else all day. Don't—don't say you've failed!"

"No," she said, opening her purse, "I haven't failed. Here's a cheque from Lord Caylesham. It's post-dated, but only a day or two. That doesn't matter?"

She came to him and gave him the cheque. He put it on the table and rested his head on his arm. He seemed almost dazed; the stiffness had gone out of his body.

"By Jove, he's a good sort! By Jove, he is a good sort!" he murmured.

"He was very kind indeed. He made no difficulties. He said he was sure he could trust you, and was glad to help you. And he sent his remembrances and good luck to you, John."

She had taken off her fur coat and her hat as she was speaking, and now sank down into a chair.

"By Jove, he is a good sort!" John suddenly sprang up. "It means salvation!" he cried. "That's what it means—salvation! I can pay my way. I can look people in the face. I shan't bring the business to ruin and shame. Oh, I've had my lesson—I go steady now! And if I don't pay these good chaps every farthing call me a scoundrel! They are good chaps, Grantley and old Caylesham—devilish good chaps!"

"Don't go quite off your head, John dear! Try to take it quietly."

"Ah, you take it quietly enough, don't you, old girl?" he exclaimed, coming up to her. "But you've done it all—yes, by heaven you have! I know you didn't like it; I know you hated it. You're so proud, and I like that in you too. But it wasn't a time for pride, and you put yours in your pocket for my sake—yes, for my sake, I know it. We've had our rows, old girl, but if ever a man had a good wife in the end, I have, and I know it."

He caught hold of her hands and pulled her to her feet, drawing her towards him at the same time.

"Quietly, John," she said, "quietly."

"What, don't you want to give me a kiss?"

"I'll give you a kiss, but quietly. Poor old John!"

She kissed him lightly on the cheek.

"Now let me go! I—I'm tired."

"Well, you shall rest," he said good-naturedly, and let her go.

She sank back in her seat and watched him turn to the cheque again.

"It's salvation!" he repeated, and paid no heed to a sudden quick gasp of breath from her throat.

Even Caylesham would have allowed that he had no suspicion. But Christine sat a prey to vague forebodings. She felt as though the thing were not finished yet. The dead would not bury its dead.

CHAPTER X

THE FLINTY WALL

There was one point about Jeremy Chiddingfold's system of philosophy—if that name may be allowed to dignify the rather mixed assortment of facts and inferences which he had gathered from his studies: This point was that there was no appeal against facts. Nature was nature, feelings were feelings, and change was development. One thing was right to-day; it became wrong to-morrow without ceasing to have been right yesterday. Let there be an end of ignorant parrot-like chatter about inconsistency. Is evolution inconsistency? Inconsistency with what? He put this question and kindred ones quite heatedly to Mrs. Mumple, who did not at all understand them, and to whom they savoured of unorthodoxy; she had ever distrusted a scientific education. If Jeremy could have put his case in a concrete form, he would have won her sympathy. But she did not know where such general principles would stop, and she had heard that there were persons who impugned the authority of Moses.

Jeremy did not care much about Mrs. Mumple's approval, though he tried his arguments on her as a boxer tries his fists on a stuffed sack (she suggested the simile). He did not expect to convince her, and would have been rather sorry if he had. In her present mental condition she was invaluable as a warning and a butt. But it was exasperating that Mrs. Hutting should hold antique, ludicrous, and (in his opinion) in the end debased views about social intercourse between the sexes—in fact (to descend to that concrete which Jeremy's soul abhorred) about girls of seventeen taking walks with young men of twenty-two. Mrs. Hutting's views on this point imposed on Jeremy proceedings which he felt to be unbecoming to a philosopher. He had to scheme, to lie in wait, to p!an most unlikely accidents, on occasion to palter with truth, to slip behind a waggon or to hide inside a barn. A recognition on Mrs. Hutting's part of nature, of facts, and of development would have relieved Jeremy from all these distasteful expedients.

But Mrs. Hutting was an old-fashioned woman. She obeyed her husband—usually, however, suggesting on what points he might reasonably require obedience. She expected her daughter to obey her. And she had her views, which she had enforced in a very quiet but a very firm way. Modern tendencies were not in favour at the rectory; that being established as a premise, it followed that anything which was disapproved of at the rectory was a modern tendency; wherefore clandestine and spuriously accidental meetings between young men and young women were a modern tendency, or, anyhow, signs of one—and of a very bad one too. No ancient instances would have shaken Mrs. Hutting on this point; the train of logic was too strong. Certainly Dora never tried to shake her mother's judgment, or to break the chain. For Dora was old-fashioned too. She admitted that clandestine and spuriously accidental meetings were wrong. But sometimes the clandestine character or the spuriousness of the accident could be plausibly questioned; besides, a thing may be wrong, and yet not be so very, very bad. And the thing may be such fun and so amusing that—well, one goes and tries not to be found out. On these ancient but not obsolete lines Miss Dora framed her conduct, getting thereby a spice of excitement and a fearful joy which no duly licensed encounters could have given her. But she had no doubt that Mrs. Hutting was quite right. Anna Selford's critical attitude towards her parents was not in the rectory way.

"Suppose she'd seen us!" Dora whispered behind the barn, as the rectory pony-chaise rolled slowly by.

"We're doing nothing wrong. I should like to walk straight out and say so."

"If you do, I'll never speak to you again."

"I hate this—this dodging!"

"Then why don't you take your walks the other way? You know I come here. Why do you come if you feel like that about it?"

Thus Dora fleshed her maiden sword. It was an added joy to make Jeremy do things which he disliked. And all this time she was snubbing him and his tentative approaches. Lovers? Certainly not—or of course she would have told mamma! Accepted Jeremy? No—she liked to think that she was trifling with him. In fine, she was simply behaving shamefully badly, in a rapturously delightful way; and to see a pretty girl doing that is surely a refreshing and rejuvenating sight!

Well, the word pretty is perhaps a concession to Jeremy. The only girl in the place is always pretty. Dora was, at any rate, fresh and fair, lithe and clean-limbed, gay and full of fun.

A dreadful peril threatened, with which Dora appalled her own fancy and Jeremy's troubled heart. At seventeen school is still possible—a finishing-school. Mrs. Hutting had brandished this weapon, conscious in her own mind that the rectory finances would hardly suffice to put an edge on it. Dora did not realise this difficulty.

"You remember that time we were seen? Well, there was an awful row, and mamma said that if it happened once again I should go—for a year!"

Jeremy felt that something must be done, and said so.

"What could I do?"

That was a little more difficult for Jeremy.

"You must take pains to avoid me," said Dora, schooling her lips to primness. "You don't want to get me sent away, do you?"

Certainly these spring months were very pleasant to Miss Dora. But, alas, calamity came. It happened in Milldean just as it might have happened in the West End of London. The school-teacher said something to the post-mistress. There was nobody much else to say anything—for the wise-eyed yokels, when they met the youth and the maid, gave a shrewd kindly nod, and went on their way with an inarticulate but appreciative chuckle. However the school-teacher did say something to the post-mistress, whence the something came to Mrs. Hutting's ears. There was another "row," no doubt even more "awful." The finishing-school was brandished again, but, after a private consultation on finance, put aside by the rector and Mrs. Hutting. Another weapon was chosen. Mrs. Hutting dictated a note, the rector wrote and sealed it; it was sent across to Old Mill House by the gardener, addressed to "Jeremy Chiddingfold, Esq." In fact no circumstance of ceremony was omitted, and Dora watched the messenger of tyranny from her bedroom window. In the note (which began "Sir") Jeremy was plainly given to understand that he was no gentleman, and that all relations between the rectory and himself were at an end.

Jeremy stumped up and down the room, furiously exclaiming that he did not care whether he was a gentleman or not. He was a man. That was enough for him, and ought to be enough for anybody. Mrs. Mumple was positively frightened into agreeing with him on this point. But however sound the point may be, relations with the rectory were broken off! What was to be done? Jeremy determined to go to town and lay before Grantley and Sibylla the unparalleled circumstances of the case. But first there was—well, there would be—one more stolen meeting. But it was not quite of the sort which might have been anticipated. Dora's levity was gone; she played with him no more. But neither did she follow the more probable course, and, under the influence of grief and the pain of separation, give the rein to her feelings, acknowledge her love, and exchange her vows for his. The old-fashioned standards had their turn; evidently the rectory upbraidings had been very severe. Every disobedience, every trick, every broken promise rose up in judgment, and declared the sentence to be just, however severe. Jeremy was at a loss how to face this. He had been so convinced that nature was with them, and that nature spelt rectitude. He was aghast at a quasi-theological and entirely superstitious view that no good or happiness could come out of a friendship (Dora adhered obstinately to this word) initiated in such a way. He refused to recognise her wickedness and even his own. When she announced her full acceptance of the edict, her determination to evince penitence by absolute submission, he could only burst out:

"They haven't been cruel to you?"

"Cruel? No! They've been most—most gentle. I've come to see how wrong it was."

"Yet you're here!" He could not resist the retort.

"For the last time—to say good-bye. And if you really care at all, you must do as I wish."

"But—I may write to you?"

"No, no, you mustn't."

"You can't stop me thinking about you."

"I shan't think of you. I shall pray to be able not to. I'm sure I can be strong."

She had got this idea in her head. It was just the sort of idea that Sibylla might have got. She wanted to immolate herself. For such views in Sibylla Jeremy had always had denunciations ready. He had no denunciation now—only a despairing puzzle.

"I can't accept that, and I won't! Do you love me?"

"I'm going to keep my promise to say nothing. I've told you what I must do and what you must. I made up my mind—and—and then I went to the Sacrament to-day."

Jeremy rubbed his wrinkled brow, eyeing this determined penitent very ruefully. A sudden return to rectitude is disconcerting in an accomplice. He did not know what to do. But his bulldog persistence was roused and his square jaw set obstinately.

"Well, I shall consider what to do. I believe you love me, and I shan't sit down under this."

"You must," she said. "And now, good-bye."

He came towards her, but her raised hand stopped him.

"Good-bye like this? You won't even shake hands?"

"No, I can't. Good-bye."

Of course he was sorry for her, but he was decidedly angry too. He perceived a case of the selfishness of spiritual exaltation. His doggedness turned to surliness.

"All right, then, good-bye," he said sulkily.

"You're not angry with me?"

"Yes, I am."

She accepted this additional cross, and bore it meekly.

"That hurts me very much. But I must do right. Good-bye."

And with that she went, firm to the last, leaving Jeremy almost as furious with women as in the palmiest days of his youth, almost as angry with her as he had ever been with the long-legged rectory girl.

Pursuing (though he did not know it) paths as well trodden as those which he had already followed, he formed an instant determination in his mind. She should be sorry for it! Whether she should sorrow with a lifelong sorrow or whether she should ultimately, after much grief and humiliation, find forgiveness, he did not decide for the moment; both ideas had their attraction. But at any rate she should be sorry, and that as soon as possible. How was it to be brought about? Jeremy conjectured that a remote and ill-ascertained success in original research would not make her sorry, and his conclusion may be allowed to pass; nor would a continuance of shabby clothes and an income of a hundred a year. This combination had once seemed all-sufficient. Nay, it would suffice now for true and whole-hearted love. But it was not enough to make a cruel lady repent of her cruelty, nor to convict a misguided zealot of the folly of her zeal. It was not dazzling enough for that. In an hour Jeremy threw his whole ideal of life to the winds, and decided for wealth and mundane fame—speedy wealth and speedy mundane fame (speed was essential, because Jeremy's feelings were in a hurry). Such laurels and fruits were not to be plucked in Milldean. That very night Jeremy packed a well-worn leather bag and a square deal box. He was going to London, to see Grantley and Sibylla, to make them acquainted with the state of the case, and to set about becoming rich and famous as speedily as possible. His mind o'erleapt the process and saw it already completed—saw his return to Milldean rich and famous—saw his renewed meeting with Dora, the confusion of the rector and Mrs. Hutting, the unavailing—or possibly at last availing—regret and humiliation of Dora. It cannot truthfully be said that he went to bed altogether unhappy. He had his dream, even as Dora had hers; he had his luxury of prospective victory as she had hers of unreserved and accepted penitence; and they shared the conviction of a very extraordinary and unprecedented state of things.

So to town came Jeremy, leaving Mrs. Mumple in Old Mill House. She was not idle. She was counting months now—not years now, but months; and she was knitting socks, and making flannel shirts, and hemming big red handkerchiefs, and picturing and wondering in her faithful old heart what that morning would be like for whose coming she had waited so many many years. Great hopes and great fears were under the ample breast of her unshapely merino gown.

In the Imason household the strain grew more intense. With rare tenacity, unimpaired confidence, and unbroken pride, Grantley maintained his attitude. He would tire out Sibylla's revolt; he would outstay the fit of sulks, however long it might be. But the strain told on him, though it did not break him: he was more away; more engrossed in his outside activities; grimmer and more sardonic when he was at home; careful to show no feeling which might expose him to rebuff; extending the scope of this conduct from his wife to his child, because his wife's grievance was bound up with the child. And Sibylla, seeing the attitude, seeing partially only and therefore more resenting the motives, created out of it and them a monster of insensibility, something of an inhuman selfishness, seeming the more horrible and unnatural from the unchanging, if cold, courtesy which Grantley still displayed. This image had been taking shape ever since their battle at Milldean. It had grown with the amused scorn which was on his face as he told her of the specialist's judgment, and made her see how foolish she had been, what an unnecessary fuss she had caused, how dangerous and silly it was to let one's emotions run away with one. It had defined itself yet more clearly through the months before and after the boy's birth, as Grantley developed his line of action and adhered to it, secure apparently from every assault of natural tenderness. Now the portentous shape was all complete in her imagination, and the monster she had erected freed her from every obligation. By her hypothesis it was accessible by no appeal and sensitive to no emotion. Why, then, labour uselessly? It would indeed be to knock your head—yes, and your heart too—against a flinty wall. As for trying to show or to cherish love for it—that seemed to her prostitution itself. And she had no tenacity to endure such a life as Grantley, or her image of Grantley, made for her. In her headlong fashion she had already pronounced the alternatives—death or flight.

And there was the baby boy in his helplessness; and there was young Blake with his ready hot passion, masked by those aspirations of his, and his fiery indignation seconding and applauding the despair of her own heart. For Blake knew the truth now—the truth as Sibylla's imaginings made it; and in view of that truth the thing his passion urged him to became a holy duty. His goddess must be no more misused; her misery must not be allowed to endure.

Knowing his thought and what his heart was towards her, Sibylla turned to him as a child turns simply from a hard to a loving face. Here was a life wanting her life, a love asking hers. She had always believed people when they said they loved and wanted her—why, she had believed even Grantley himself!—and was always convinced that their love for her was all they said it was. It was her instinct to believe that. She believed all—aye, more—about young Blake than he believed about himself, though he believed very much just now; and she would always have people all white or all black. Grantley was all black now, and Blake was very white, white as snow, while he talked of his aspirations and his love, and tempted her to leave all that bound her, and to give her life to him. He tempted well, for he offered not pleasure, but the power of doing good and bestowing happiness. Her first natural love seemed to have spent itself on Grantley; she had no passion left, save the passion of giving. It was to this he made his appeal; this would be enough to give him all his way. Yet there was the child. He had not yet ventured on that difficult uncertain ground. That was where the struggle would be; it was there that he distrusted the justice of his own demand on her, there that his passion had to drown the inward voices of protest.

It might have happened that Jeremy, with his fresh love and fresh ambitions, would have been a relief to such a position; that his appeal both to sympathy and to amusement would have done something to clear the atmosphere. So far as he himself went, indeed, he was irresistible; his frankness and his confidence were not to be denied. Trusting in the order of nature, he knew no bashfulness; trusting in himself, he had no misgivings. Without a doubt he was right. They all agreed that the old ideal of original research and a hundred a year must be abandoned, and that Jeremy must become rich and famous as soon as possible.

"Though whether you ought to forgive her in the end is, I must say, a very difficult point," remarked Grantley with a would-be thoughtful smile. "In cases of penitence I myself favour forgiveness, Jeremy."

"But there is the revelation of her character," suggested Sibylla, taking the matter more seriously, or treating its want of seriousness with more tenderness.

"I'm inclined to think the young lady's right at present," said Blake. "What you have to do is to give her ground for changing her views—and to give her mother ground for changing hers too."

Jeremy listened to them all with engrossed interest. Whatever their attitude, they all confirmed his view.

"You once spoke of a berth in the City?" he said to Grantley.

"Not much fame there; but perhaps you may as well take things by instalments."

"I don't like it, you know. It's not my line at all."

Blake came to the rescue. The Selfords drew their money from large and important dyeing-works, although Selford himself had retired from any active share in the work of the business. There was room for scientific aptitude in dyeing-works, Blake opined rather vaguely. "You could make chemistry, for instance, subserve the needs of commerce, couldn't you?"

"That really is a good suggestion," said Jeremy approvingly.

"Capital!" Grantley agreed. "We'll get at Selford for you, Jeremy; and, if necessary, we'll club together, and send to Terra del Fuego, and buy Janet Selford a new dog."

"I begin to see my way," Jeremy announced.

Whereat the men laughed, while Sibylla came round and kissed him, laughing too. What a very short time ago, and she had been even as Jeremy, as sanguine, as confident, seeing her way as clearly, with just as little warrant of knowledge!

"Meanwhile you mustn't mope, old chap," said Grantley.

"Mope? I've no time for moping. Do you think I could see this Selford to-morrow?"

"I'll give you a letter to take to him," laughed Grantley. "But don't ask for ten thousand a year all at once, you know."

"I know the world. When I really want a thing, I can wait for it."

But it was evident that he did not mean to wait very long. Grantley said ten thousand a year: a thousand would seem riches to the Milldean rectory folk.

"That's right. If you want a thing, you must be ready to wait for it," agreed Grantley, with smiling lips and a pucker on his brow.

"So long as there's any hope," added Sibylla.

These hints of underlying things went unheeded by Jeremy, but Blake marked them. They were becoming more frequent now as the tension grew and grew.

"There's always a hope with reasonable people."

"Opinions differ so much as to what is reasonable."

"Dora's not reasonable at present, anyhow."

Jeremy's mind had not travelled beyond his own predicament.

The contrast he pointed, the mocking memories he stirred, made his presence accentuate and embitter the strife, confirming Sibylla's despair, undermining even Grantley's obstinate self-confidence; while to Blake his example, however much one might smile at it, seemed to cry, "Courage!" He who would have the prize must not shrink from the struggle.

That night Sibylla sat long by her boy's cot. Little Frank slept quietly (he had been named after his godfather, Grantley's friend, that Lord Caylesham who was also the Fanshaws' friend), while his mother fought against the love and the obligation that bound her to him—a sad fight to wage. She had some arguments not lacking speciousness. To what life would he grow up in such a home as theirs! Look at the life the Courtland children led! Would not anything be better than that—any scandal in the past, any loss in present and future? She called to her help too that occasional pang which the helpless little being gave her, he the innocent cause and ignorant embodiment of all her perished hopes. Might not that come oftener? Might it not grow and grow till it conquered all her love, and she ended by hating because she might have loved so greatly? Horrible! Yes, but had it not nearly come to pass with one whom she had loved very greatly? It could not be called impossible, however to be loathed the idea of it might be. No, not impossible! Her husband was the child's father. Did he love him? No, she cried—she had almost persuaded herself that his indifference screened a positive dislike. And if it were not impossible, any desperate thing would be better than the chance of it. But for Grantley she could love, she could go on loving, the child. Then why not make an end of her life with Grantley—the life that was souring her heart and turning all love to bitterness? Grantley would not want the child, and, not wanting it, would let her have it. She did not believe that he would burden himself with the boy for the sake of depriving her of him. She admitted with a passing smile that he had not this small spitefulness—his vices were on a larger scale. She could go to Grantley and say she must leave him. No law and no power could prevent her, and she believed that she could take the boy with her.

Why not do that? Do that, and let honour, at least, stand pure and unimpeached?

The question brought her to the issue she had tried to shirk, to the truth she had sought to hide. Her love for the boy was much, but it was not enough, it did not satisfy. Was it even the greatest thing? As it were with a groan, her spirit answered, No. The answer could not be denied, however she might stand condemned by it. Of physical passion she acquitted herself—and now she was in no mood for easy self-acquittal; but there was the greater passion for intercourse of soul, for union, for devotion, for abandonment of the heart. These asked a responding heart, they asked knowledge, feelings grown to full strength, a conscious will, an intellect adult and articulate. They could be found in full only where she had thought to find them—in the love of woman and man, of fit man for fit woman, and of her for him. They could not be found in the love for her child. Christine Fanshaw had asked her if she could not be wrapped up in the baby. No. She could embrace it in her love, but hers was too large for its little arms to enfold. She cried for a wider field and what seemed a greater task.

And for what was wrong, distasteful, disastrous in the conclusion? She had the old answer for this. "It's not my fault," she said. It was not her fault that her love had found no answering love, had found no sun to bloom in, and had perished for want of warmth. Not on her head lay the blame. So far as human being can absolve human being from the commands of God or of human society, she declared that by Grantley's act she stood absolved. The contract in its true essence had not been broken first by her.

Ah, why talk? Why argue? There were true things to be said, valid arguments to use. On this she insisted. But in the end the imperious cry of her nature rang out over all of them and drowned their feebler voices. Come what might, and let the arguments be weak or strong, she would not for all her life, that glorious life Heaven had given her, beat her heart against the flinty wall.

CHAPTER XI

THE OLIVE BRANCH

Suzette Bligh was staying at the Courtlands'—that Suzette who had been at Mrs. Raymore's party, and was, according to Christine Fanshaw, a baby compared with Anna Selford, although ten years her senior. She had neither father nor mother, and depended on her brother for a home. He had gone abroad for a time, and Lady Harriet had taken her in, partly from kindness (for Lady Harriet had kind impulses), partly to have somebody to grumble to when she was feeling too conscientious to grumble to the children. This did happen sometimes. None the less the children heard a good deal of grumbling, and in Suzette's opinion knew far too much about the state of the household. They were all girls, Lucy, Sophy, and Vera, and ranged in age from thirteen to nine. They took to Suzette, and taught her several things about the house before she had been long in it; and she relieved Lady Harriet of them to a certain extent, thereby earning gratitude no less than by her readiness to listen to grumblings. Tom was little seen just now; he came home very late and went out very early; he never met his wife; he used just to look in on the children at schoolroom breakfast, which Suzette had elected to share with them, Lady Harriet taking the meal in her own room. It was not a pleasant house to stay in, but it was tolerably comfortable, and Suzette, not asking too much of life, was content enough to be there, could tell herself that she was of use, and was happy in performing an act of friendship.

Of course the question was how long Lady Harriet would stand it. The little girls knew that this was the question; they were just waiting for mamma to break out. They had not disliked their mother in the past; occasional fits of temper are not what children hate most. They endure them, hoping for better times, or contrive to be out of the way when the tempest arises. Cracks with any implement that came handy were the order of the day when the tempest had risen; but on calm days Lady Harriet had been carelessly indulgent, and, in her way, affectionate to the girls. But now the calm days grew rarer, the tempests more frequent and violent. Fear grew, love waned, hatred was on its way to their hearts. They had never disliked their father; though they had no great respect for him, they loved him. They regarded him with compassionate sympathy, as the person on whom most of the cracks fell; and they quite understood why he wanted to keep out of the way. This was a bond of union. They had even vague suspicions as to where he went in order to get out of the way. They had listened to their mother's grumbling; they had listened to the talk of the servants too. Suzette was no check on their speculations; they liked her very much, but they were not in the least in awe of her.

"Will you take us for a walk this afternoon, Miss Bligh?" asked Sophy, at schoolroom breakfast on Sunday. "Because Garrett says mamma's not well to-day, and we'd better not go near her—she's going to stay in her own room till tea-time."

"Of course I will, dears," said Suzette Bligh.

"Oh, there's nothing the matter with mamma, really," declared Lucy—"only she's in an awful fury. I met Garrett coming out of her room, and she looked frightened to death."

"Ah, but you don't know why!" piped up Vera's youthful voice in accents of triumph. "I do! I was in the hall, just behind the curtain of the archway, and I heard Peters tell the new footman. Papa was expected last night, and mamma had left orders that she should be told when he came in. But he didn't——"

"We know all that, Vera," Sophy interrupted contemptuously. "He sent word that he'd been called out of town and wouldn't be back till Monday."

"And the message didn't get here till twelve o'clock. Fancy, Miss Bligh!"

"Well, I'm glad you're going to take us to church, and not mamma, Miss Bligh."

"I hope she won't send for any of us about anything!"

"I hope she won't send for me, anyhow," said Vera, "because I haven't done my French, and——"

"Then I shouldn't like to be you if you have to go to her," said Lucy, in a manner far from comforting.

Lady Harriet was by way of teaching the children French, and had not endeared the language to them.

"I wonder what called papa away!" mused Sophy.

"Now, Sophy, that's no business of yours," said poor Suzette, endeavouring to do good. "You've no business to——"

"Well, I don't see any harm in it, Miss Bligh. Papa's always being called away now."

"Especially when mamma's——"

"I can't listen to any more, dears. Does the vicar or the curate preach in the morning, Lucy dear?"

"Don't know, Miss Bligh. I say, Vera, suppose you go and ask mamma to let us have some of that strawberry jam at tea."

"Yes, let's make her go," Sophy chimed in gleefully.

"You may do anything you like," declared Vera, "but you can't make me go—not if you kill me, you can't!"

The two elder girls giggled merrily at her panic.

Poor Suzette was rather in despair about these children—not because they were unhappy. On the whole they had not been very unhappy. Their mother's humours, if alarming, were also the cause of much excitement. Their father's plight, if sorrowful, was by no means wanting in the comic aspect. The suspense in which they waited to see how long Lady Harriet would stand it had a distinct spice of pleasure in it. But the pity of it all! Suzette's training, no less than her fidelity to Lady Harriet, inclined her to lay far the heavier blame on Tom Courtland. But she did have a notion that Lady Harriet must be very trying—and the more she listened to the children the more that idea grew. And, between them, the mother and the father were responsible for such a childhood as this. The children were not bad girls, she thought, but they were in danger of being coarsened and demoralised; they were learning to laugh where they had better have cried. It was Suzette's way to be rather easily shocked, and she was very much shocked at this.

They were just starting for their afternoon walk, when John Fanshaw arrived and found them all in the hall. He was an old friend—Vera's godfather—and was warmly welcomed. John was very cheery to-day; he joked with the children, and paid Suzette Bligh a compliment. Then Vera wanted to know why he had called:

"Because papa's not at home, you know."

"Never mind that, puss. I've come to see your mamma."

"You've come to see mamma!" exclaimed Lucy.

Glances were exchanged between the three—humorous excited glances; admiring amused eyes turned to John Fanshaw. Here was the man who was going to enter the lion's den.

"Shall we start, dears?" suggested Suzette Bligh apprehensively.

No notice was taken. Sophy gave John a direct and friendly warning.

"You'd better look out, you know," she said; "mamma's just furious because papa's not come back."

"But it's not my fault, pussie," said John. "She can't put me in the corner for it."

"Well, if you happen to be there——" began Lucy, with an air of experience.

"We must really start, Lucy dear," urged Suzette.

"What have you come to see mamma about?" asked Vera shrilly.

"To find out how to keep little girls in order," answered John, facetiously rebuking curiosity.

"I expect you've come about papa," observed Vera, with disconcerting calmness and an obvious contempt for his joke.

"I'm going to start, anyhow," declared poor Suzette. "Come along, dears, do!"

"Well, if there's a great row, Garrett'll hear some of it and tell us," said Sophy, consoling herself and her sisters as they reluctantly walked away from the centre of interest.

John Fanshaw's happiness was with him still—the happiness which Caylesham's cheque had brought. It was not banked yet, but it would be to-morrow; and in the last two days John had taken steps to reassure everybody, to tell everybody that they would be paid without question or difficulty, to scatter the cloud of gossip and suspicion which had gathered round his credit in the City. It was now quite understood that John's firm had weathered any trouble which had threatened it, and could be trusted and fully relied on again. Hence John's happy mind, and, a result of the happy mind, a sanguine and eager wish to effect some good, to bring about some sort of reconciliation and a *modus vivendi* in the Courtland family. His hopes were not visionary or unreasonable: he did not expect to establish romantic bliss there; a *modus vivendi* commended itself to him as the best way of expressing what he was going to suggest to Lady Harriet. In this flush of happy and benevolent feeling he was really glad that he had consented to undertake the embassy.

Lady Harriet liked John Fanshaw. She called him John and, though he did not quite venture to reciprocate the familiarity, he felt that it gave him a position in dealing with her. Also he thought her a very handsome woman; and since she was aware of this, there was another desirable element in their acquaintance. And he thought that he knew how to manage women—he was sure he would not have made such a bad job of it as poor Tom had. So he went in without any fear, and found justification in the cordiality of his welcome. Indeed the welcome was too cordial, inasmuch as it was based on an erroneous notion.

"You're the very man of all men I wanted to see! I was thinking of sending for you. Come and sit down, John, and I'll tell you all about it."

"But I know all about it," he protested, "and I want to have a talk to you."

"Nobody can know but me; and I believe you're the best friend I have. I want to tell you everything and take your advice how I'm to act."

Evidently she didn't suppose that he was in any sense an ambassador from her husband. He was to be her friend. John found it difficult to correct this mistake of hers.

"I'm at the end of my patience," she said solemnly. "I'm sure anybody would be. You know what's happening as well as I do, and I intend to put an end to it."

"Oh, don't say that! I—well, I'm here just to prevent you from saying that."

"To prevent me? You know what's happening? Do you know he's staying away from home again? What do the servants think? What must the children begin to think? Am I to be exposed to that?"

She looked very handsome and spirited, with just the right amount of colour in her cheeks and an animated sparkle in her eyes.

"Why, I could name the woman!" she exclaimed. "And so could you, I daresay?"

"Don't make too much of it," he urged. "We're not children. He doesn't really care about the woman. It's only because he's unhappy."

"And whose fault is it he's unhappy?"

"And because of that he's being foolish—wasting all his money too, I'm afraid."

"Oh, I've got my settlement. I shall be all right in case of proceedings."

"Now pray don't think of proceedings, Lady Harriet."

"Not think of them! I've made up my mind to them. I wanted to ask you how to set about it."

"But it would ruin his career; it would destroy his public position."

"I can't help that. He should have thought of that for himself."

"And then think of the girls!"

"Anything would be better than going on like this—yes, better for them too."

John saw that he must face an explanation of his embassy. He got up and stood on the hearthrug.

"I'm here as the friend of you both," he began.

The colour and the sparkle both grew brighter.

"Oh, are you?" said Lady Harriet.

"It comes to this. Tom's friends—I and one or two more—have been speaking seriously to him. We've got him to say that he's ready to drop—to drop what you very properly object to—and to make another effort to find a—a *modus vivendi.*"

"I'm glad he's got so much decent feeling! Only it comes rather late. He wants me to forgive him, does he?"

"I don't think we can put it quite so simply as that." John risked a timid smile. "There must be a give-and-take, Lady Harriet—a give-and-take, you know."

"Well?" She was relapsing into that dangerous stillness of hers. She was very quiet, but her eyes shone very bright. Tom Courtland would have known the signs, so would the girls.

"We've got him to say what I've told you; but there must be something from your side."

"What am I to do, John?" she asked, with deceptive meekness.

"Well, I think you might—well—er—express some regret that—that things haven't gone more harmoniously at home. You might hold out an olive branch, you know."

"Express regret?"

"Don't stand on a point of pride now. Haven't you sometimes been—well, a little exacting—a little quick-tempered?"

"Oh, you're in that old story, are you? Quick-tempered? Suppose I am! Haven't I enough to make me quick-tempered?"

"Yes, now you have. But what about the beginning?"

"Do you mean it was my fault in the beginning?"

"Don't you think so yourself? Partly, at all events?"

Lady Harriet took up a tortoiseshell paper-knife and played with it. Her eyes were set hard on John, who did not like the expression in them. He became less glad that he had undertaken the embassy.

"May a man desert and deceive his wife because she's a little quick-tempered?"

"No, no, of course not; that's absurd."

"It's what you're saying, isn't it?"

"We must look at it as men and women of the world."

"I look at it as a wife and a mother. Do you mean to say it was my fault in the beginning?"

John was losing patience; he saw that some plain speaking would be necessary, but his want of patience made it hard for him to do the plain speaking wisely.

"Well, yes, I do," he said. "In the beginning, you know. Tom's a good-natured fellow, and he was very fond of you. But you—well, you didn't make his home pleasant to him; and if a man's home isn't pleasant, you know what's likely to happen."

"And you're the friend I meant to send for!"

"I am your friend—that's why I venture to speak to you freely. There's no hope unless you both realise where you've been wrong. Tom acknowledges his fault and is ready to change his ways. But you must acknowledge yours and change too."

"What is my fault?"

John took a turn up and down the room.

"I must let her have it," he decided, as he came back to the hearthrug.

"You make everybody afraid of you with your lamentable fits of temper," he told her. "Tom's afraid of you, and afraid of what you might drive him into. Your children are afraid of you. Everybody's afraid of you. You make the house impossible to live in. You're even violent sometimes, I'm afraid, Lady Harriet."

If breaking a paper-knife in two be violence, she was violent then. She threw the pieces down on the table angrily.

"How dare you come to me and talk like this? I've done nothing; I've nothing to blame myself with. What I've had to put up with would have spoilt anybody's temper! Express regret? I shall do nothing of the kind. If that's what you came to ask, you can take your answer and go."

She was working herself up to the full tide of her rage. John's undertaking was quite hopeless now, but he would not recognise it yet; he determined to "let her have it" a little more still.

"Look at that!" he said, pointing to the broken paper-knife. "Just try to think what that—that sort of thing—means! What man can be expected to stand that? The state of things which has arisen is your fault. You've made no effort to govern your temper. You're reaping the fruit of what you've sown. If poor Tom had shown more firmness it might have been better."

"You'd have shown more firmness, I suppose?"

"Yes, I should; and I believe it would have done some good. You may suppose it gives me great pain to speak like this, but really it's the only way. Unless you realise how greatly you've been to blame, unless you determine to conquer this deplorable failing, there's no hope of doing any good."

She sat quiet for a moment or two longer with shining eyes, while John, now confident again and very masculine, developed the subject of the real truth about her. Then she broke out.

"You fool!" she said. "You silly fool! You come to me with this nonsense! You tell me you'd have shown more firmness! You tell me it's my fault Tom's gone off after this creature! Much you know about it all! Wonderfully wise you are! Leave other men's wives alone, and go back and look after your own, John."

"There's nothing that I'm aware of wrong in my house, Lady Harriet. We needn't bring that into the question."

"Oh, we needn't, needn't we? And there never was anything wrong, I suppose? I'm such a bad wife, am I? Other men have bad wives too."

"Do you attach any particular meaning to that?" he asked coldly, but rather uneasily.

"Do I attach——? Oh, what an idiot you are! You to come and lecture me as if I was a child! I may be anything you like, but I've never been what your wife was, John Fanshaw."

He turned on her quickly.

"What do you mean by that?"

"That's my affair."

"No, it isn't. You've dared to hint——"

"Oh, I hint nothing I don't know!"

"You shall give me an explanation of those words. I insist upon that."

"You'd better not," she laughed maliciously.

John was moved beyond self-control. He caught her by the wrist. She rose and stood facing him, her breath coming quick. She was in a fury that robbed her of all judgment and all mercy; but she had no fear of him.

"You shall withdraw those words or explain them!"

"Ask Christine to explain them!" she sneered. "What a fool you are! Here's a man to give lectures on the management of wives, when his own wife——" She broke off, laughing again.

"You shall tell me what you mean!"

"Dear me, you can't guess? You've turned very dull, John. Never mind! Don't make too much of it! Perhaps you were quick-tempered? Perhaps you didn't make her home pleasant? And if a woman's home isn't pleasant—well, you know what's likely to happen, don't you?"

Perspiration was on John Fanshaw's brow. He pressed her wrist hard.

"You she-devil!" he said. "Tell me what you mean, I say!"

"Oh, ask Christine! And if she won't tell you, I advise you to apply to Frank Caylesham, John."

"Is that true?"

"Yes, it is. Don't break my wrist."

"Caylesham!"

He held her wrist a moment longer, then dropped it, and looked aimlessly round the room.

She rubbed her wrist and glared at him with sullen eyes, her fury dying down into a malicious rancour.

"There, that's what you get from your meddling and your preaching!" she said. "I never meant to give Christine away, I never wanted to. It's your doing; you made me angry, and I hit out at you where I could. I wish to God you had never come here, John! Christine's one of the few women who are friendly to me, and now I've—— But you've yourself to thank for it."

He sank slowly into a chair; she heard him mutter "Caylesham!" again.

"If you know I've a quick temper, why do you exasperate me? You exasperate me, and then I do a thing like that! Oh, I'm not thinking of you; I'm thinking of poor Christine. I hate myself now, and that's your doing too!"

She flung herself into her chair and began to sob tempestuously. John stared past her to the wall.

"It's just what Tom's always done," she moaned through her sobs—"making me lose my temper, and say something, and then——" Her words became inarticulate.

Presently her sobs ceased; her face grew hard and set again.

"Well, are you going to sit there all day?" she asked. "Is it so pleasant that you want to stay? Do you still think you can teach me the error of my ways?"

From the first moment John Fanshaw had not doubted the truth of what she said. Things forced out by passion in that way were true. Her stormy remorse added a proof—a remorse which did not even attempt retractation or evasion. And his memory got to work. He knew now why Christine had been so reluctant to go to Caylesham. There were things back in the past too, which now became intelligible—how that acquaintance had grown and grown, how constant the companionship had been, one or two little things which had seemed odd, and then how there had been a sudden end, and they had come to see very little of Caylesham, how neither of them had seen him for a long while, till John had sent Christine to borrow fifteen thousand pounds.

"For God's sake, go!" she cried.

He rose to his feet slowly, and her fascinated eyes watched his face. His eyes were dull, and his face seemed to have gone grey. He asked her one question:

"How long ago?"

"Oh, all over years ago," she answered, with an impatient groan, drumming her fingers on the arms of her chair.

He nodded his head in a thoughtful way.

"Good-bye, Lady Harriet," he said.

"Good-bye, John." Suddenly she sprang up. "Stop! What are you going to say to Christine?"

He looked bewildered still.

"I don't know. Oh, really I don't know! My God, I never had any idea of this, and I don't know! I can't—can't realise it all, you know—and Caylesham too!"

"Are you going to tell her I told you?"

"I don't know what I'm going to do, Lady Harriet—I don't know."

"Ah!"

With a cry of exasperation she turned away and sat down in her chair again.

"Good-bye," he muttered, and slouched awkwardly out of the room.

She sat on where she was, very still, frowning, her hand holding her chin, only her restless eyes roving about the room. She was like some handsome, fierce, caged beast. There she sat for close on an hour, thinking of what she was and of what she had done—of how he had shown her the picture of herself, and of how, from malice and in her wrath, she had betrayed Christine. Once only in all this time her lips moved; they moved to mutter:

"What a cursed woman I am!"

CHAPTER XII

IMAGES AND THEIR WORK

By this time young Walter Blake had not only clearly determined what he wanted and meant to do, he had also convinced himself of his wisdom and courage in wanting and meaning to do it. He was not blind, he declared, to the disagreeable and distressing incidents. There were painful features. There would be a scandal, and there would be an awkward and uncomfortable period—a provisional period before life settled down on its new and true lines. That was inevitable, since this case—the case of himself and Sibylla—was exceptional, whereas laws and customs were made for the ordinary cases. He did not condemn the laws and customs wholesale, but he was capable of seeing when a case was exceptional, and he had the wisdom and the courage to act on what he perceived. He even admitted that very few cases were really exceptional, and took the more credit for perceiving that this one really was. He did not take Grantley into account at all, neither what he was nor what he might do. Grantley seemed to him negligible. He confined his consideration to Sibylla and himself—and the exceptional nature of the case was obvious. He was a prey to his ready emotions and to his facile exaltation. Desires masqueraded as reasons, and untempered impulses wore the decent cloak of a high resolve. If he could have put the case like that to himself, it might not have seemed so plainly exceptional.

He was never more convinced of his wisdom and courage than when he listened to Caylesham's conversation. They were racecourse and club acquaintances, and had lunched together at Caylesham's flat on the Sunday on which John Fanshaw went to Lady Harriet's house in order to show her the error of her ways. Blake glowed with virtue as he listened to his friend's earthly views and measured his friend's degraded standards against his own.

"The one duty," said Caylesham, somewhat circumscribing the domain of morality, as his habit was, "is to avoid a row. Don't get the woman into a scrape." From gossiping about Tom Courtland they had drifted into discussing the converse case. "That really sums it all up, you know." It was a chilly day, and he warmed himself luxuriously before the fire. "I don't set myself up as a pattern to the youth, but I've never done that, anyhow."

Virtuous Blake would have liked to rehearse to him all the evil things he had done—the meanness, the hypocrisy, the degradation he had caused and shared; but it is not possible to speak quite so plainly to one's friends.

"Yes, that's the gospel," he said sarcastically. "Avoid a row. Nothing else matters, does it?"

"Nothing else matters in the end, I mean," smiled Caylesham, good-naturedly conscious of the sarcasm and rather amused at it. "As long as there's no row, things settle down again, you see. But if there's a row, see where you're left! Look what you've got on your hands, by Jove! And the women don't want a row either, really, you know. They may talk as if they did—in fact they're rather fond of talking as if they did, and they may think they do sometimes. But when it comes to the point, they don't. And what's more, they don't easily forgive a man who gets them into a row. It means too much to them, too much by a deal, Blake."

"And what does it mean when there's no row?"

"Oh, well, there, of course, in a certain sense you have me," Caylesham admitted with a candid smile. "If you like to take the moral line, you do have me, of course. I was speaking of the world as we know it; and I don't suppose it's ever been particularly different. Not in my time anyhow, I can answer for that."

"You're wrong, Caylesham, wrong all through. If the thing has come to such a point, the only honest thing is to see it through, to face it, to undo the mistake, to put things where they ought to have been from the beginning."

"Capital! And how are you going to do it?"

"There's only one way of doing it."

Caylesham's smile broadened; he pulled his long moustache delicately as he said:

"Bolt?"

Blake nodded sharply.

"Oh, my dear boy!"

He laughed in a gentle comfortable way, and drew his coat right up into the small of his back.

"Oh, my dear boy!" he murmured again.

Nothing could have made Walter Blake feel more virtuous and more courageous.

"The only honest and honourable thing," he insisted—"the only self-respecting thing for both."

"You convert the world to that, and I'll think about it."

"What do I care about the world? It's enough for me to know what I think and feel about it. And I've no shadow of doubt."

His face flushed a little and he spoke rather heatedly.

"I wouldn't interfere with your convictions for the world, and, as I'm a bachelor, I don't mind them." He was looking at Blake rather keenly now, wondering what made the young man take the subject so much to heart. "But if I were you I'd keep them in the theoretical stage, I think."

He laughed again, and turned to light a cigar. Blake was smoking too, one cigarette after another, quickly and nervously. Caylesham looked down on him with a good-humoured smile. He liked young Blake in a half-contemptuous fashion, and would have been sorry to see him make a fool of himself out and out.

"I'm not going to ask you any questions," he said, "though I may have an idea about you in my head. But I'm pretty nearly twenty years older than you, I fancy, and I've knocked about a good bit, and I'll tell you one or two plain truths. When you talk like that, you assume that these things last. Well, in nine cases out of ten, they don't. I don't say that's nice, or amiable, or elevated, or anything else. I didn't make human nature, and I don't particularly admire it. But there it is—in nine cases out of ten, you know. And if you think you know a case that's the tenth——"

This was exactly what Blake was sure he did know.

"Yes, what then?" he asked defiantly.

"Well," answered Caylesham slowly, "you be jolly sure first before you act on that impression. You be jolly well sure first—that's all." He paused and laughed. "That's not moral advice, or I wouldn't set up to give it. But it's a prudential consideration."

"And if you are sure?"

"Sure for both, I mean, you know."

"Yes, sure for both."

"Well, then you're in such a bad way that you'd better pack up and go to the Himalayas or somewhere like that without an hour's delay, because nothing else'll save you, you know."

Blake laughed rather contemptuously.

"After all, there have been cases——"

"Perhaps—but I don't like such long odds."

"Well, we've had your gospel. Now let's hear how it's worked in your case. Are you satisfied with that, Caylesham?"

He spoke with a sneer that did not escape Caylesham's notice. It drew another smile from him.

"That's a home question—I didn't question you as straight as that. Well, I'll tell you. I won't pretend to feel what I don't feel; I'll tell you as truly as I can." He paused a moment. "I've had lots of fun," he went on. "I've always had plenty of money; I've never had any work to do; and I took my fun—lots of it. I didn't expect to get it for nothing, and I haven't got it for nothing. Sometimes I got it cheap, and sometimes, one way and another, it mounted to a very stiff figure. But I didn't shirk settling day; and if there are any more settling days, I won't shirk them if I can help it. I don't think I've got anything to complain about." He put his cigar back into his mouth. "No, I don't think I have," he ended, twisting the cigar between his teeth.

What a contempt for him young Blake had! Was ever man so ignorant of his true self? Was ever man so sunk in degradation and so utterly unconscious of it? Caylesham could look back on a life spent as his had been—could look back from the middle-age to which he had now come, and find nothing much amiss with it! Blake surveyed his grovelling form from high pedestals of courage and of wisdom—absolutely of virtue pure and undefiled.

"Nothing very ideal about that!"

"Good Lord, no! You wanted the truth, didn't you?"

"Well, I suppose I thought like that once—I was contented with that once."

"You certainly used to give the impression of bearing up under it," smiled Caylesham. "But things are changed now, are they?"

"Yes, thank God! Imagine going on like that all your life!"

Caylesham threw himself into a chair with a hearty laugh.

"Now we've gone just as far as we can with discretion," he declared.

"What do you mean by that?" asked Blake rather angrily.

"Well, I'm not an idiot, am I, as well as a moral deformity?"

"I don't know what you are talking about."

"Yes, but I know what you've been talking about, Blake. I know it all except one thing—and that I don't propose to ask."

Blake rose with a sulky air and tossed away the end of his cigarette.

"And what's that?"

"The lady's name, my boy," said Caylesham placidly.

This talk was fuel to Blake's flame. It showed him the alternative—the only alternative. (He forgot that suggestion about the Himalayas, which did not, perhaps, deserve to be forgotten.) And the alternative was hideous to him now—hideous in its loss of all nobility, of all the ideal, in its cynically open-eyed acceptance of what was low and base. He would have come to that but for Sibylla. But for him, even Sibylla—Sibylla mated to Grantley—might have come to it also. It was from such a fate as this that they must rescue one another. One wise decision, one courageous stroke, and the thing was done. Very emotional, very exalted, he contrasted with the life Caylesham had led the life he and Sibylla were to lead. Could any man hesitate? With a new impetus and with louder self-applause he turned to his task of persuading Sibylla to the decisive step.

Part of the work was accomplished. Sibylla had cast Grantley out of her heart; she disclaimed and denied both her love and her obligation to him. The harder part remained: that had been half done in her vigil by the baby's cot. But it was ever in danger of being undone again. A cry from the boy's lips, the trustful clinging of his arms from day to day, fought against Blake. Only in those gusts of unnatural feeling, those spasms of repugnance born of her misery, was she in heart away from the child. On these Blake could not rely, nor did he seek to, since to speak of them brought her to instant remorse; but, left to be brooded over in silence, they might help him yet. He trusted his old weapons more—his need of her love and her need to give it. Caylesham's life gave him a new instance and added strength to his argument. He told her of the man, though not the man's name, sketching the life and the state of mind it brought a man to.

"That was my life till you came," he said. "That was what was waiting for me. Am I to go back to that?"

He could attack her on another side too.

"And will you lead the sort of life that man has made women live? Is that fit for you? You can see what it would do to you. You would get like what he's like. You would come down to his level. First you'd share his lies and his intrigues, perforce, while you hated them. Gradually you'd get to hate them less and less: they'd become normal, habitual, easy; they'd become natural. At last you'd see little harm in them. The only harm or hurt at last would be discovery, and you'd get cunning in avoiding that. Think of you and me living that life—aye, till each of us loathed the other as well as loathing ourselves. Is that what you mean?"

"Not that, anyhow not that," she said in a low voice, her eyes wide open and fixed questioningly on him.

"If not that and not the other, what then? Am I to go away?" But he put Caylesham's alternative in no sincerity. He put it to her only that she might thrust it away. If she did not, he would spurn it himself. "And where should I go? Back to where I came from—back to that life?"

She could not tell him to go away, nor to go back to that life. She sat silent, picturing what his life and what her own life would be through all the years, the lifelong years, when even the boy's love would be bitterness, and she could have a friend in nobody because of the great sad secret which would govern all her life.

"I can't tell you. I can't decide to-day."

Again and again she had told him that, fighting against the final and the irrevocable.

But Blake was urgent now, wrought up to an effort, very full of his theories and his aspirations, full too of a rude natural impatience which he called by many alien names, deceiving his very soul that he might have his heart's desire, and have it without let or hindrance. He launched his last argument, a last cruel argument, whose cruelty seemed justice to a mind absorbed in its own selfishness. But she had eyes for no form of selfishness save Grantley's. To ask all did not seem selfishness to her; it was asking nothing or too little that she banned.

"You've gone too far," he told her. "You can't turn back now. Look what you've done to me since you came into my life. Think what you've taught me to hope and believe—how you've let me count on you. You've no right to think of the difficulties or the distress now. You ought to have thought of all that long ago."

It was true, terribly true, that she ought to have thought of all that before. Was it true that she had lost the right to arrest her steps and the power to turn back?

"You're committed to it. You're bound by more than honour, by more than love. You'll be untrue to everybody in turn if you falter now."

It was a clever plea to urge on a distracted mind. Where decision is too difficult, there lies desperate comfort in being convinced that it is already taken, that facts have shaped it, and previous actions irrevocably committed the harassed heart.

"You've made my love for you my whole life. You knew you were doing it. You did it with full knowledge of what it meant. I say you can't draw back now."

He had worked himself up to a pitch of high excitement. There was nothing wanting in his manner to enforce his words. His case was very exceptional indeed to him; and so it seemed to her—believing in his love because of the love she had herself to give, yearning to satisfy the hunger she had caused, to make happy the life which depended utterly on her for joy.

The long fight, first against Grantley, latterly against herself, had worn and almost broken her. She had no power left for a great struggle against her lover now. Her weariness served his argument well. It cried out to her to throw herself into the arms which were so eagerly ready for her. One way or the other anyhow the battle must be ended, or surely it would make an end of her.

But where was an end if she stayed with Grantley? That life was all struggle, and must be so long as it endured. Who could find rest on a flinty wall?

She was between that monstrous image she had made of her husband, and the shape which Blake presented to her as himself—far more alluring, not a whit less false. But for the falseness of either she had no eyes.

"I want your promise to-day," he said. "Your promise I know you will keep."

He had become quiet now. There was an air of grave purpose about him. The excitement and ardour had done their work with her; this succeeding mood, or manner (for he had lost all distinction between what he felt and what he made himself seem to feel), had its place, and was well calculated to complete his victory.

"I will send you my answer to-night," she said.

"It means all that I am—everything in the world to me. Remember that."

And he urged her no more, leaving with her these simple sincere-sounding words to plead for him.

That was what the answer meant to him. What would it mean to Grantley Imason? She asked herself that as she sat silent opposite to him at dinner. It chanced that they were alone, though of late she had schemed to avoid that. And to-night she could not speak to him, could say nothing at all, though his raised brows and satirical glance challenged her. Things might be uncomfortable, but why lose either your tongue or your manners, Grantley seemed to ask. You might have a grievance (Oh, real or imaginary, as you please!) against your husband, but why not converse on topics of the day with the gentleman at the other end of the table? He seemed to be able to do his part without any effort, without any difficulty to avoid open war, and yet never to commit himself to any proposition for peace. All through the years, thought Sibylla, he would go on suavely discussing the topics of the day, while life went by, and love and joy and all fair things withered from the face of the earth.

The servants disappeared, and Grantley's talk became less for public purposes.

"I wonder how old John has got on with Harriet Courtland!" he said in an amused way. "He was uncommonly plucky to face her. But, upon my word, the best thing from some points of view would be for him to fail. At least it would be the best if old Tom wasn't such a fool. But as soon as Tom sees a chance of getting rid of one woman, he saddles himself with another."

"Could he have got rid of Lady Harriet?"

"They might have arranged a separation. As it is, there'll be an open row, I'm afraid."

"Still if it puts an end to what's intolerable——?" she suggested, as she watched him drinking his coffee and smoking his cigarette with his delicate satisfaction in all things that were good.

"A very unpleasant way out," he said, shrugging his shoulders.

"Would you have endured what Mr. Courtland couldn't?"

He smiled across at her; the sarcastic note was strong in his voice as he asked:

"Do you think me an impatient man? Do you think I've no power of enduring what I don't like, Sibylla?"

She flushed a little under his look.

"It's true," he went on, "that I endure vulgarity worst of all; and Harriet Courtland's tantrums are very vulgar, as all tantrums are."

"Only tantrums? Aren't all emotions, all feelings, rather vulgar, Grantley?"

He thought a smile answer enough for that. It is no good arguing against absurd insinuations, or trying to show them up. Let them alone; in time they will die of their own absurdity.

"Grantley, would you rather I went away? Don't you find life unendurable like this?"

"I don't find it pleasant," he smiled; "but I would certainly rather you didn't go away. If you want a change for a few weeks, I'll endeavour to resign myself."

"I mean, go away altogether."

"No, no, I'm sure you don't mean anything so—— Forgive me, Sibylla, but now and then your suggestions are hard to describe with perfect courtesy."

She looked at him in a wondering way, but made no answer; and he too was silent for a minute.

"I think it would be a good thing," he went on, "if you and Frank betook yourselves to Milldean for a few weeks. I'm so busy that I can see very little of you here, and country air is good for nerves."

"Very well, we'll go in a day or two. You'll stay here?"

"Yes, I must. I'll try to get down now and then, and bring some cheerful people with me. Blake will come sometimes, I daresay. Jeremy won't till he's rich and famous, I'm afraid."

In spite of herself, it flashed across her that he was making her path very easy. And she wondered at the way he spoke of Blake, at his utter absence of suspicion. Her conscience moved a little at this.

"Yes, I'm sure you'll be better at Milldean," he went on; "and—and try to think things over while you're there."

It was his old attitude. He had nothing to think over—that task was all for her. The old resentment overcame her momentary shame at deceiving him.

"Are they so pleasant that I want to think them over?"

"I think you know what I mean; and in this connection I don't appreciate repartee for its own sake," said Grantley wearily, but with a polite smile.

A sudden impulse came upon her. She leant across towards him and said:

"Grantley, have you seen Frank to-day?"

"No, I haven't to-day."

"I generally go and sit by him for a little while at this time when I'm free. Did you know that?"

"I gathered it," said Grantley.

"You've never come with me, nor offered to."

"I'm not encouraged to volunteer things in my relations with you, Sibylla."

"Will you come with me now?" she asked.

She herself could not tell under what impulse she spoke—whether it were in hope that at the last he might change, in the hope of convincing herself that he would never change. She watched him very intently, as though much hung on the answer that he gave.

Grantley seemed to weigh his answer too, looking at his wife with searching eyes. There was a patch of red on his cheeks. Evidently what she had said stirred him, and his composure was maintained only by an effort. At last he spoke:

"I'm sorry not to do anything you ask or wish, but as matters are, I will not come and see Frank with you."

"Why not?" she asked in a quick half-whisper.

His eyes were very sombre as he answered her.

"When you remember that you're my wife, I'll remember that you're the mother of my son. Till then you are an honoured and welcome guest in this house or in any house of mine."

Their eyes met; both were defiant, neither showed a hint of yielding. Sibylla drew in her breath in a long inhalation.

"Very well, I understand," she said.

He rose from his chair.

"You're going upstairs now?" he suggested, as though about to open the door.

"I'm going, but I'm not going upstairs to-night," she answered as she rose. "I shall go and write a letter or two instead."

He bowed politely as she passed out of the room. Then he sat down at the table again and rested his head on both his hands. It took long—it took a very long while. She was hard to subdue. Hard it was too to subdue himself—to be always courteous, never more than permissibly ironical, to wait for his victory. Yet not a doubt crossed his mind that he was on the right track, that he must succeed in the end, that plain reason and good sense must win the day. But the fight was very long. His face looked haggard in the light as he sat alone by the table and told himself to persevere.

And Sibylla, confirmed in her despair, bitterly resentful of the terms he had proposed, seeing the hopelessness of her life, fearing to look on the face of her child lest the pain should rend her too pitilessly, sat down and wrote her answer to Walter Blake. The answer was the promise he had asked.

The images had done their work—hers of him and his of her—and young Blake's fancy picture of himself.

CHAPTER XIII

THE DEAD AND ITS DEAD

"Well, have you managed to amuse yourself to-day?" asked Caylesham, throwing himself heavily on a sofa by Tom Courtland, and yawning widely.

He had dropped in at Mrs. Bolton's, after dinner. Tom had spent the day there, and had not managed to amuse himself very much, as the surly grunt with which he answered Caylesham's question sufficiently testified. He had eaten too much lunch, played cards too long and too high, with too many "drinks" interspersed between the hands; then had eaten a large dinner, accompanied by rather too much champagne; then had played cards again till both his pocket and his temper were the worse. There had been nothing startling, nothing lurid about his day; it had just been unprofitable, boring, unwholesome. And he did not care about Mrs. Bolton's friends—not about Miss Pattie Henderson, nor about the two quite young men who had made up the card-party. His face was a trifle flushed, and his toothbrushy hair had even more than usual of its suggestion of comical distress.

"Been a bit dull, has it?" Caylesham went on sympathetically. "Well, it often is. Oh, I like our friend Flora Bolton, you know, so long as she doesn't get a fit of nerves and tell you how different she might have been. People should never do that. At other times she's a good sort, and just as ready to ruin herself as anybody else—nothing of the good old traditional harpy about her. Still perhaps it works out about the same."

It certainly worked out about the same, as nobody knew better than Tom Courtland. He was thinking now that he had paid rather high for a not very lively day. The only person he had won from was Miss Henderson, and he was not sure that she would pay.

"Must spend your time somewhere," he jerked out forlornly.

"A necessity of life," Caylesham agreed; "and it doesn't make so much difference, after all, where you do it. I rather agree with the fellow who said that the only distinction he could see between—well, between one sort of house and the other sort—was that in the latter you could be more certain of finding whisky and soda on the sideboard in the morning; and now I'm hanged if that criterion isn't failing one! Whisky and soda's got so general."

The card-party at the other end of the room was animated and even a little noisy. Mrs. Bolton was prone to hearty laughter. Miss Henderson had a penetrating voice, and usually gave a little shriek of delight when she won. The two young men were rather excited. Caylesham regarded the whole scene with humorous contempt. Tom Courtland sat in moody silence, doing nothing. He had even smoked till he could smoke no more. He had not a pleasure left.

Presently Miss Pattie threw down her cards and came across to them. She was a tall ladylike-looking young woman; only the faintest trace of Cockney accent hung about the voice. She sat down by Caylesham in a friendly way.

"We hardly ever see you now," she told him. "Are you all right?"

"All right, but getting old, Pattie. I'm engaged in digging my own grave."

"Oh, nonsense, you're quite fit still. I say, have you heard about me?"

"Lots of things."

"No, don't be silly. I mean, that I'm going to be married?"

"No, are you, by Jove? Who's the happy man?"

"Georgie Parmenter. Do you know him? He's awfully nice."

"I know his father. May I proffer advice? Get that arrangement put down in writing. Then at the worst it'll be worth something to you."

Miss Pattie was not at all offended. She laughed merrily.

"They always said you were pretty wide-awake, and I believe it!" she observed. "He'll have ten thousand a year when his father dies."

"In the circumstances you mention he won't have a farthing a year till that event happens, I'm afraid, Pattie. A man of strong prejudices, old Sir George."

"Well, I'm sure I've got letters enough to——"

"That's all right. I shall watch the case with interest."

He yawned again and rose to his feet.

"Tom's pretty dull, isn't he?" asked Miss Pattie with a comical pout.

"Yes, Tom's pretty dull, certainly."

"I'm sleepy," said Tom Courtland.

"So am I. I shall go home," and Caylesham walked off to bid the lady of the house good-night.

The lady of the house came into the hall and helped him on with his coat. It appeared that she wanted to have a word with him—first about the wisdom of backing one of his horses, and secondly about Tom Courtland. Caylesham told her on no account to back the horse, since it wouldn't win, and waited to hear what she had to say about Tom.

"I'm distressed about him, Frank," she said. "You know I do like Tom, and I never saw a man so down in the mouth." Her face was rather coarse in feature and ruddy in tint, but kindly and good-natured; her concern for Tom was evidently quite genuine. "What a devil that wife of his must be!"

"She has her faults. Perhaps we have ours. Be charitable, Flora."

"Oh, you can be as sarcastic as you like. Heaven knows I don't mind that! But I'm worried to death about him, and about what she'll do. And then there's the money too. I believe he's hard up. It's very tiresome all round. Oh, I don't care much what people say of me, but I don't want to go through the court again, if I can help it."

"Which of the two courts do you refer to?" he asked, as he buttoned his coat. "Bankruptcy or——?"

"Either of them, Frank, you old fool!" she laughed.

"Send him back to his wife. You'll have to soon, anyhow—when the money's gone, you know. Do it now—before those two men come and stand opposite to see who goes in and out of the house."

"But the poor chap's so miserable, Frank; and I like him, you see."

"Ah, I can't help you against honest and kindly emotions. They're not part of the game, you know."

"No, they aren't; but they come in. That's the worst of it," sighed Mrs. Bolton. "Well, good-night, Frank. We shall get through somehow, I suppose."

"That's the only gospel left to this age, Flora. Good-night."

He had not been able to help poor Mrs. Bolton much; he had not expected to be able to. That things could not be helped and must be endured was, as he had hinted, about the one certain dogma of his creed. The thing then was to endure them as easily as possible, to feel them as little as one could either for oneself or for other people. There was Flora Bolton's mistake, and a mistake especially fatal for a woman in her position. She would probably have been much happier if she had not been just as ready to ruin herself as she was to ruin anybody else—if she had, in fact, been the old traditional harpy through and through.

In truth it was not the least use distressing himself about Tom Courtland. Still he was rather worried about the affair, because Tom, again, was not thoroughly suited to the part he was now playing. Plenty of men were, and they demanded no pity. But poor old Tom was not. He could not spend his money without thinking about it; he could not do things without considering their bearings and their consequences; he could not forget to-morrow. He had none of the qualifications. His tendencies were just as little suited to the game as were Flora Bolton's honest and kindly emotions. Tom was pre-eminently fitted to distribute the bacon at the family breakfast and to take the children for their Sunday walk; to work away at his politics in a solid undistinguished way, and to have a good margin in hand when he came to make up the annual budget of his household. But Lady Harriet had prevailed to rout all these natural tendencies. A remarkable woman, Lady Harriet!

Suddenly Caylesham saw ahead of him a figure which he recognised by the light of the street lamps. It was John Fanshaw going in the direction of his home. It was rather late for John to be about, and Caylesham's first idea was to overtake him and rally him on his dissipated hours. He had already quickened his steps with this view, when it struck him that, after all, he would not accost John. It might look as if he wanted to be thanked for his loan. Anyhow John would feel bound to thank him, and he did not desire to be thanked. So he fell behind, and followed in that fashion till his road home diverged from John's. But the encounter had turned his thoughts in a new direction. Tom and Lady Harriet were no more in his mind, nor was Flora Bolton. He was thinking about Christine as he turned into his flat, and being sorry that she had felt so much dislike to taking the money from him. It was all right that she should dislike it, but still he was sorry for her. Christine's small dainty face had always kept so much of the child about it that it had the power of making him very sorry for her just because she was sorry for herself, apart from any good reasons at all. His feelings, however well schooled they might be, would not easily have faced a great distress on Christine's face. But as he got into his dressing-gown the sombre hue passed from his mind. Either there was nothing to worry about, or it was no good worrying. Everybody would get through somehow.

John Fanshaw pursued his homeward way heavily and slowly. He had gone straight from the Courtlands' house to the quietest of his clubs, and sent a messenger to his wife to say that he was going to dine there, and that she was not to sit up in case he were late back. He wanted to think the thing over, and he did not want to see Christine. He could not even try to doubt; Harriet Courtland's passionate taunt and her passionate remorse—her remorse most of all—had carried, and continued to carry, absolute conviction; and memory, hideously active and acute, still plied him with confirmatory details. After these six years he remembered things which at the time he could hardly have been said to know; they emerged from insignificance and took on glaring meanings. How had he been so blind? Yet he had been utterly blind. He had had many quarrels with Christine—over money and so forth; he had blamed her for many faults, sometimes justly, sometimes not. This one thing he had never suspected—no, nor dreamed of her. It seemed to shatter at one blow all his conceptions of their married life. He was confused and bewildered at the thought of it—so it cut away foundations and tore up deep-grown roots. Christine do that? Orderly, cool, sarcastic, self-controlled Christine! She seemed the old Christine no more. He did not know how to be towards her. He would hate to have her near him—she would not seem to be his.

He found himself wishing he had known of the thing at the time. It would have been a fearful shock, but by now he would have grown used to it. Something would have been done, or, if nothing had been done, the thing would have become ancient history—a familiar fact to which they would have adjusted themselves. It was awful to be told of it now, when it seemed too late to do anything, when the wound was so old, and yet the smart of it so fresh!

And she had been such a good wife—yes, on the whole. Their bickerings had been only bickerings, and he had often been as much to blame as she. On the whole, she had been such a loyal friend and such a comforting companion. He had liked even her acid little speeches—on the whole. He had always thought her not very demonstrative perhaps, but very true—true as steel. Cold perhaps—he had felt that and resented it sometimes—but always true. He had never had a misgiving as to that in all his married life.

When he got home he went straight to his study and sat down at his writing-table. It was one o'clock, and Christine would have gone to bed—he was glad of that. He made an effort to collect his mind, because the immediate question was not of what Christine had done, not of the blow to him, not whether he wanted to see Christine or even could bear to see her, not of the change all his life and all his ideas had undergone. There was plenty of time to think of all that later on. He must think now of the other thing—of how he stood and of what he was going to do.

He took out his keys and unlocked the despatch-box that stood on the table. After pausing to take a drink of whisky and water, he opened the upper drawer and drew forth Caylesham's cheque for fifteen thousand pounds. It had been post-dated to the Monday—it was already Monday now. In nine hours it was to have been credited to his account at the bank, ready to answer his obligations, to discharge his commitments, to reassure his creditors, to drive away all the clouds which had obscured the fair fame of his firm. Caylesham's cheque and Grantley's were to have been salvation. Grantley's alone was no use. And Caylesham's—he held it in his fingers and looked at it with a poring scrutiny.

Twice he reached for an envelope, in the mind to send it back—to send it back either with the truth or with a lie. Once he took hold of either end, as though to tear it across. But a paralysis fell on his fingers. How should he send back, how should he destroy, that all-potent little slip of paper? It meant credit, honour, comfort, peace—perhaps even life. His imagination pictured two scenes—going to the City, to his office, next day, with that slip of paper; and going without it. The sketch was enough—his thoughts were too busy to fill in the details.

One picture meant a gradual ascent from out of all his troubles; the other, a fall into a gulf of calamity unfathomable. His hands refused to destroy or to send back the cheque.

But if he kept it, used it, owed salvation to it—what would that mean? The question bewildered him. He could not make out what that would mean as regarded either himself or Caylesham or Christine—least of all what it would mean as regarded Christine. He was duly conscious that the act would be in some sort a condonation. A condonation going how far? Imposing what attitude and what course of conduct on him? How far would it condition his bearing towards Caylesham, how far affect his estimate of himself? Above all, how far dictate his relations to Christine? He knew very well what would come of destroying the cheque or of sending it back. He could not reason out what he would stand committed to if he kept and used it.

Ah, this horrible question could not have arisen, either, if he had known of the thing at the time. It was fearful to be told of it now.

"It's a terrible situation for a man to be placed in—terrible!" he said aloud.

The thought flashed across his mind that he could pretend not to know. He could give Lady Harriet a caution; he could tell her he attached no importance to her words; she would take the hint and be glad. Caylesham would suspect nothing. He could keep the cheque. And Christine? Could he make that pretence to Christine?

He was sitting shrunk low into his chair, the cheque still in his fingers, when the door opened softly, and Christine came in. She had heard him open and close the front door, and had wondered why he did not come upstairs. His delay, taken with his staying out all the evening, made her ask whether anything had happened. She was in a white dressing-gown, which she had thrown on when she got out of bed, and little slippers of white fur. She looked very small, very dainty, very childish; her hair was like a child's too, brushed smoothly away from the forehead.

"Why, John, what's kept you so late? And what are you doing here?"

She came some steps towards him, before she saw what it was that he held in his hand. Then she smiled, saying:

"You're gloating over that cheque, you foolish man!"

He raised dull slow eyes to her.

"Yes, I've got it here," he muttered.

Christine walked to the rug; his table was on one side of the fireplace, and she was within five or six feet of him.

"What are you doing with it?" she asked, with an impatient ring in her voice. She did not enjoy the sight of the cheque, and had hoped to be able by degrees to forget it.

"It's dated for Monday. I ought to pay it in in the morning."

"Well, why not? Of course you'll pay it in." A sudden hope rose in her. "Nothing's occurred to make it unnecessary?"

He shook his head heavily, and laid the paper down on the table.

"No, nothing," he said, and then his eyes rested on her again.

"John, aren't you well?" she asked.

Her littleness and her childishness made no appeal to his tender feelings. Their contrast with what she had done, with the way she had deceived and betrayed him, roused all his repulsion again, and with it came now a man's primitive fierce anger. It was impossible for him to pretend not to know.

"Go away!" he said in a thick harsh whisper. "Go to bed—I don't want you. I want to be alone."

Her eyes seemed to grow large; a fearful apprehension dawned in them.

"What's the matter? What have I done?" she asked, trying to summon her wits, wondering at what point she was attacked. Already her thoughts were on Caylesham, but she did not yet see whence suspicion could have come.

He gave her no clue. His eyes had fallen to the cheque again; he kept shuffling his legs about and fidgeting with his short stiff beard.

"Ah," she cried suddenly, "you went to Harriet Courtland's to-day! Has she said something about me? John, you wouldn't believe what she said against me?"

He made no answer. In truth she needed none. She knew Harriet Courtland, who had been her friend and in her confidence. It had not been considered safe to send Raymore, because Harriet would have taunted him about his erring son. She knew what Harriet, blind with rage, had found to taunt John Fanshaw with. She was hardly conscious of resentment against the traitor. It was all too hopeless for that, and it all seemed too inevitable. From the moment she had agreed to go to Caylesham for the money, her forebodings had told her that calamity would come. That was opening the grave. Now the dead bones had come to life. She felt as though she could not struggle against it—could not protest nor deny. She did not see how anybody could believe her denial.

"Why haven't you gone? I told you to go. In God's name, go!" he growled threateningly. "Leave me alone, I tell you."

She gathered her dressing-gown closer round her. She felt as though the cold struck through it to her body. She felt utterly prostrated—and, oh, so terribly, so helplessly sorry for poor old John! She hated leaving him alone, and wished there was somebody else there to console him. She made an advance towards him, holding out her hands.

"Don't come here! Don't come near me!" he said in a low voice.

She drew back; her eyes were on him and full of pity. Now the cheque came into her mind.

"And that?" she whispered.

"I think I shall kill you if you don't go," he said, with a sudden unsteadiness in his voice.

"Oh, I'll go!" she murmured disconsolately. "I'll leave you alone." She put her hands up before her face and gave a choking sob. "It's all no use now."

She began to walk across the room, her face covered in her hands, her dressing-gown trailing on the floor behind her. But when she had got half-way, she turned on him in a fit of weak petulance.

"I didn't want to go to him; I tried not to. I did all I could to avoid going to him. It was you who insisted. You made me go. How could I help it? I hated it! And now——" She came a step towards him, and her voice changed to a very humble sad pleading: "It's very long ago, dear John, many years ago. It was all over many years ago."

He did not speak. He motioned her away with his hand; her appeal did not seem to reach him at all. For all he did, he might not have heard it. With a long sigh she turned away, and walked unsteadily to the door. When she reached it, she turned again, and looked at him. He was putting the cheque back in the despatch-box with awkward trembling hands. She went slowly up to her room and sat down before the dying embers of the fire there.

John would send back the cheque! He must send it back now; it would be a fearful thing to keep it, knowing what he did. And if he sent it back, all that happened then would be on her head! He mustn't send it back! She started up once in a panic, ready to rush down and implore him to keep it—implore him to commit the baseness of keeping it. No, she could not do that. If she were never to speak with him again, her last word ought to be to beseech him to send it back. But to send it back was ruin. Between the remorseless alternatives of calamity and degradation her mind oscillated in helpless indecision.

Through long hours of the night John Fanshaw wrestled with himself; and when at last he crawled up to his dressing-room, flung off his coat and waistcoat, put on his slippers, and stretched himself exhausted on his bed, he declared that he could come and had come to no conclusion—that it was too hard for him. He was trying to deceive himself. There was a conclusion which he would not own, which had crept and insinuated itself into his mind, while he struggled against it and denied it to himself.

He could not send back nor destroy the cheque. Still his hands had refused that office. He could not face the City without it, could not endure the calamity and the ruin which the loss of it would mean. But neither would he face that fact and what it meant—that he was to become a party to the transaction, to recognise, to condone, and to pardon. He had no right to keep his anger, his indignation, the repulsion which made him drive Christine from his presence, if he were her accomplice. If he kept and used the cheque, what right had he to moral indignation, to a husband's just anger, to a true man's repulsion at the shame and the deceit? Yet he would not give up these things. He hugged them in his heart, even while he hugged the idea of the cheque, and all the virtue of the cheque, in his mind. He would be saved, but he would not touch the hand that saved him. That conclusion did not bear thinking of. But conclusions which do not bear thinking of are none the less thought out; they take possession of the protesting mind; they establish themselves there. Then they seek sophisms, excuses, pleas for themselves; they point to the good results which spring from them. Time and familiarity rob them of some of their ugliness; they grow habitual; they govern actions, shape lives, and condition character. John Fanshaw would have it both ways—salvation by his wife's sin, and horror at it.

So Harriet Courtland would have love and loyalty, though she bridled not her evil rage. So Mrs. Bolton would think honest and kindly emotions could flourish in a life like hers. So Grantley Imason asked all her inmost life and love of another, though the lock was kept turned on his own. So Sibylla would give the rein to impulse, and persuade herself that she performed a duty. So young Blake would seek to be made good by the enjoyment of his darling sin. Only dainty little Christine looked open-eyed at the pleasure she had won and at the ruin it had made. She saw these things clearly as she sat sleepless through the night. And when she watched her husband start for his work the next morning, though he had told her nothing, though not a word had passed between them, she knew well that Caylesham's cheque was in his pocket and would find its way to the bank that day. John would have his salvation—with or without its price.

CHAPTER XIV

FOR HIS LOVE AND HIS QUARREL

Jeremy Chiddingfold had established himself in London greatly to his satisfaction. He had hired a bedroom in Ebury Street, an attic, and had made friends with one Alec Turner, a journalist, who lodged in the same house. Alec Turner took him often to the Metropolitan Radical Club, and had proposed him for membership. Here he could eat at moderate charges, play chess, smoke, and argue about all things in heaven (assuming heaven) and earth (which, anyhow, was full of matter for argument). And at Ebury Street he was not only within easy reach of the Imasons in Sloane Street, but equally well in touch with the Selfords in Eccleston Square, and the Raymores in Buckingham Gate. A third-class on the Underground Railway from Victoria carried him to Liverpool Street, whence he proceeded to the dyeing-works near Romford, in Essex. For the dyeing-works project was taking shape. Jeremy had been down to Romford several times to look round and see what the processes were like. He had digested the article on dyeing in the *Encyclopædia Britannica*, and had possessed himself of the *Dictionary of Dyeing* and the *Manual of Dyeing*. His talk both at the Metropolitan Radical Club and at the houses he frequented was full of the learning and the terminology of dyeing—things you dyed, and things you dyed the things with, and the things you did it in, and so forth. He fascinated Eva Raymore by referring airily (and at this stage somewhat miscellaneously) to warm vats, and copperas, and lime vats, to insoluble basic compounds, to mordants and their applications, to single and double muriate of tin. You could go so far on the article without bothering about the *Dictionary* or the *Manual* at all; but then Eva did not know that, and thought him vastly erudite. In fact Jeremy was in love with dyeing, and rapidly reconsidered his estimate of the Beautiful—the Beautiful as such, even divorced from Utility—in the scheme of nature and of life. On Alec Turner's recommendation he read Ruskin and William Morris, and thought still better of the Beautiful.

He soon made himself at home both at the Selfords' and at the Raymores', dropping in freely and casually, with an engaging confidence that everybody would be glad to see him and pleased to allow him to deposit his long angular body in an armchair, and talk about dyeing or the Social Armageddon. He was, however, interested in other things too—not so much in pictures, but certainly in dogs. He had country lore about dogs and their diseases, and so won Mrs. Selford's respect. He found Anna Selford's keen mind an interesting study, and delighted to tease the pretty innocence of Eva Raymore. In neither house was there a young man—no son at the Selfords', and the Raymores' house was empty of theirs; and Jeremy, in his shabby coat, with his breezy jollity and vigorous young self-assertion, came like a gust of fresh wind, and seemed to blow the dust out of the place. Mrs. Raymore, above all, welcomed him. He went straight to her heart; she was for ever comparing and contrasting him with her own boy so far away—and only just the inevitable little to his disadvantage. Jeremy, in his turn, though unconsciously, loved the atmosphere of the Raymores' house—the abiding sense of trouble, hard to bear, but bravely borne, and the closeness of heart, the intimacy of love which it had brought. Being at the Selfords' amused him; but being at the Raymores' did more than that.

And what of his broken heart? Anna Selford had heard the story and asked him once in her mocking way.

"You seem so very cheerful, Mr. Chiddingfold!" said she.

Jeremy explained with dignity. His heart was not broken; it had merely been wounded. Not only did he consider it his, and any man's, duty to be cheerful, but as a fact he found no difficulty in being cheerful, occupied as he was with the work of life, and sustained by a firm purpose and an unshaken resolve.

"Only I don't care to talk about it," he added, by which he meant, really, that he did not care to talk about it to persons of a satirical turn. Mrs. Raymore could get him to talk about it very freely, while to Eva he would sometimes (usually for short times) be so moody and melancholy as to excite an interest of a distinctly sentimental nature. It is to be feared that, like most lovers, Jeremy was not above a bit of posing now and then. He was having a very full and happy life, and, without noticing the fact, began gradually to be more patient about the riches and the fame.

None the less, affairs were in train. Selford's working partners were disposed to be complaisant about Jeremy and the dyeing-works; they were willing to oblige Selford, and found themselves favourably impressed by the young man himself. But business is business. They could give him a pittance for ever, no doubt. If he wanted that very different thing—an opening—other considerations came to the front. Good openings are not lightly given away.

In fine, Jeremy could come and try his hand at a nominal salary. If he proved his aptitude, they would be willing to have him for a junior partner; but in that case he must put five thousand pounds into the business. The sum was not a large one to ask, they said; and with all their good opinion of Jeremy and all their desire to oblige Selford, they could not, in justice to themselves, their wives, and their families, put the figure any lower.

It was rather a shock to Jeremy, this first practical illustration of the pervading truth that in order to get money you must have some first. He might give all he had in the world, and not realise five thousand pounds. He went to tea at the Raymores' that evening with his spirits dashed. He had consulted Alec Turner, but that young man had only whistled, implying thereby that Jeremy might whistle for the money too. The journalistic temperament was not, Jeremy felt, naturally sympathetic; so he laid the question before Mrs. Raymore.

To her it was the opening of the sluice-gates. She was full of maternal love, dammed up by distance and absence. She was tender and affectionate towards Eva, but her love for her daughter was pale and weak beside her feeling for her only son; and now a portion of the flow meant for far-off Charley was diverted to Jeremy. She loved and could have wept over his brave simplicity, his sincere question as to how he could speedily make five thousand pounds. He was not a fool; he knew he could not break the bank at Monte Carlo, or write a play or a novel, or get the desired sum thereby if he did; but he had the great folly which clings to men older than he was—the belief that blind impartial fortune may show special divine favour. Kate Raymore smiled and sighed.

"Have you no friends who would guarantee it—who would advance it? You could pay interest, and pay off the capital gradually," she suggested.

That was not at all Jeremy's idea.

"No, I don't want to do that. I don't want to be indebted to anybody."

"But it's a pity to let the chance slip, from a feeling of that sort," she urged.

"Besides there's nobody in our family who ever had such a lot of money to spare," said Jeremy, descending to the practical. He sighed too, and acknowledged the first check to his ardent hopes, the first disillusionment, in the words: "I must wait."

When a man says that he must wait, he has begun to know something of the world. The lesson that often he must wait in vain remains behind.

"But I shall find out some way," he went on (the second lesson still unlearnt). "I've got a fortnight to give my answer in. They'll keep it open for me till then."

Eva came in, with her large learning eyes, and her early charming girl's wonder at the strength and cleverness of the young men she liked. In a very few minutes Jeremy was confident and gay, telling her how he had the prospect of a partnership in quite a little while. Oh, yes, a junior partnership, of course, and a minor share. But it ought to be worth four or five hundred a year anyhow—yes, to start with. And what it might come to—in vigorous hands, with new blood, new intellect, new energy—well, nobody could tell. Mr. Thrale's casks and vats were not really—as a potentiality of growing rich beyond the dreams of avarice—comparable to Jeremy's vats and mordants and muriates. Eva was wonderfully impressed, and exclaimed, in childish banter:

"I hope you'll know us still, after you're as rich as that?"

Jeremy liked that. It was just the sort of feeling which his wealth was destined to raise in Dora Hutting. Meanwhile, pending the absence and obduracy of Dora, it was not unpleasant to see it reflected in Eva's wondering eyes. Mrs. Raymore listened and looked on with a fixed determination to lose no time in telling Grantley Imason that for a matter of five thousand pounds the happiness of a life—of a life or two—was to be had. The figure was often cheaper than that, of course; less than that often meant joy or woe—far less. Witness Charley in Buenos Ayres, over youthful folly and a trifle of a hundred and fifty! But Grantley was rich—and she did not know that he had recently lent John Fanshaw fifteen thousand pounds.

In requital for services rendered at the Metropolitan Radical, Jeremy had introduced his friend, Alec Turner, to the Selfords. Alec had come up to town from the staff of a provincial journal, and found very few houses open to him in London, so that he was grateful. He had a native, although untrained, liking for art, and could talk about pictures to Selford, while Jeremy talked about dogs to Mrs. Selford; and both the young men sparred with Anna, whose shrewd hits kept them well on their defence. Alec went about his avocations in a red tie, a turned-down collar, and lively mustard-coloured clothes. A dress suit he assumed reluctantly when he was sent to report the speeches of prosperous Philistine persons at public dinners. He hated prosperous Philistine persons, especially if their prosperity (and consequent Philistinity) came from art or letters, and delighted in composing paragraphs which should give them a little dig. He was, however, not really ill-natured, and would not have hurt the prosperous persons seriously, even if he could have; he was anxious to declare that neither he nor anybody else could, in fact, hurt them seriously, owing to the stupidity of the public—which was incalculable. He was a decided assistance to Jeremy in enlivening the Selford household and in keeping Anna's wits busy and bright.

"I suppose nothing would induce you to be successful?" she said to him with malicious simplicity.

"Success for me means something quite different," Alec explained. "It lies in influencing the trend of public opinion."

"But the public's hopelessly stupid! It seems to me rather foolish to spend your time trying to influence hopelessly stupid people."

Jeremy chuckled. He did not see how Alec was going to get out of that.

"I spoke of the bulk. There is a small intelligent minority on whom one can rely."

"If you can rely on them already, why do they want influencing?" objected Anna.

"On whom one can rely for a hearing and for intelligent appreciation, Miss Selford."

"Then the fewer people who care what you say, the more successful you really are?"

"That's hardly the way I should put it——"

"No, I don't suppose you would," interrupted Anna. "But it comes to that, doesn't it, Jeremy?"

"Of course it does," agreed Jeremy. "The fact is, writing about things is all rot. Go and do something—something practical."

Dyeing was doing something practical.

"Oh, yes, go into business, of course, and get rich by cheating. Trading's only another name for cheating."

"Well, you're right there for once," said Anna.

"Right?" cried Jeremy fiercely. "Well, then, why isn't it cheating when he" (he pointed scornfully at Alec) "charges a ha'penny for his beastly opinion about something?"

"Oh, it's not for me to say! You must ask Mr. Turner that."

In fact the discussions were of a most spirited order, since everybody was always quite wrong, and each in turn could be rapidly and ignominiously refuted, the other two uniting in a warm but transient alliance to that end.

This young and breezy society was good for Selford and for his wife too. It gave them something to think about, and did not leave each so much time to consider the unreasonableness of the other. Tiffs became less frequent, the false sentimentalism of their reconciliations was less in demand; and as they watched Anna's deftness and brightness, they began to ask whether they had been as proud of her as they ought to be.

"She's got brains, that girl of ours," said Selford, nodding his head complacently.

"And a taking manner, don't you think, Dick?"

"Those boys find her attractive, or it looks like it, anyhow!"

"Of course she's not exactly pretty, but I do think she's rather distinguished somehow."

"Your daughter would be sure to be that, my dear Janet," he remarked gallantly.

"No, I really think she's more like you," insisted Janet amiably. "I must make an effort" (Mrs. Selford was fond of that phrase) "and take her out into society more. I don't think we're quite giving her her chance."

"Ah, you've begun to think of match-making!" he cried in playful reproof.

But it pleased him highly to think that he had, after all, an attractive daughter. He took much more notice of her than he had been used to take, and Mrs. Selford eyed her with critical affection. Decidedly the increase of human interest, as opposed to artistic and canine, was a good influence in the Selford household.

Anna soon saw how her position had improved. She was not demonstrative about it, but she appreciated it. She was also sharp enough to use it. The next time an invitation to a party came, she refused to go unless she might have a frock of her own choosing.

"I won't go if I'm to look a guy!" she said.

There was a battle over that; a battle between her and Mrs. Selford, and a tiff between father and mother to boot. For Selford was with Anna now. They won the day, and Anna, with a cheque in her pocket, went off to consult Christine Fanshaw, nursing in her heart that joy which only the prospect of being dressed really just as you'd like to be dressed seems able to excite.

"Merely a malicious desire to cut out the other girls," commented Alec loftily.

"I really don't think you ought to talk about dress," retorted Anna, eyeing the mustard suit.

But when Anna appeared in the frock which Christine had sedulously and lovingly planned, she carried all before her. She was most undoubtedly distinguished.

"Well, I suppose you've come to an age when that charming simplicity which used to suit you so well must give way to something more stylish," even Mrs. Selford admitted, capitulating and marching out—but with the honours of war.

Grantley Imason was rich; yet fifteen thousand pounds is a solid sum of money. To put that sum at John Fanshaw's disposal had not caused him serious inconvenience, but it had entailed a little contriving. To lay out another five thousand in Jeremy's service would involve more contriving, and the return of the money rested, of necessity, in a distant and contingent future. Nevertheless, when Kate Raymore suggested that the happiness of a life should be secured, he found the proposition attractive. He was a man lavish of money and appreciative of all the various pleasures of giving it away—both those of a more and those of a less self-regarding order. He enjoyed both the delight of the recipient and the sense of his own generosity and his own power. He would like Jeremy to be indebted to him for the happiness of his life—of course that was an exaggerated way of putting it, but it was a telling exaggeration. He also liked Jeremy very much for his own sake. And it would be altogether a handsome thing to do—under present circumstances a peculiarly handsome thing. For Sibylla had left him and gone down to Milldean, accompanied by the boy, without a word of friendship or a hint of reconciliation; and Jeremy's welfare was very dear to his sister. To help Jeremy, and thereby prepare for her the pleasure of seeing Jeremy prosper, to do this secretly, to have it as a private merit and a hidden claim on her, was an idea which appealed strongly to Grantley. In his imaginings she was to discover what he had done in the future, but not till after their reconciliation. Would it not have an effect then? One effect it was to have was, in plain words, to make Sibylla feel ashamed; but Grantley did not put it so simply or so nakedly as that—that would have been to recognise the action as almost pure revenge. He blinked that side of it, and gave prominence to the other sides. But that side was there among the rest, and he would suffer wrong at her hands with the more endurance the greater were the obligations she was under to him. His love for her and his quarrel with her joined hands to urge him. Commanding Kate Raymore to respect his desire for secrecy, he undertook to consider the matter. But his mind was really made up; and since the thing was to be done, it should be done liberally and splendidly. He had lent his money to Fanshaw, as Caylesham had surmised, with a very satisfactory prospect of repayment; to Jeremy he was ready to lend it on no security, careless about repayment, because he loved Sibylla and because he had so grievous a quarrel against her. It was all a part of his broad and consistent plan of conquering her by his unchanging patience, unchanging love, unchanging persistence in being just what he had always been to her from the beginning, however sore a trial her unreasonableness and her vagaries might put him to. This generosity to Jeremy would be a fine example of his chosen attitude, a fine move in the strategy on which he had staked the ultimate success of his campaign against Sibylla.

"If I decide to do it, I'll tell Sibylla myself, at my own time, and in my own way—remember that," he said to Kate Raymore.

She had an idea that things had not been going quite smoothly, and nodded in a wise fashion. She was picturing a pretty scene of sentiment when Grantley confessed his generosity. Of the real state of his mind she had no idea, but her own conception of the case was enough to ensure her silence.

Grantley went to work quietly, saying nothing to Jeremy, approaching the working partners through Selford, learning what they thought of Jeremy, not letting them suppose that the sum required was lightly to be come by, or was considered a small one, making, like a good man of business, the best bargain that he could for the object of his bounty. These negotiations took some days, and during those days Jeremy's heart lost something of its buoyancy, though nothing of its courage. London was having its effect on his receptive mind—the crowd, the stress, the push, the competition. Courage and brains enough to rise by? Perhaps, but not enough to rise by quickly. A walk about the streets, a look at the newspapers, the talk at the Metropolitan Radical, all taught him that. Wait and work—wait and work! That was what they all said—and they none of them said that it was easy to lay your hands on five thousand pounds.

The light of truth began to glimmer through those folds of young self-confidence. Jeremy grew sober; he was no more so gay and so assured in talking with Eva Raymore. He allowed himself to dwell less on that mythical return to Milldean with fame and riches. Now and then, it must be confessed, he had to brace himself up lest his very courage should falter. He contrived to keep it; but with it there came now a feeling new to Jeremy—a humility, a sense that he was, after all, as other men were, and neither by natural endowment nor by any rare caprice of fortune to be different from them or to find his life other than theirs. He too was not above the need of a helping hand; for want of it he too might have to tread very long and very dreary paths before he made much impression on the hill which he had set out to climb so gaily, and with so little provender for the journey. In such a mood as this he was as incapable of expecting any sudden interposition of outside aid as of refusing it when it came. He would protest, he would declare that he must refuse, but refuse in the end he could not. The fierce jealousy of his independence was cooled by his new experience of the world.

He heard first of what was being done from one of the partners down at Romford. The matter was practically concluded, he was told; in two years' time he was to have the junior partnership, and the share allotted to him at that date would be somewhat larger in consideration of the stipulated capital being paid immediately—it happened to be wanted for an extension of the buildings. Jeremy threw over work for that day, and hurried back to London—to refuse. But all the way he was thinking of the incredible difference this benevolent interposition would make.

He found Grantley in his study after lunch. The deed regulating the arrangements between the partners on the one side and Jeremy and himself on the other was before him. A look at Jeremy's face told him that Jeremy knew.

"I—I can't take it, you know," Jeremy blurted out.

"You can't escape the obligations Sibylla has brought on you by marrying me," smiled Grantley.

"Of course Sibylla's been at you—told you she couldn't be happy unless——"

"Nothing of the kind. Sibylla knows nothing about it; and, what's more, she isn't to know till I choose to tell her—till I choose, not you—that's part of the bargain, Jeremy."

Jeremy sat down. Anxious to avoid a formal talking-over of the matter, Grantley got up and lit a cigarette.

"Then why have you done it?" asked Jeremy.

Grantley shrugged his shoulders.

"Of course it's the one thing in the world for me; but—but I wanted to do it for myself, you know." Grantley still smiled on him, with a touch of mockery now. "Yes, well, I know I couldn't." He looked at Grantley in a puzzled way. "What makes it worse," he went on, "is that I've been doing you an injustice in a kind of way. I knew you were always kind and—and jolly, but somehow I thought you were a fellow who wouldn't put himself out very much for—for anybody else."

"I am not putting myself out. I like it."

"Planking down five thousand, and not knowing when you'll get it back, if you ever do? If you like that for its own sake, it's rather a rare taste."

"Now don't jaw any more," said Grantley with friendly impatience. "I was just going to sign the deed when you came in—I should have done it by now, but I must have a witness, and I didn't want to ring Thompson up from his dinner. We'll ring for him now."

"I'm not an ass," said Jeremy. "I don't think that because a man marries a woman he's bound to provide for her family—or to like them either."

"You grow in worldly wisdom."

"Yes, I fancy I do. I know a bit more about myself too. I might have worked ten years and not got this money."

"Oh, thank my forefathers! I've not worked ten years, or ten minutes either, for you!" His back had been to Jeremy. He turned round now as he said slowly, "You may consider it as a thanksoffering for my happiness with Sibylla."

"And why isn't she to know?"

"I like it better that way for the present. I'm entitled to make that condition."

Jeremy went back to his defence of himself against himself.

"A week ago I—I'd have backed myself to make it somehow. But—well, one soon learns how devilish hard it is to get what one wants. What a conceited young idiot you must have thought me when we used to talk down at Milldean!"

"You were always an excellent companion. Let's ring for Thompson and execute the deed."

Jeremy could not refuse, and could not yet consent. Grantley stood smoking airily and looking at him with a whimsical smile. Then the door opened and the butler came in, unsummoned.

"Ah, the fates decide!" exclaimed Grantley with a laugh. "Where's a pen, Jeremy?"

"For you, sir," said Thompson, holding out a salver with a letter on it.

"Oh!" Grantley laid down his pen, took the letter, and sat down at the writing-table. "Wait a minute; I want you to witness something for me," he said to the butler.

Thompson stood in serene immobility. His thoughts were far away, engrossed in a discussion he had been having with the groom as to the "form" of that same horse of Caylesham's about which Mrs. Bolton had wanted to know. Jeremy sat making up his mind to endure being helped, and poignantly remorseful about the view he had taken of Grantley. The view was earnestly disclaimed now; the help seemed very fine and wonderful. He did so want hope, scope, a chance, a start, and that all his talk of what he would do should not come to naught. In turn Dora, Eva, and Anna passed through his mind, each bringing her own influence to bear, giving him a new picture of the future. And why refuse? If ever a gift had been freely, grandly offered, this was. Would it not be even churlish to refuse? Reasons or no reasons, his heart and his hand went out instinctively; he could not refuse the beginning of all things.

Giving his head a restless little jerk as at last he accepted this decision, he chanced to turn his eyes on Grantley's face. Their attention was caught and arrested by it. There was something strange there. The cheeks were rather pale, the jaw set rigidly. Grantley read his letter with a curious engrossment—not hurriedly nor off-hand, as a man generally reads when other business is at a standstill till he reaches the end. He turned back, it seemed, once or twice, to look at another sentence again. Jeremy could not stop staring at him. Even Thompson awoke to the fact that he was being kept waiting a long while, and that the groom would probably finish the beer and go away, leaving their important discussion unfinished and the proper odds unascertained.

Grantley had recognised Christine Fanshaw's large irregular handwriting, and had expected nothing more serious than an invitation to dinner. But he was not reading an invitation to dinner now.

"I have just heard from Sibylla—from Milldean. She encloses a letter for you, which she says I am to send on to you *to-morrow*. She insists that I am not to send it before; and if I won't do as she asks, I am to burn it. You are *not* to have it to-day. I cannot disobey her in this; but she says nothing about my telling you she has sent a letter; the only thing is that I must not deliver it to you till to-morrow. I had no idea you had let her go down to Milldean alone. How could you let her do this? There is one other thing I must say to you. Walter Blake was to have dined here to-night. This morning he wired excuses, saying he was going for a cruise in his yacht. You must consider what that means. I beg you not to wait for the letter, but to go to Milldean *this afternoon*. Say nothing of having heard from me. Just go as if it was by accident; say you got your work done sooner than you expected, or anything you like; but go. I believe you'll be sorry all your life if you don't go. Let nothing stop you, for your own sake, and still more for *hers*.—C.F."

That was the letter; the sentence he had turned back to re-read was the one in which Walter Blake's movements were mentioned.

Grantley looked across to Jeremy.

"Have you heard from Sibylla since she went to Milldean?" he asked.

"Not a line. But she doesn't write much to me."

Again Grantley looked at the paper. Then he laid it down and took up his pen.

"Now for the deed," he said, and drew it to him.

He signed. Thompson fulfilled the formality for which he was required, and then left them alone. Jeremy did not break out into new thanks. That unexplained something in Grantley's face forbade him.

"I can only say that I'll try to justify your extraordinary kindness," he said soberly.

Grantley nodded absently, as he rose and put Christine's letter into the fire. It was better there—and there was no danger that he would forget the contents.

"I say, there's no bad news, is there?" Jeremy could not help asking.

"No news at all, good or bad," answered Grantley, as he held out his hand. "Good-bye and good luck, Jeremy."

Jeremy took his hand and gripped it hard, emotion finding a vent that way. Grantley returned the pressure more moderately.

"Remember, under no circumstances, a word about it to Sibylla!" he said.

"I give you my honour."

"Good."

He released Jeremy's hand and turned away. He had much self-control, but he could not be sure of what was showing on his face.

Jeremy had his great good-fortune, but his joy was dashed. Grantley looked like a man whom heavy calamity finds unprepared.

"All the finer of him to sign the deed then and there," Jeremy muttered as he left the house. "Whatever has happened, he didn't forget his word to me."

But it had not been of Jeremy or of his word that Grantley had been thinking when he signed. His signature was a defiance of his wife and of his fate.

CHAPTER XV

IN THE TEETH OF THE STORM

An instinct of furtiveness, newly awakened by the suggestion of Christine Fanshaw's letter, had led Grantley Imason to send no word of his coming. He hired a fly at the station, and drove over the downs to Milldean. It was a wild evening. A gale had been blowing from the south-west all day, and seemed to be increasing in violence. A thick rain was driven in sharp spats against the closed windows. The old horse toiled slowly along, while the impatient man chafed helplessly inside.

At last he stopped at Old Mill House and dismissed the carriage. Mrs. Mumple's servant-girl came to the door, and said her mistress was up at his house, and was, she thought, to stay there all night. Grantley nodded, and began to trudge up the hill. He had no thought but to seek and find Sibylla. It was now between seven and eight, and dusk had fallen.

He saw a light in the dining-room windows. He walked into the hall and took off his hat. A servant saw him and ran to help him. Saying briefly that he would want some dinner, he went into the dining-room. Mrs. Mumple sat there alone over a chop.

"You come home, Mr. Imason!" she exclaimed. "Sibylla didn't expect you, did she?"

"No, I didn't expect to come. I didn't think I could get away, and it wasn't worth wiring. Where is Sibylla?"

"How unlucky! She's gone away—to Fairhaven. She didn't expect you. She's to sleep the night there."

He came to the table and poured himself out a glass of sherry. He was calm and quiet in his manner.

"To sleep at Fairhaven? Why, who's she going to stay with?"

"Mrs. Valentine. You know her? She lives by the church—a red house with creepers."

Mrs. Valentine was, as he knew, an old, but not an intimate, acquaintance. He shot a keen glance at Mrs. Mumple's simple broad face.

"I'm here to look after baby. But of course since you've come——"

"No, no, you stay here; and go on with your dinner. They'll bring something for me directly."

He pulled up a chair and sat down.

"To sleep at Mrs. Valentine's? Has she often done that before when I've been away?"

"She used to as a girl sometimes, Mr. Imason; but no, never lately, I think—not since she married."

There were no signs of disturbance or distress about Mrs. Mumple. Grantley sat silent while the servant laid a place for him and promised some dinner in ten minutes.

"Has Sibylla been all right?"

"Oh, yes! A little fretful the last day or two, I think. But Mr. Blake came over from Fairhaven yesterday, and she had a nice walk with him; and she was with baby all the morning."

"All the morning? When did she go to Fairhaven?"

"I think it was about three o'clock. It's a terrible evening, Mr. Imason."

"Very rough indeed."

"The wind rose quite suddenly this morning, and it's getting worse every minute."

Grantley made no answer. After a pause the old woman went on—

"I've got some news."

"News have you? What news?"

He was suddenly on the alert.

She glanced at the door to make sure the servant was not within hearing.

"Very great news for me, Mr. Imason. My dear husband's to come home three months sooner than I thought. I got a letter to say so just after Sibylla started."

"Oh, really! Capital, Mrs. Mumple!"

"It's only a matter of six months now. You can't think what I feel about it—now it's as near as that. I haven't seen him for hard on ten years. What will it be like? I'm full of joy, Mr. Imason; but somehow I'm afraid too—terribly afraid. The thought of it seems to upset me, and yet I can't think of anything else."

Grantley rubbed his hand across his brow. Old Mrs. Mumple's talk reached him dimly. He was thinking hard. This sleeping at Mrs. Valentine's sounded an unlikely story.

Mrs. Mumple, in her turn, forgot her chop. She leant back in her chair, clasping her fat hands in front of her.

"We shall have to pick up the old life," she went on, "after seventeen years! I was thirty-five when he left me, and nearly as slight as Sibylla herself. I'm past fifty now, Mr. Imason, and it's ten years since I saw him; and he's above sixty, and—and they grow old soon in there. It'll be very different, very different. And—and I'm half afraid of it, Mr. Imason. It's terribly hard to pick up a life that's once been broken."

The servant brought in Grantley's dinner, and Mrs. Mumple pretended to go on with her chop.

"Nurse said I was to tell you Master Frank is sleeping nicely," the servant said to Mrs. Mumple, as he placed a chair for Grantley.

That was a strange story about Mrs. Valentine.

"We must have patience, and love on," said Mrs. Mumple. "He's had a grievous trial, and so have I. But I don't lose hope. All's ready for him—his socks and his shirts and all. I'm ahead of the time. I've nothing to do but wait. These last months'll seem very long, Mr. Imason."

Grantley came to the table.

"You're a good woman, Mrs. Mumple," he said.

She shook her head mournfully. He looked at the food, pushed it away, and drank another glass of sherry.

"Don't think I've no sympathy with you, but—but I'm worried."

"Nothing gone wrong in town, I hope, Mr. Imason?"

"No."

He stood there frowning. He did not believe the story about Mrs. Valentine. He walked quickly to the bell and rang it loudly.

"Tell them to saddle Rollo, and bring him round directly."

"You're never going out on such a night?" she cried.

"I must"; and he added to the surprised servant, "Do as I tell you directly."

"Where are you going?" she asked wonderingly.

"I'm going to Mrs. Valentine's."

"But you've no cause to be anxious about Sibylla, Mr. Imason; and she'll be back to-morrow."

Grantley was convinced that she, at least, was innocent of any plot. Simple sincerity spoke on her face, and all her thoughts were for herself and her dearly cherished fearful hopes.

"I must see Sibylla on a matter of urgent business to-night," he said.

"It'll be hardly safe up on the downs," she expostulated.

"It'll be safe enough for me," he answered grimly. "Don't sit up for me; and look after the baby." He smiled at her kindly, then came and patted her hand for a moment. "Yes, it would be hard to pick up a life that's once broken, I expect," he said.

She looked up at him with a sudden apprehension in her eyes. His manner was strangely quiet; he seemed to her gentler.

"There, I mean nothing but what I say," he told her soothingly. "I must go and get ready for my ride."

"But, Mr. Imason, you'll take something to eat first?"

"I can't eat." He laughed a little. "I should like to drink, but I won't. Good night, Mrs. Mumple."

Ten minutes later he was walking his horse down the hill to Milldean, on his way to Fairhaven. But he had little thought of Mrs. Valentine; he had no belief in that story at all. It served a purpose, but not the purpose for which it had been meant. What it did was to remove the last of his doubts. Now he knew that Christine's suggestion was true. He was going to Fairhaven not to find Sibylla at Mrs. Valentine's, but to seek Sibylla and Blake he knew not where.

He thought not much of Sibylla. He had taught himself to consider his wife incalculable—a prey to disordered whims, swept on by erratic impulses. This whim was more extraordinary, more disorderly, more erratic than any of the others; but it was of the same nature with them, the same kind of thing that she had done when she determined to hold herself aloof from him. This blow had fallen entirely and utterly unforeseen, but he acknowledged grimly that it had not been unforeseeable. He thought even less of young Blake, and thought of him without much conscious anger. The case there was a very plain one. He had known young Blake in the days when aspirations did not exist, and when the desire to be good was no part of his life. He took him as he had known him then, and the case was very simple. Whatever an attractive woman will give, men like Blake will take, recking of nothing, forecasting nothing, careless of themselves, merciless to her whom they are by way of loving. In regard to Blake the thing had nothing strange in it.

Here too it was unexpected, but again by no means unforeseeable.

No, nothing had been unforeseeable; and in what light did that fact leave him? What flavour should that give to his meditations? For though he rode as quickly as he could against the gale and the rain which now blinded and scorched his eyes, his mind moved more quickly still. Why, it set him down as a fool intolerable—as the very thing he had always laughed at and despised, as a dullard, a simpleton, a dupe. He could hear the mocking laughter and unashamed chuckling, he could see the winking eyes. He knew well enough what men had thought of him. They had attributed to him successes with women; they had joked when he married, saying many husbands would feel safer; they had liked him and admired him, but they had been of opinion that he wanted taking down a peg. How they would laugh to think that he of all men had made such a mess of it, that he had let young Blake take away his wife—young Blake, whom he had often chaffed for their amusement or instructed for their entertainment! Imason had got a pretty wife, but he couldn't keep her, poor old boy! That would be the comment—an ounce of pity to a hundredweight of contempt, and—yes, a pound of satisfaction. And it would be all true. Somehow—even allowing for Sibylla's vagaries and unaccountable whims, he could not tell how—somehow he had been a gross dupe, a blockhead blindly self-satisfied, a dullard easily deluded, a fool readily abandoned and left, so intolerable that not all his money, nor his houses, nor his carriages could make it worth while even to go on with the easy task of deceiving him. He was not worth deceiving any more; it was simpler to be rid of him. In the eyes of the world that fact would be very significant of what he was. And that same thing he was in his own eyes now. The stroke of this sharp sword had cloven in two the armour of his pride; it fell off him and left him naked.

Could he endure this fate for all his life? It would last all his life; people have long memories, and the tradition does not die. It would not die even with his life. No, by heaven, it would not! A new thought seized him. There was the boy to whom he had given life. What had he given to the boy now? What a father would the boy have to own! And what of the boy's mother? The story would last the boy's life too. It would always be between him and the boy. And the boy would never dare speak of his mother. The boy would be kept in ignorance till ignorance yielded, perforce, to shame. His son's life would be bitterness to him, if it meant that—and bitterness surely to the boy too. As he brooded on this his face set into stiffness. He declared that it was not to be endured.

He came to where Milldean road joined the main road by the red villas, and turned to the right towards Fairhaven. Here he met the full force of the gale. The wind was like a moving rushing wall; the rain seemed to hit him viciously with whips; there was a great confused roar from the sea below the cliffs. He could hardly make headway or induce his horse to breast the angry tempest. But his face was firm, his hand steady, and his air resolute as he rode down to Fairhaven, sore in the eyes, dripping wet, cold to the very bone. His purpose was formed. Fool he might be, but he was no coward. He had been deluded, he was not beaten. His old persistence came to his rescue. All through, though he might have lost everything else, he had never lost courage. And now, when his pride fell from him, and his spirit tasted a bitterness as though of death, his courage rose high in him—a desperate courage which feared nothing save ridicule and shame. These he would not have, neither for himself nor for his boy. His purpose was taken, and he rode on. His pride was broken, but no man was to behold its fall. In this hour he asked one thing from himself—courage unfearing, unflinching. It was his, and he rode forward to the proof of it. And there came in him a better pride. In place of self-complacency there was fortitude; yet it was the fortitude of defiance, not of self-knowledge.

He rode through the gale into Fairhaven, thinking nothing of Mrs. Valentine's house, waiting on fate to show him the way. Just where the town begins, the road comes down to the sea, and runs along by the harbour where a sea-wall skirts deep water. A man enveloped in oilskins stood here, glistening through the darkness in the light of a gas-lamp. He was looking out to sea, out on the tumble of angry waves, stamping his feet and blowing on his wet fingers now and then. It was no night for an idle man to be abroad; he who was out to-night had business.

"Rough weather!" called Grantley, bringing his horse to a stand.

The man answered, not in the accents of the neighbourhood, but with a Cockney twang and a turn of speech learnt from board schools and newspapers. He was probably a seaman then, and from London.

"Terribly severe," he said. "No night to keep a man on the look-out."

He looked at Grantley, evidently not knowing him.

"A bad night for a ride too, sir," he added; "but it's better to be moving than standing here, looking for a boat that's as likely to come as the Channel Squadron!" He spat scornfully as he ended.

"Looking for a boat?"

For the moment Grantley was glad to talk; it was a relief. Besides he did not know what he was going to do, and caught at a brief respite from decision.

"Aye," the man grumbled, "a boat to come from Portsmouth. Best luck for her if she's never started, and next best if she's put in for shelter on the way. She'd never make Fairhaven to-night."

"Then what's the good of looking for her?"

"Because I get five shillings for it. The owner's waiting for her—waiting at the Sailors' Rest there." He pointed to the inn a hundred yards away. "She was to have been here by midday, and he's in a hurry. Best for him if she doesn't come, if he means to sail to-night, as he says he does." He paused and spat again. "Pretty weather for a lady to go to sea, ain't it?" he ended sarcastically.

The fates were with Grantley Imason. They sent guidance.

"What boat is it?" he asked quietly.

"The *Ariadne*" ("Hairy Adny," he pronounced the name).

"Ah, yes! Mr. Blake's yacht?"

"You know him, sir? Well, you'll find him and his lady at the 'Rest' there; and if you're a friend of theirs, you tell 'em not to expect her to-night, and not to go on board her if she comes."

"Here's another shilling for you, and good-night."

Grantley rode on to the inn, thanking fate, realising now how narrow the chance had been. But for the storm, but for the wind that had buffeted and almost beaten him, no pride, no resolution, would have been of any avail. With fair weather the yacht would have come and gone. He saw why Christine Fanshaw was not to deliver his letter till the morrow. Without the storm, no pride, no resolution, no courage would have availed him. The *Ariadne* would have put to sea, and Sibylla would have been gone for ever. Now, thanks to fate, she was not gone. Grantley drew a long breath—the breath of a man whom a great peril has narrowly passed by. The plan had been well laid, but the storm had thwarted it. There was time yet.

Was there? That question could not but rise in his mind. He faced it fairly and squarely, and jogged on to the Sailors' Rest.

"Praise to this fine storm!" he cried within himself—to the storm which beat and raged, which had feigned to hinder his coming, but was his ally and friend. Good luck to it! It had served his turn as nothing else could. And how it was attuned to his mood—to the fierce stern conflict which he had to wage! This was no night for gentleness. There were nights when nature's gentleness mocked the strife to which her own decrees condemned the race of men. But to-night she herself was in the fight. She incited, she cheered, she played him on; and she had given him his field of battle. The sense of helplessness passed from him. He was arrayed for the fight. He drank in the violent salt air as though it were a potion magic in power. His being tingled for the struggle.

There was a light in an upper window of the Sailors' Rest. The blinds were not drawn. No, the pair in that room were looking out to sea, looking for the boat which did not come, looking in vain over the tumbling riot of waves. But stay! Perhaps they looked no more now; perhaps they had abandoned that hope for the night. Christine was not to deliver his letter till the morrow; they would think that they had to-night. The thought brought back his pain and his fierceness. They would think that they had to-night! They were wrong there; but it was ten o'clock. "Ten o'clock!" he muttered, as he drew rein at the door of the Sailors' Rest and cast his eyes up to the light in the window over his head.

Within, young Blake was turning away from the window.

"She won't come to-night," he said. "I suppose they started, or I should have had a wire. They must have put back or put in for shelter somewhere. And if she did come, I couldn't take you to sea to-night." He came across to where Sibylla sat over the fire. "It's no use expecting her to-night. We must get away to-morrow morning. There's plenty of time." He meant time before Grantley Imason would receive Sibylla's letter and come to Fairhaven, seeking his wife.

"It's too perverse," Sibylla murmured forlornly.

Her vision of their flight was gone. The rush through the waves, the whistling wind, the headlong course, the recklessness, the remoteness from all the world, the stir, the movement, the excitement—all were gone. On the yacht, out in mid-sea, no land in sight, making for a new world, they two alone, with all that belonged to the old life out of view and out of thought—the picture had caught and filled her fancy. In her dream the sea had been as Lethe, the stretch of waters a flood submerging all the past and burying the homes of memory. She had stood arm in arm with him, revelling in the riot of the open seas. No further had the vision gone. The room in the inn was very different. It was small, stuffy, and not too clean. The smell of stale tobacco and of dregs of liquor hung about it. The fire smoked, sending out every now and then a thick dirty cloud that settled on her hands and hair. Her dainty cleanliness rose in revolt. It was a sordid little room. It was odious then; it would never be pleasant in retrospect. Somehow it carried a taint with it; it brought into prominence all that her thoughts had forgotten; its four dingy walls shut out the glowing picture which her fancy had painted.

Blake came and stood behind her chair, laying his hand on her shoulder. She looked up at him with a sad smile.

"Nothing's quite what you expect," she said. "I wanted my voyage! I suppose I didn't want—reality! But I'm not a child, Walter. I have courage. This makes no difference really."

"Of course it doesn't—so long as we're together."

"I didn't come to you to make the good times better, but to make the bad times good—to do away with the bad times. That's what you wanted me for; that's what I wanted to do." She rose and faced him. "So I'll always welcome trouble—because then I'm wanted, then I can do what I've come to do."

"Don't talk about trouble, Sibylla. We're going to be very happy."

"Yes, I think so," she said, looking at him with thoughtful eyes. "I think we shall be."

"By God, I love you so!" he burst out suddenly, and then walked off to the window again.

She spread out her hands in an instinctive gesture of deprecation, but her smile was happy.

"That's how I can do what I want to do for you," she said. "That's how I can change your life, and—and find something to do with mine."

He came slowly back towards her, speaking in a low restrained voice:

"It's really no use waiting for the boat. She won't come."

Sibylla stood very still; her eyes were fixed on his face. He met her gaze for a moment, then turned away, sat down by the table, and lit a cigarette—doing it just by habit, and because he was so restless, not because he wanted to smoke.

She stood there in silence for two or three minutes. Once she shuddered just perceptibly. She was striving to yield, to do what he asked, to live up to her gospel of giving everything so that she might make happy him whom she had chosen to receive her gifts—might make him happy, and so fill, enrich, and ennoble his life and hers. She had not thought there would be a struggle; that had got left out in the visions—the visions which were full of the swish of the wind, the dance of the waves, and the sailing to worlds new and beautiful. What struggled? Old teachings, old habits, instincts ingrained. She was acting in obedience to ideas, not to feeling. And feeling alone has power to blot such things out of being.

But for good and evil she was a fanatic—she owned her ideas as masters, and forced herself to bend to them as a slave. What they asked must be given—whatever the sacrifice, the struggle, the repulsion. That they might realise what her nature craved, they must be propitiated by what her nature did not love. On that condition alone would they deal with her. And now these ideas, with all their exacting relentless claims, had found embodiment in Walter Blake.

Blake turned his head and looked at her. She came quickly to him and fell on her knees by him. His hand rested on the table, and she laid hers lightly on it.

"Walter, it's hard!"

"If you love me——" he murmured.

She knew by now that love can be unmerciful. With a little sigh she raised his hand and kissed it. She was half reconciled to her surrender, because she hated it. Had anyone been there to interpose and forbid, her reluctant acceptance would have been turned into an ardent desire to complete her sacrifice.

Young Blake flung away his cigarette and sprang to his feet. He was not thinking of his aspirations now. Wanting to be good was not present to his mind, nor the leading of a new life. He was full of triumph. He forgot the yacht that had not come, and anything there might be uncongenial in the surroundings. He caught Sibylla's hands. She looked at him with a smile half of wonder, half of pity. She had put away her shrinking, though it might come back; but it was a little strange that good could be done only on conditions.

They were standing thus when they heard a voice, the loud gruff voice belonging to the retired merchant-skipper who kept the inn. He was rather a rough customer, as indeed the quality of his patrons rendered necessary; he did not hesitate to throw a man out or (as Fairhaven's report averred) to lay a stick across the back of the saucy buxom daughter who served the bar for him if her sauciness became too pronounced. On the whole he was the sort of character popular in the nautical quarter of Fairhaven.

The loud voice came from a distance—from the bottom of the stairs apparently. The landlord was talking to himself, for all that appeared—no other voice made itself heard. He was saying that he had made a promise, and that he was a man of his word. He said this several times. Blake and Sibylla stood hand in hand, their eyes turned in the direction of the door. Then the landlord observed that "times were hard, and that he was a poor man." Blake and Sibylla heard that too. Then the landlord's heavy step came half-way up the stairs. "A poor man," they heard him say with strong emphasis. Still they could hear no other voice and no other step. But they had dropped one another's hands by now, and stood quite still a couple of paces apart.

"Oh, he's bargaining with somebody for the price of a bed!" said young Blake, with an attempt at lightness.

The landlord's steps were heard descending the stairs again. And now another step drew near.

Suddenly young Blake darted towards the door and locked it. He turned a scared face round on Sibylla. The steps sounded along the passage. His eyes met hers. He did not know the step, but he knew the one thing that he feared, and his uneasy mind flew to the apprehension of it.

"Can it be—anybody?" he whispered.

"It's Grantley," she answered quietly. "Unlock the door. I'm not afraid to meet him. In the end I believe I'm glad."

"No, no! You're mad! You mustn't see him. I'll see him. You go into the other room." There was a communicating door which led to a bedroom. "I'll not let him come near you. I'll stand between you and him."

"I must see him. I'm not afraid, Walter. Unlock the door."

"Oh, but I shan't let him come in. I shall——"

"If it's Grantley, he'll come in. Unlock the door. At any rate we can't have the door broken in."

She smiled a little as she said this, and then sat down in the chair by the table where Blake had been sitting when she kissed his hand and gave him her surrender.

A knock came on the door. Young Blake unlocked it, and stood opposite to it. His face was pale now.

"He shan't come near you," he whispered to Sibylla over his shoulder.

She made no sign. She sat resting her clasped hands on the table and gazing intently towards the door. There was no sign of confusion or of guilt about her. Her face was composed and calm. Young Blake's fists were clenched. He seemed to keep himself still with an effort.

The door opened, and Grantley appeared on the threshold. He was very wet; the rain dripped from his hat as he took it off his head; salt spray hung on the hair over his ears. He shook himself as he shut the door behind him. Then he looked from Sibylla to Blake, and back to Sibylla, at last fixing his eyes on her.

"You can't come in here," said Blake. "I'll come outside with you, if you like, but you can't come in here."

Grantley took no notice. His eyes were on Sibylla.

"Am I too late, Sibylla?" he asked.

"Yes," she answered tranquilly, "too late."

A sudden flush swept over Grantley's face, but in an instant his usual pallor had returned.

"In the sense in which I spoke, is that true, Sibylla?"

She shrugged her shoulders a little. She seemed composed and almost careless as she answered, with a touch of contempt:

"No; but it is true, for all that."

CHAPTER XVI

THE UPPER AND THE NETHER STONE

"Then you must come back with me," said Grantley. Young Blake sprang forward a step, crying—"By God, no!"

Neither of them heeded him; their eyes were on one another. Already the fight was between the two, and the two only.

"Do you really think that?" she asked. "I don't know how you come to be here—I suppose Christine warned you somehow; but it's by mere accident that you are here, and that I haven't gone before now. It makes no difference. You're not in time, as you call it. The thing is settled already; it was settled when I planned to come, not when I came. What you meant doesn't count. Do you really think I shall come back now?"

"Yes, you must come back now."

"Back to that life? Never! Of course you don't know what it was to me, and I don't suppose I could tell you. You wouldn't understand."

Blake threw himself into a chair by the window. He was helplessly impatient of the situation. Grantley came a little nearer the table and stood there, to all seeming impassive. The appearance was not very deceptive. He was not now dominated by emotion; he was possessed by a resolve. His love for his wife was far buried in his heart; his set purpose was all he knew.

"I don't see what you had to complain of," he said coldly. "The way we lived was your choice, not mine. But I'm not going to discuss that. I'm here to take you home to your husband's house and to your child."

"I've faced all that a thousand times, and answered it a thousand times. It can't move me now. You'd better go away, Grantley."

Again Blake rose; he did not lack physical courage.

"I'll go with you. I'm at your service," he said. "But outside; you shan't stay here."

He waited a moment for an answer, but, getting none, nor so much as a look, sank awkwardly into his seat again.

Grantley spoke to his wife.

"I know what happened. Before you did this, you fogged your mind with all sorts of fantastic ideas. You're not the woman to do this kind of thing easily."

"Fantastic ideas! Yes, they seem so to you. The fantastic idea of having something to live for, some life, something else than a prison, than repression, than coldness. I had lots of those fantastic ideas, Grantley."

"You had your child."

"I tell you I've faced it." She pressed her fingers hard into her cheek and frowned. "The child made it worse," she jerked out fiercely. "Seeing you with the child was——" She shook her head with a shiver.

Grantley raised his eyebrows.

"As bad as that?" he asked mockingly. He paused, and went on: "But this is all beside the point. Supposing it was as bad as you say, what then? You had made your bargain; you chose to take me; you relied on your own opinion. Say it was a mistaken opinion—what difference does that make?"

"It does make a difference. I'm not called upon to throw away every chance of happiness because of one mistake."

"That's just what you are called upon to do—in civilised society."

"You don't actually propose an abstract argument," she asked, "now—under these circumstances?" She smiled derisively.

"Oh, no! But your point of view compelled a protest. I'm not here to argue; I'm here to take you back—or, if you won't come, to tell you the consequences."

"I'm prepared for the consequences."

That gave young Blake another chance. He rose and came forward.

"Yes, she is—and so am I," he said; "and that ought to end the matter between us. We're prepared for the trouble and the scandal and all that; and I'm prepared for anything else you may think proper to ask. We've weighed all that, and made up our minds to it. That's the answer we have to give."

He spoke in a low voice, but very quickly and with passion; evidently he had hard work to keep control of himself. When he finished speaking, there was a moment's silence. He looked from Grantley to Sibylla, then went back to his chair; but he drew it nearer and listened intently.

"It is so," said Sibylla. "We've made up our minds to all that."

Grantley passed his hand across his brow—almost the first movement that he had made. He was about to speak when another short fit of vehemence caught hold of Sibylla.

"Yes," she cried, striking the table with her hand, "and it's better than that life of sham and fraud and failure and heartbreak! Yes, a thousand, thousand times better!"

He let the gust pass by, and then spoke slowly, as though he weighed his words.

"Those are the consequences to you and your—your friend here," he said. "Have you thought of the consequences to me?"

"To you? Am I so necessary?" She laughed bitterly.

"And to the boy?"

"Not so bad as growing up in such a home as ours!" she flashed out fiercely again.

"Oh, that's the way you argued that?" he said with a smile. "I was rather wondering. However there are other consequences still." He came yet a pace nearer to her, so that he was close to the table, and rested one hand on it. "There will be other consequences still," he said. "I don't accept the position you propose for me. I don't accept these consequences which you have been so good as to face and decide upon. I refuse them totally—both for myself and for my son I refuse them utterly. It's fair you should understand that. I refuse them root and branch."

Blake leant forward, ready to spring up. The idea of violence came into his head, the idea that Grantley might be armed. Grantley noticed his movement, and at last addressed a word to him.

"Don't be afraid. I don't mean that," he said with a short laugh.

Sibylla spoke to him, sadly now.

"You can't refuse. It's put out of your power. This thing must be. It has become inevitable. There's no use in talking of refusing the consequences. They won't be as bad as you think."

"It's not inevitable; it's not out of my power. It's entirely in my power to accept your consequences or not to accept them, to face them or not to face them; and I have decided. I won't be, and I won't be known as, what you're making me; and your son shan't have to confess you his mother before men."

Young Blake looked at him with a puzzled impatience; Sibylla with a slow pondering glance. She twisted a ring on her finger as she asked:

"What do you mean by that?"

"In this world nothing need happen to us that we don't choose to bear, and nothing to those who are in our power that we don't choose to accept for them."

"What are you talking about?" asked Blake fretfully. "It sounds all nonsense to me."

He leant back with a scornful toss of his head. This sort of thing had lasted long enough, in his opinion.

"Tell me what you mean," said Sibylla, leaning forward across the table.

Grantley announced the resolve that possessed him, born of those bitter meditations, of those intolerable pictures of the future which had formed themselves in his mind as he battled through the storm to Fairhaven. He uttered it not as a threat, but as a warning; it was, as he had said, fair that she should understand.

"If you persist, I shall kill Frank and myself to-night."

Blake broke into a loud scornful laugh, sticking his hands in his pockets. Grantley turned towards him, smiling slightly.

"Oh, this isn't a melodrama, you know," Blake said, "and we're not to be bluffed like that. Don't be so damned absurd, Imason! On my soul, I've had enough of this business without having to listen to stuff like that!"

"Do you think it's bluff and melodrama?" Grantley asked Sibylla. "Do you think I've no real intention of doing it?"

She looked up at him intently.

"You love yourself more than the boy, and your pride more than life or happiness," she said slowly. He frowned, but heard her without interruption. "So I think you might do it," she ended.

"Sibylla!" cried Blake, leaning forward again.

A gesture from her arrested his speech. He rose slowly to his feet and stood listening.

"I may be made a fool of. I don't make a fool of myself. If I pledge myself to you to do it, you know I shall do it, Sibylla?"

"Yes, then you would do it," she agreed.

"Oh, but it's nonsense, it's rank madness, it's—it's inconceivable!" Blake broke out.

"I do now so pledge myself," said Grantley.

Sibylla nodded; she understood. She leant back in her chair now, regarding her husband thoughtfully.

Grantley's pale face was set in a fixed smile; he met her gaze steadily.

"It's madness—you'll be stopped!" Blake burst out. "I can't believe you mean it. Anyhow, you'll be stopped."

"By you? Will you send for a policeman? or will you come to my house and stop me? Nothing can stop me unless you kill me. Is that your choice?"

He spoke to Blake, but he looked still at Sibylla. Blake came near and scrutinised the pale face with eyes whose expression grew from wonder and incredulity into a horrified apprehension. The silence now seemed long.

"Yes," said Sibylla at last, "it's like you. That's what you'd do. I never thought of it; but I'm not surprised. It's you. It's just that in you which has made my life an impossible thing. You sacrificed me to it. You would sacrifice yourself and your son. Yes, it's you."

She put her hands up before her face for a moment, pressing her fingers on her eyelids. Then her eyes sought his face again.

"But, Sibylla——" cried Blake.

"Yes, he'd do it, Walter," she interrupted, not turning round.

Blake took two restless paces to and fro, and sank into his chair again.

"You understand now. It lies with you," said Grantley to his wife. "I've told you. I was bound to tell you. Now it lies with you."

Again passion seized her.

"No, no, that's false! It doesn't lie with me! It lies at your door, both the crime—the hideous crime—and, I pray God, the punishment!"

"I'm not talking about the crime or the punishment," he said coldly. "I take those on myself as much as you like. What depends on you is whether the thing happens. That's all I meant to say."

Young Blake was staring at him now as if fascinated by his firm and hideous resolve. Slowly it had been driven into Blake's brain that the man meant what he said, that he would do the thing. The man looked like it, and Sibylla believed he would. He would kill himself—yes, and the pretty child with whom Sibylla had been used to play. He could see the picture of that now—of Sibylla's beautiful motherhood. His heart turned sick within him as he began to believe Grantley's sombre pledge.

"It's a lie," said Sibylla in grim defiance. "Nothing depends on me. It's the evil of your own heart. I've nothing to do with it."

"It's with you to bring it about or to prevent it."

"No!" she cried, rising to her feet in the agonised strain of her heart—"no, no! That's a lie—a lie! On your head be it! Ah, but perhaps it would be best for him! God knows, perhaps it would be best!"

"So I think," said Grantley quietly. "And you accept that?"

"No, I acknowledge no responsibility—not a jot."

"Well, leave the question of responsibility. But it's your will that this shall happen sooner than that you should leave this man?"

"Sooner than that I should come back to you, that life of ours begin again, and Frank grow up to a knowledge of it!"

"And it's my will, sooner than that he should grow up to a knowledge of how his mother ended it. That's settled then?"

"It's no bargain!" she protested fiercely. "You have settled it."

"But it is settled?" he persisted.

"If you do it, may God never pardon you!"

"Perhaps. But you know that it is settled?"

She made no answer.

"You can't deny that you know. So be it."

He faced her for a moment longer; her figure swayed a little, but she stood her ground. She was not beaten down. And she knew the thing was settled, unless by chance, at the last, pity should enter Grantley's heart. But she did not believe pity could enter that heart; he had never shown her that there was a way.

The smile rested still on Grantley's face as he regarded his wife. She looked very beautiful in her fierce defiance, her loathing of him, her passionate protest, her refusal to be beaten down, her facing of the thing. She had a fine spirit; it did not know defeat or cravenness. She was mad with her ideas. Perhaps he was mad with his. And the ideas clashed—with ruin to her life, and his, and the child's. But she did not bow her head any more than he would bend his haughty neck.

"At least you have courage," he said to her. "It is settled. And now I'll say good-bye and go. I'll interrupt you no more."

It was his first taunt of that kind. It seemed to pass unheeded by Sibylla; but young Blake's face turned red, and he clenched his hands; but not in anger. A wave of horror passed over him. He would not interrupt longer what his coming had interrupted—that was what Grantley Imason meant. He would leave them to themselves while he went back alone to his home, and there found the sleeping child. But the idea of that—the picture of the one house and the other—was too fearful. How could the two bear to think of that? How could they stand there and decide on that? It was unnatural, revolting, alien from humanity. Yet they meant it. Blake doubted that no more, and the conviction of it unmanned him. He had been prepared for scandal, he had been ready to risk his life. Those things were ordinary; but this thing was not. Scandal is one thing, tragedy another. This grim unyielding pair of enemies threw tragedy in his appalled face. It was too much. A groan burst from his lips.

"My God!" he moaned.

They both turned and looked at him—Sibylla gravely, Grantley with his rigid smile.

"My God, I can't bear it!" He was writhing in his chair, as though in keen bodily pain. "It's too awful! We—we should think of it all our lives. I should never get rid of it. I should see the poor little beggar's face. I can't stand that. I never thought of anything like that. I never meant anything like that. Poor little Frank! My God, you can't mean it, Imason?"

"You know I mean it. It's nothing to you. The responsibility is ours. What do you count for? It was you or another—that's all. Neither my life nor my son's is anything to you."

"But it would—it would always be there. I could never sleep at nights. I should feel like—like a murderer. For pity's sake——"

He came towards Grantley, stretching out his hands for mercy. Grantley made no sign. Blake turned to Sibylla. She too was stiff and still, but her eyes rested on him in compassion. He turned away and threw himself into the chair again. A convulsive movement ran through his body, and he gave a loud sob.

Sibylla walked slowly away to the hearthrug, and stood looking at the agonised young man. Grantley waited in immovable patience. The thing was not finished yet.

"The horror of it!" Blake moaned almost inarticulately. He turned to weak rage for an instant and hissed across to Grantley: "If I had a revolver, I'd shoot you where you stand."

"That would be better for me, but not better for the boy," said Grantley.

"I can't understand you," Blake gasped, almost sobbing again.

"Why should you? My account is not to be rendered to you. If I've ruined my wife's life—and you've heard her say I have—if I take my own and my son's, what is it to you?"

In Grantley's slow measured words there breathed a great contempt. What, he seemed to say, were any great things, any stern issues, to this unmanned hysterical creature, who dressed up his desires in fine clothes, and let them beguile him whither he knew not, only to start back in feeble horror at the ruin that he had invited? What was it all to him, or he to it? It was he or another. The real battle was still between himself and Sibylla. With what eyes was she looking on this young man? He turned from the collapsed figure and faced his wife again.

But her eyes were now on Walter Blake, with a pleading, puzzled, pitying look. The next moment she walked quickly across the room and knelt down by his side, taking one of his hands in both of hers. She began to whisper consolation to him, praying him not to distress himself, to be calm and brave, tenderly reproaching his lack of self-control. She was with him as Grantley had seen her with the child. He wondered to see that, and his wonder kept his temper under command. There did not seem enough to make a man's passion rage or his jealousy run wild, even though she whispered close in Blake's ear, and soothingly caressed his hand.

"Don't be so distressed," he heard her murmur. "It's not your fault, dear. Don't be frightened about it."

He tried to shake her off with a childish petulance, but she persevered. Yet she could not calm him. He broke from her and sprang to his feet, leaving her kneeling.

"I can't face it! By God, I can't!" he cried.

"It will happen," said Grantley Imason. "If not to-night—if anything prevents me to-night—still very soon. You'll hear of it very soon."

The young man shuddered.

"The poor little chap—the poor innocent little chap!" he muttered hoarsely. He turned to Grantley. "For Heaven's sake, think again!"

"It's you who have to think. I have thought. I've little time for more thought. You've all your life to think about it—all your life with that woman, who is the mother of the child."

"Why do you torment him?" broke out Sibylla angrily.

But she rose slowly and drew away from Blake as she spoke.

Grantley shrugged his shoulders scornfully.

"The fellow has no business in an affair like this," he said. "He'd better get back to his flirtations."

"I never thought of anything like this."

The repetition came from Blake like some dull forlorn refrain.

He put his hand to his throat and gulped with a hard dry swallow. He looked round the room, made for a table where some whisky stood, and took a drink of it. Then he half staggered back to his chair, and sat down all in a heap. His limit was reached. He was crushed between the upper and the nether stone—between Grantley's flinty pride and the ruthless fanaticism of Sibylla's ideas. Between them they would make him, who had wanted to be good, who had had such fine aspirations, such high-coloured dreams, such facile emotions, so impulsive a love—between them they would make him a murderer—a murderer in his own eyes. Whatever hands did the deed, to the end of his days conscience would cry out that his were red.

Sibylla sighed. Her eyes were very mournful. She spoke, as it seemed, more to herself than to either of them.

"I wanted to make him happy, and I've made him very unhappy. I can do it, but he can't do it. I mustn't ask it of him. He would never be happy, I could never make him happy. Even if I could be happy, he couldn't; it's too hard for him. I don't know what to do now."

Grantley neither spoke nor moved.

"I've no right to ask it of any man. Nobody could agree to it, nobody could endure it. There's misery both ways now."

She went to Blake, who was sitting in the apathetic stupor which had followed his raving outburst. Again she knelt by him and whispered to him soothingly. At last Grantley spoke.

"It would be well if we were home before it's light and the servants up," he said.

She looked across at him from beside Blake's knee. She looked long and searchingly. His smile was gone; his manner and air were courteous, however peremptory.

"Yes, it would be well," she said. She rose and came a little way towards him. "There's no help for it. I can't escape from you. I'm bound to you in bonds I can't loosen. I've tried. I've stood at nothing. I wish to Heaven I could! Going back is like going back to death. But perhaps he's right. Better my living death than the thing you meant to do." She paused and ended: "I'll go back to the child, but I will not come back to you."

"You give all I've asked," said Grantley with cold politeness.

She looked round at young Blake with a pitiful smile.

"It's the only way, my dear. With this man what he is, it's the only way. I must leave you alone."

Blake leaned towards her with a passionate cry of pain. She reasoned gently with him.

"But you know the alternative—you've heard it. We can't help it. This man is capable of doing it, and he would find out a way. I don't see that we could do anything at all to stop him. Then when you heard it, it would be so terrible to you. You'd hate yourself. Oh, and, my dear, I think you'd hate me! And I couldn't bear that. No, you must be reasonable. There's no other way."

Blake hid his face in his hands. He made no further effort. He knew that her words were true.

Sibylla walked into the bedroom, leaving the two alone. Neither now moved nor spoke. The storm outside seemed to have abated, for the rain dashed no more against the windows, and the wind was not howling round the walls of the house. It was very still. Grantley Imason presently began to button his coat, and then to dust the wet off his hat with his coat sleeve.

Sibylla came back in her hat and cloak.

"We must get something to carry you," said Grantley. "I wonder if we could raise a cart here!"

"How did you come?"

"I rode over."

"I don't want a cart. I shall walk beside your horse."

"Impossible! At this time of night! And such a night!"

"I shall walk—I must walk! I can't sit in a cart and——"

Her gesture explained the rest. Struggling along on foot, she might keep her wits. Madness lay in sitting and thinking.

"As you will," said Grantley.

She had begun to draw on her gloves; but when she looked at Blake she drew them quickly off again, and thrust them into a pocket of her cloak. She walked past Grantley to Blake, and took hold of both his hands. Bending over him, she kissed him twice.

"Thank you for having loved me, Walter," she said. "Good-bye."

Blake said nothing. He held her hands and looked up imploringly in her face. Then she disengaged herself from his grasp and turned round to her husband.

"I'm ready," she said. "Let us go."

Grantley bowed slightly, went to the door, and opened it for her. She looked back once at Blake, murmuring:

"For having loved me, Walter," and kissed her hand to him.

With no sign of impatience Grantley waited. Himself he took no heed of Blake, but followed Sibylla out of the room in unbroken silence.

When he found himself alone, young Blake sprang towards the door, giving a cry like some beast's roar of rage and disappointment. But his feet carried him no more than half-way. Half-way was all he ever got. Then he reeled across tc where the liquor was, and drank some more of it, listening the while to the paces of Grantley's horse on the stone flags outside the inn. As they died away, he finished his liquor and got back to his chair. He sat a moment in dull vacancy; then his nerves failed him utterly, and he began to sob helplessly, like a forsaken frightened child. As Grantley Imason said, he had no business in an affair like that.

CHAPTER XVII
WANDERING WITS

Grantley's pride was eager to raise its crest again. It caught at the result of the struggle and claimed it as a victory, crying out that there was to be no pointing of scornful fingers, no chuckles and winks, no shame open and before the world. The woman who walked by his horse was a pledge to that. He was not to stand a plain fool and dupe in the eyes of men. If that thought were not enough, look at the figure young Walter Blake had cut! Who had played the man in the fight? Not the lover, but the husband. Who had won the day and carried off the prize? The woman who walked by his horse was the evidence of that. Who had known his will, and stood by it, and got it? The woman answered that. He bore her off with him; young Blake was left alone in the dingy inn, baulked in his plan, broken in spirit, disappointed of his desire.

The night was still and clear now. Broad puddles in the low-lying road by the sea, and the slipperiness of the chalky hill up to the cliffs, witnessed to the heaviness of the recent downpour, as the flattened bushes in the house gardens proved the violence of the tempest. But all was over now, save the sulky heaving of big rollers. A clear moon shone over all. They met nobody: the man who had vainly watched for the yacht had gone home. Sibylla did not speak. Once or twice she caressed Rollo, who knew her and welcomed her. For the rest she trudged steadily through the puddles, and set her feet resolutely to climb the sticky road. She never looked up at her companion. The brutality of his pride rejoiced again to see her thus. Here was a fine revenge for her scornful words, for the audacity with which she had dared to bring him within an ace of irremediable shame—him and the child she had borne to him! She was well punished; she came back to him perforce. Was she weary? Was she cruelly weary? It was well. Did she suffer? It was just. Woe to the conquered—his was the victory! Even in her bodily trial his fierceness found a barbaric joy.

But deep within him some mocking spirit laughed at all this, and would not let its gibes be silenced. It derided his victory, and made bitter fun of his prancing triumph. "I'll go back to the child, but I will not come back to you." "Going back is like going back to death." "Thank you for having loved me, Walter." The mischievous spirit was apt at remembering and selecting the phrases which stung sharpest. Was this triumph? it asked. Was this victory? Had he conquered the woman? No, neither her body nor her soul. He had conquered—young Blake! The spirit made cheap of that conquest, and dared Grantley to make much of it. "Rank, blank failure," said the spirit with acrid merriment. "And a lifetime of it before you!" The world would not know, perhaps, though it can generally guess. But his heart knew—and hers. It was a very fine triumph that!—a triumph fine to win against the woman who had loved him, and counted her life worth having because it was hers to give to him! Through the blare of the trumpets of his pride came this piercing venomous voice. Grantley could not but hear. Hearing it, he hated Sibylla, and again was glad that she trudged laboriously and painfully along the slimy oozing road. The instinct of cruelty spoke in him. She had chosen to trudge. It was her doing. That was excuse enough. Whatever the pain and labour, she had her way. Who was to blame for it?

They passed the red villas, and came where the Milldean road branched off to the left at the highest point of the downs. From here they looked over the cliffs that sloped towards their precipitous fall to the sea. The moon was on the heaving waters; a broad band of silver cut the waves in two. Grantley brought his horse to a stand, and looked. At the instant Sibylla fell against the horse's shoulder, and caught at his mane with her hands, holding herself up. Rollo turned his head and nosed her cloak in a friendly fashion. A stifled sob proclaimed her exhaustion and defeat. She could walk no more. The day had been long, full of strain, compact of emotion and struggle; even despair could inspire no more exertion. In a moment she would fall there by the horse's side. Grantley looked down on her with a frowning face, yet with a new triumph. Again she failed; again he was right.

"Of course you couldn't do it! Why did you try?" he asked coldly. "The result is—here we are! What are we to do now?"

She made no answer; her clutch on Rollo's mane grew more tenacious—that alone kept her up.

"You must ride. I'll get down," he said surlily. Then he gave a sudden laugh. "No, he can carry us both—he's done it once before. Put your feet on the stirrup here—I'll pull you up."

She made no sign of understanding his allusion. He saw that she was dazed with weariness. He drew her up, and set her behind him, placing her arm about his waist.

"Take care you don't let go," he warned her curtly, as he jogged the horse on again, taking now to the turf, where the going was better.

Her grasp of his waist was limp.

"Hold on, hold on!" he said testily, "or you'll be slipping off." There was no hint of tenderness in his voice.

But Sibylla recked nothing of that now. With a long-drawn sigh she settled herself in her place. It was so sweet to be carried along—just to be carried along, to sit still and be carried along. She tightened her grip on him, and sighed again in a luxury of content. She let her head fall against his shoulder, and her eyes closed. She could think no more and struggle no more; she fell into the blessed forgetfulness, the embracing repose, of great fatigue.

The encircling of her arm, the contact of her head, the touch of her hair on his neck moved him with a sudden shock. Their appeal was no less strong because it was utterly involuntary, because the will had no part in the surrender of her wearied-out body. Memory assailed him with a thousand recollections, and with one above all. His face set in a sullen obstinate resistance; he would not hear the voice of his heart answering the appeal, saying that his enemy was also the woman whom he loved. He moved the horse into a quicker walk. Then he heard Sibylla speaking in a faint drowsy whisper: "Good Rollo, good Rollo, how he carries us both—as easily as if we were one, Grantley!" She ended with another luxurious sigh. It was followed by a little shiver and a fretful effort to fold her cloak closer about her. She was cold. She drew nearer to him, seeking the warmth of contact. "That's a little better," she murmured in a childish grumbling voice, and sought more comfortable resting for her head on his shoulder.

He knew that her wits wandered, and that the present was no more present to her. She was in the past—in the time when to be near him was her habit and her joy, the natural refuge she sought, her rest in weariness, the end of her every journey, when his arms had been her home. Certainly her wits must be wandering, or she would never rest her head on his shoulder, nor suffer her hair to touch his neck, nor speak nor sigh like that, nor deliver herself to his charge and care in this childish holy contentment. Wandering wits, and they alone, could make her do anything of this. So it was not to be regarded. How should any sane man regard it from the woman who had forsaken her child and sought to dishonour her home, whom he had but just torn from the arms of a lover?

He was afraid. Hence came his summoning of the hardest thoughts, his resort to the cruellest names. He braced himself to disregard the appeal she made, to recall nothing of all that her intimate presence thrust upon his mind. He would not be carried back across the gulf of the last year, across the chasm which those months had rent between them. For here was no such willing submission as he asked. It was all unconscious; it left her rebellion unquelled and her crime unexpiated. Yet he waited fearfully to hear her voice again. Whither would the errant wits next carry her? Whither must they carry her? He seemed to be able to answer that question in one way only. They must go right back to the beginning. With a sense of listening to inevitable words, he heard her soft drowsy whisper again:

"Let's ride straight into the gold, Grantley, straight into the gold, and let the gold——"

The faint happy murmur died away in a sigh, and her head, which had been raised a moment, nestled on his shoulder again.

It had come—the supreme touch of irony which he had foreseen and dreaded. The errant wits had overleapt the stupendous gulf; they crimsoned the cold rays of the moon into the glory of summer sunset; they coloured desolate ruins with the gleaming hues of splendid youth. Her soul was again in the fairy ride, the fairy ride which had led whither? Which had led to this? Nothing that waking wits, or an ingenuity pointed by malice, might have devised, could have equalled this. She might have searched all her armoury in vain for so keen a weapon. Nay, she would have rejected this, the sharpest of all; no human being could have used it knowingly. It would have been too cruel. He listened in dull terror for a repetition of the words. They did not come again. What need? He heard them still, and a groan broke the seal of his lips.

"My God, must she do that?" he muttered to himself. "Get on, Rollo, get on!"

For now the triumph faded away, the unsubstantial pageant was no more. There was no blare of trumpets to deaden the mocking voice. The little victory stood in its contemptible dwarfishness beside the magnitude of his great defeat. That the past had been, that the present was—that was enough. The fairy ride and the struggle in the inn—they stood side by side and bade him gaze on the spectacle. Beside this it seemed as though he had suffered nothing that day and night—nothing in the thought of ridicule and shame, nothing in the dishonour of his house and home, nothing in the jealousy and anger of a forsaken man. This thing alone seemed to matter—that the past had been that, and that the present was this, and that they had been so shaped in the hands of him, the fashioner of them.

Then suddenly, with a quick twist of thought, he was bitterly sorry for Sibylla: because words and memories which come back like that, unbidden and of themselves, when the wits are wandering, must have meant a great deal and had a great place once. At such a time the mind would not throw up trifles out of an unconscious recollection. The things which have been deepest in it, which have filled—yes, and formed it—those were the things that it would throw up. In themselves they might sound wild trifles, but they were knit to great deep things, towards which they stood as representatives. They expressed nethermost truths, however idle and light they sounded. When she babbled of riding into the gold, and sank her spirit in the memory of the fairy ride, she went back all unconsciously to the great moment of her life and to its most glorious promise. She spoke of the crown of all her being.

It was strange to him, this new sorrow for Sibylla. He had never felt that yet. It was odd he should feel it now—for the woman who had forsaken her child and sought to dishonour her husband and her son. But the feeling was very strong on him. It found its first utterance in words of constrained civility. He turned his head back, saying:

"I'm afraid you're very tired?"

She answered nothing.

"I hope you're not very cold?"

A little shiver of her body ran into his.

"We shall be home very soon."

"Home!" she murmured sleepily. "Yes, soon home now, Grantley!"

"God help me!" he muttered.

He could not make it out. Somehow his whole conception of her, of the situation, of himself, seemed shaken. This guilty woman behind him (was she not guilty in all that was of consequence, in every decision of her will and every impulse of her nature?) seemed to accuse not herself, but him. He was torn from the judgment-seat and set rudely in the dock, peremptorily bidden to plead, not to sentence, to beg mercy in lieu of pronouncing doom. Her wandering wits and drowsy murmurs had inexplicably wrought this transformation. And why? And how?

Was it because she had been capable of the fairy ride and able to make it eternal? Capable—yes, and confident of her ability. So confident that, in the foolhardiness of strength, she had engaged herself to try it with young Blake—with that poor light-o'-love, who was all unequal to the great issues which he himself had claimed as the kernel of the fight. Where lay the failure of the fairy ride? Where resided its nullity? How came it that the bitter irony of contrast found in it so fair, so unmatched a field? Who had turned the crimson of the glorious sunset to the cold light of that distant unregarding moon?

On a sudden her grasp of him loosened; her arm slipped away. She gave a little groan. He wrenched himself round in the saddle, dropping the reins. Old Rollo came to a standstill; Grantley darted out his hands with a quick eager motion. Another second, and she would have fallen heavily to the ground. With a strain he held her, and brought her round and set her in front of him. She seemed deathly pale under the blue-white moon rays. Her lips opened to murmur "Grantley!" and with a comfortable sigh she wreathed her arms about his neck. He almost kissed her, but thought of young Blake, and took up his reins again with a muttered oath.

So they rode down the hill into Milldean, old Rollo picking his steps carefully, since the chalk was slimy and there were loose flints which it behoved a careful and trusted horse to beware of. The old scene dawned on Grantley, pallid and ghostly in the moonlight—the church and the post-office; Old Mill House, where she had lived when he wooed her; his own home on the hill beyond. Sibylla's cold arms about his neck prayed him to see it again as he had seen it once—nay, in a new and intenser light; to see it as the place where his love had been born, whence the fairy ride had started and whither returned. He did not try to loosen her grasp about his neck. She seemed a burden that he must carry, a load he bore home from out the tempest of the winds and waves which he had faced and fought that night. And ever, as he went, he sought dimly, saying, "Why, why?" "How did it come about?" "Haven't I loved her?" "Hasn't she had everything?" Or exclaiming, "Blake!" Or again, "And the child!"—trying to assess, trying to judge, trying to condemn, yet ever feeling the inanimate grasp, looking on the oblivious face, returning to pity and to grieve.

A groom was waiting up for him. Grantley roused himself from his ponderings to give the man a brief explanation. Mrs. Imason had meant to stay at Mrs. Valentine's, but he had wanted to talk to her on business, and she had insisted on coming back with him. Unfortunately she had attempted to walk, and it had been too much for her; her bag would be sent home to-morrow. He had arranged this with the gruff innkeeper, and paid him a good sum to hold his tongue. But he was conscious that tongues would not be held altogether, and that the groom was puzzled by the story, and certainly not convinced. This seemed to matter very little now—as little as young Blake had mattered. Let them guess and gossip—what was that compared to the great unexplained thing between himself and Sibylla, compared to the great questioning of himself by himself which had now taken possession of him? What the outside world might think seemed now a small thing—yes, although he had been ready to kill himself and the child because of it.

He bore Sibylla into the hall of the house. One lamp burned dimly there, and all was quiet—save for a shrill fractious cry. The child was crying fretfully. The next moment old Mrs. Mumple came to the top of the stairs, carrying a bedroom candle and wrapped in a shabby voluminous dressing-gown.

"You're back, Mr. Imason?" She did not see Sibylla, and held up her hand. "Hark to poor little Frank!" she said. "He's been crying all the evening. I can't quiet him. He misses his mummy so."

Could words more sorely condemn Sibylla—the woman who had forsaken her child? But Grantley gathered her gently into his arms and began to carry her upstairs. Then Mrs. Mumple saw, and turned on him eyes full of wonder.

"She's unconscious, I think," he said. "She can do nothing for herself. I'll take her to her room, and you must put her to bed. She's very cold too. You must make her warm, Mrs. Mumple."

The old woman followed him into the bedroom without a word. He laid Sibylla down on the bed. For an instant she opened her eyes and smiled tenderly at him; then she fell into oblivion again. Mrs. Mumple moved quickly to her. Standing by her, ranged on her side in a moment by some subtle instinct, she faced Grantley with an air of defiance.

"Leave her to me, Mr. Imason. Leave the poor child to me."

"Yes," he answered. "Get her to bed as soon as you can. Good night."

Mrs. Mumple was feeling Sibylla's face, her hands, her ankles. She began to unbutton the wet boots hastily.

"What have you done to her?" she asked in motherly indignation. "Poor lamb!"

She pulled off the boots, and felt the damp stockings with low exclamations of horror. She was in her element, fussing over somebody she loved. She got a rough towel, and knelt down to strip off the stockings.

"I can leave her to you now," said Grantley, and he walked out of the room, closing the door behind him.

In the stillness of the house he heard the little peevish cry again; the complaint in it was more intense, as though the child missed old Mrs. Mumple's care and feared to be alone. Grantley went along the passage and into the nursery. A night-light burned by the cot. The door of the adjoining room stood open a few inches, but all was dark and quiet in there. When Grantley came near, the child saw him, and stretched out his little arms to him in a gesture which seemed to combine welcome and entreaty. Grantley shook his head, smiling whimsically.

"I wonder what the little beggar wants! I'm devilish little use," he murmured. But he lifted little Frank from the cot, wrapped him in a blanket, and carried him to the fireside. "I wonder if I ought to feed him?" he thought. "What's the nurse up to? Oh, I suppose she's left him to old Mumple. Why didn't she feed him?"

Then it struck him that perhaps Frank had been fed too much, and he shook his head gravely over such a trying situation as that. Frank was lamenting still—more gently, but in a remarkably persevering way. "He must want something," Grantley concluded; and his eye fell on a cup which stood just within the fender. He stooped down and stuck his finger into it, and found it half-full of a warm, thick, semi-liquid stuff.

"Got it!" he said in lively triumph, picking up the cup and holding it to Frank's lips. The child sucked it up. "Well, he likes it anyhow; that's something. I hope it won't kill him!" mused Grantley, as he gently drew the cup away from the tenacious little fingers.

Frank stuck one of the fingers in his mouth, stopped crying, and in an instant, seemingly, was sound asleep. Grantley got him into a position that he guessed would be comfortable, and lay back in the chair, nursing him on his knees.

In half an hour Mrs. Mumple came in and found them both sound asleep in front of the fire. She darted to them, and shook Grantley by the shoulder. He opened his eyes with a start.

"My gracious, you might have dropped him!"

"Not a bit of it! Look how he's holding on!" He showed the little hand clenched tightly round his forefinger. "He could hang like that, I believe!"

"Hang indeed!" muttered Mrs. Mumple resentfully. "Give him to me, Mr. Imason."

"Oh, by all means! But, by Jove, he doesn't want to go, you know!"

He did not want to go, apparently, and Grantley was quite triumphant about it. Mrs. Mumple was merely cross, and grumbled all the time till she got the little fingers unlaced and Frank safe in his cot again. "It's a mercy he didn't fall into the fire," she kept repeating, with a lively and aggressive thankfulness for escape from a danger excessively remote. But she made Grantley ashamed of not having thought of it. At last she spoke of Sibylla.

"She's warm and comfortable and sleeping now, poor lamb!" she said.

"It's time we all were," said Grantley, making for the door.

"You won't disturb her, Mr. Imason?"

He turned round to her, smiling.

"No," he said.

Mrs. Mumple moved her fat shoulders in a helpless shrug. She had made out nothing about the matter; she was clear only that Sibylla had somehow been disgracefully ill-used, and that Frank might very well have fallen into the fire. Of these two things she was unalterably convinced. But she spoke of one of them only; the other was declared in her hostile eyes.

Against his will—perhaps against his promise—Grantley was drawn to his wife's bedside. He trod very softly. The only light in the room came from the bright flickering flames of the fire. They lit up her face and her throat where she had torn her nightgown apart. He felt the white neck very lightly with his hand. It was warm—healthily warm, not feverish. She had taken no hurt either from storms within or from storms without. She slept deeply now; she would awake all well on the morrow. She would be herself again on the morrow. He thanked Heaven for that, and then recollected what it meant. Herself was not the woman who murmured "Grantley!" and dreamed of the gold and the fairy ride. Herself was the woman who could not live with him, who had forsaken the child, who had gone to Walter Blake. To that self she would awake to-morrow. Then was it not better that she should never awake? Ought he not to be praying Heaven for that—praying that the death which had passed by him and his son should, in its mercy, take her now?

Aye, that was the easiest way—and from his heart and soul Grantley despised the conclusion. His face set as it had when he faced her in the dingy inn and tore her from her lover's ready arms. His courage rose unbroken from the ruins of his pride. He would fight for her and for himself. But how? There must be a way.

Suddenly she raised herself in the bed. In an instant he had drawn back behind the curtains. She neither saw him nor heard. For a moment she supported herself on her hand, with the other flinging back her hair over her shoulders. Then, with one of her splendid, lithe, easy movements, she was out of bed and had darted quickly across to the door.

Grantley watched her, holding his breath, in a strange terror lest she should discover him, fearful that in such a case her delusion might still keep its hold on her—fearful too of the outrage his presence would seem if it had left her. She opened the door wider, and stood listening for fully a couple of minutes; it seemed to him that the time would never end. Then she carefully set the door half-way ajar, and turned to come back to her bed. She walked slowly now, and looked towards the fire, stretching out her hands towards it for a moment as she came opposite to it. The flames illuminated her face again, and he saw on her lips a smile of perfect happiness. All was well; there was no crying in the house; the child slept. That was all she thought of, all she cared about; her brain was dormant, but her instinct could not sleep. Now that it was satisfied, with a buoyant spring she leapt on the bed and cuddled the clothes about her happily.

In a few seconds Grantley stole silently from the room. He went downstairs, and he ate and drank: he had touched next to nothing for twelve hours. His blood stirred as warmth and vigour came back to him. He thanked Heaven that he lived, and the boy lived, that she lived and was with him still. His head was high and his courage unbroken. He looked on what he had been, and understood; yet he was not dismayed. Guided by the smile on her lips, he had found the way. He had been right to bring her back, or she could not have smiled like that—in all the plenitude of love for the little child, a love that waked while reason slept, but would not let her sleep till it was satisfied. If that was in her who had forsaken the child, so her love for him was in her who had left him to go to Walter Blake. If that were true, then there must be a way.

Somehow, he knew not how, salvation should come through the child. His mind leapt on to a vision of bonds of love joined anew by the link of those little hands.

CHAPTER XVIII
THE RISING GENERATION

The Raymores were holding up their heads again—such good reports came from Buenos Ayres. The head of Charley's department had written a letter to Raymore, speaking highly of the lad's good conduct and ability, and promising him early promotion. Raymore showed it to Kate, and she read it with tears in her eyes.

"You see he's going to give him a holiday at Christmas, and let him spend a month with us," said Raymore, pointing out a passage in the letter.

"Come on a visit, he says." She looked up with a questioning glance.

Raymore understood the question.

"Yes, my dear," he said gently. "He'll pay us a visit—many visits, I hope—but his career must lie over there. That's inevitable, and best on all grounds, I think." He came and took her hand, adding, "We must be brave about that."

"I'll try," said Kate.

She knew that was the penalty which must be paid. Over here the past would never be utterly buried. Charley would never be quite safe from it. He must buy safety and a fresh start at the price of banishment. His mother faced the bitter conclusion.

"We must make the most of the visits," she sighed. "And, yes, I will be brave."

"We must give him a splendid time while he's with us," said Raymore, and kissed her. "You've been fine about it," he whispered: "keep it up."

The penalty was high, or seemed so to a mother, but the banishment was not all evil. The boy's absence united them as his presence had never done. At home he had been an anxiety often, and sometimes a cause of distress to them. All that was gone now. He was a bond of union, and nothing else. And his own love for them came out. When he was with them, a lad's shamefacedness, no less than the friction of everyday life, had half hidden it. His heart spoke out now from across the seas; he wrote of home with longing; it seemed to grow something holy to him. He recounted artlessly the words of praise and the marks of confidence he had won; he was pleading that they made him worthy to pay his Christmas visit home. Whenever his letters came, Raymore and Kate had a good talk together over them; the boy's open heart opened their hearts also to one another—yes, and to Eva too. They paid more attention to Eva, and were quicker to understand her growth, to see how she reached forward to womanhood, and to be ready to meet her on this new ground. She responded readily, with the idea that she must do all she could to lighten the sorrow and to make Charley's absence less felt. In easy-going times people are apt to be reserved. The trouble and the worry broke up the crust which had formed over their hearts. All of them—even the boy so far away—were nearer together.

This softened mood and the gentler atmosphere which reigned in the Raymores' household, had its effect on Jeremy Chiddingfold's fortunes. It caused both Kate and Raymore to look on at his proceedings with indulgence. They were constantly asking themselves whether they had not been too strict with Charley, and whether the calamity might not have been prevented if they had encouraged him to confide in them more, and to bring his difficulties to them. They were nervously anxious to make no such mistake in regard to Eva. They were even in a hurry to recognise that Eva must consider herself—and therefore be considered—a young woman. A pretty young woman, to boot! And what did pretty young women like—and attract? Eva was not repressed; she was encouraged along her natural path. And it was difficult to encourage Eva without encouraging Jeremy too—that at least was Kate Raymore's opinion, notwithstanding that she had been made the repository of the great secret about Dora Hutting. "A boy and girl affair!" she called it once to Raymore, and made no further reference to it.

Kate was undoubtedly in a sentimental mood; the small number and the distant advent of the hundreds a year from the dyeing works did not trouble her. Half unconsciously, in the sheer joy of giving Eva pleasure, in the delight of seeing her girl spread her wings, she threw the young folk together, and marked their mutual attraction with furthering benevolence.

"We've been happy, after all," she said to Raymore; "and I should like to see Eva happily settled too."

"No hurry!" he muttered: "she's a child still."

"Oh, my dear!" said Kate, with a smile of superior knowledge; fathers were always like that.

Eva exulted in the encouragement and the liberty, trying her wings, essaying her power with timid tentative flights. Yet she remained very young; her innocence and guilelessness did not leave her. She did not seek to shine, she did not try to flirt. She had not Anna Selford's self-confidence, nor her ambition. Still, she was a young woman, and since Jeremy was very often at hand, and seemed to be a suitable subject, she tried her wings on him. Then Kate Raymore would nod secretly and significantly at her husband. She also observed that Eva was beginning to show a good deal of character. This might be true in a sense, since all qualities go to character, but it was hardly true in the usual sense. Christine Fanshaw used always to say that Eva was as good as gold—and there she would leave the topic, without further elaboration.

Well, that was the sort of girl Jeremy liked! He saw in himself now a man of considerable experience. Had he not grown up side by side with Sibylla, her whims and her tantrums? Had he not watched the development of Anna Selford's distinction, and listened to her sharp tongue? Had he not cause to remember Dora Hutting's alternate coquettishness and scruples, the one surely rather forward (Jeremy had been revising his recollections), the other almost inhuman? Reviewing this wide field of feminine variety, Jeremy felt competent to form a valid judgment; and he decided that gentleness, trustfulness, and fidelity were what a man wanted. He said as much to Alec Turner, who told him, with unmeasured scorn, that his ideas were out of date and sadly retrograde.

"You want a slave," said Alec witheringly.

"I want a helpmeet," objected Jeremy.

"Not you! A helpmeet means an equal—an intellectual equal," Alec insisted hotly. He was hot on a subject which did not seem necessarily to demand warmth because he too had decided what he wanted. He had fallen into a passion which can be described only as unscrupulous. He wanted to marry clever, distinguished, brilliant Anna Selford—to marry her at a registry office and take her to live on two pounds a week (or thereabouts) in two rooms up two pairs of stairs in Battersea. Living there, consorting with the people who were doing the real thinking of the age, remote from the fatted *bourgeoisie*, she would really be able to influence opinion and to find a scope for her remarkable gifts and abilities. He sketched this *ménage* in an abstract fashion, not mentioning the lady's name, and was much annoyed when Jeremy opined that he "wouldn't find a girl in London to do it."

"Oh, as for you, I know you're going to become a damned plutocrat," Alec said, with a scornful reference to the dyeing works.

"Rot!" remarked Jeremy, but he was by no means so annoyed at being accused of becoming a damned plutocrat as he would have been a year earlier, before he had determined to seek speedy riches and fame in order to dazzle Dora Hutting, and when he had not encountered the gentle admiring eyes of Eva Raymore. Whatever else plutocrats (if we may now omit the *epiphetus ornans*) may or may not do in the economy and service of the commonwealth, they can at least give girls they like fine presents, and furnish beautiful houses (and fabrics superbly dyed) for their chosen wives. There are, in short, mitigations of their lot, and possibly excuses for their existence.

Jeremy's state of mind may easily be gauged. The dye works were prominent, but the experience of life was to the front too. He was working hard—and had his heart in his play besides. For his age it was a healthy, and a healthily typical, existence. The play part was rich in complications not unpleasurable. The applause of large admiring brown eyes is not a negligible matter in a young man's life. There was enough of the old Jeremy surviving to make the fact that he was falling in love seem enough to support an excellent theory on the subject. But on the other hand he had meant the fame and riches for Dora Hutting—to dazzle her anyhow—whether to satisfy or to tantalise her had always been a moot point. In imagination Jeremy had invariably emerged from the process of making wealth and fame either unalterably faithful or indelibly misogynistic, Dora being the one eternal woman, though she might be proved unworthy. It had never occurred to him that he should label the fame and riches to another address. To be jilted may appear ludicrous to the rest of the world, but the ardent mind of the sufferer contrives to regard it as tragic. A rapid transference of affection tends to impair the dignity of the whole matter. Still, large brown admiring eyes will count—especially if one meets them every day. Jeremy was profoundly puzzled about himself, and did not suppose that just this sort of thing had ever occurred before.

Then a deep sense of guilt stole over him. Was he trifling with Eva? He hoped not. But of course there is no denying that the idea of trifling with girls has its own attractions at a certain age. At any rate to feel that you might—and could—is not altogether an unpleasing sensation. However Jeremy's moral sense was very strong—the stronger (as he was in the habit of assuring Alec Turner) for being based on pure reason and the latest results of sociology. Whenever Eva had been particularly sweet and admiring, he felt that he ought not to go to Buckingham Gate again until he had put his relations with Dora Hutting on an ascertained basis. He would knit his brow then, and decline to be enticed from his personal problems by Alec's invitations to general discussion. At this stage of his life he grew decidedly more careful about his dress, not aiming at smartness, but at a rich and sober effect. And all the while he started for Romford at eight in the morning. He was leading a very fine existence.

"These are very roseate hues, Kate," Christine Fanshaw observed with delicate criticism as she sipped her tea. Kate had been talking about Eva and hinting benevolently about Jeremy.

"Oh, the great trouble's always behind. No, it's not so bad now, thank heaven! But if only he could come back for good! I'm sure we want roseate hues!"

"I daresay we do," said Christine, drawing nearer the fire. It was autumn now, and she was always a chilly little body.

"Look at those wretched Courtlands! And somehow I don't believe that Grantley's marriage has been altogether successful."

She paused a moment, and there had been a questioning inflection in her voice; but Christine made no comment.

"For myself I can't complain——"

"And you won't get anything out of me, Kate."

"But we do want the young people to—to give us the ideal back again."

"I suppose the old people have always thought the young people were going to do that. And they never do. They grow into old people—and then the men drink, or the women run away, or something."

"No, no," Kate Raymore protested. "I won't believe it, Christine. There's always hope with them, anyhow. They're beginning with the best, anyhow!"

"And when they find it isn't the best?"

"You're—you're positively sacrilegious!"

"And you're disgracefully sentimental."

She finished her tea and sat back, regarding her neat boots.

"Walter Blake's back in town," she went on.

"He's been yachting, hasn't he?"

"Yes, for nearly two months. I met him at the Selfords'."

A moment's pause followed.

"There was some talk——" began Kate Raymore tentatively.

"It was nonsense. There's some talk about everybody."

Kate laughed.

"Oh, come, speak for yourself, Christine."

"The Imasons are down in the country."

"And Walter Blake's in town? Ah, well!" Kate sighed thankfully.

"In town—and at the Selfords'." She spoke with evident significance.

Kate raised her brows.

"Well, it can't be Janet Selford, can it?" smiled Christine.

"I think he's a dangerous man."

"Yes—he's so silly."

"You do mean—Anna?"

"I've said all I mean, Kate. Anna has come on very much of late. I've dressed her, you know."

"Oh, that you can do!"

"That's why I'm such a happy woman. Teach Eva to dress badly!"

Again Kate's brows rose in remonstrance or question.
"Oh, no, I don't mean it, of course. What would be the good, when most men don't know the difference?"
"You're certainly a good corrective to idealism."
"I ought to be. Well, well, Anna can look after herself."
"It isn't as if one positively knew anything against him."
"One might mind one's own business, even if one did," Christine observed.
"Oh, I don't quite agree with you there. If one saw an innocent girl——"
"Eva? Oh, you mothers!"
"I suppose I was thinking of her. Christine, did Sibylla ever——?"
"Not the least, I believe," said Christine with infinite composure.
"It's no secret Walter Blake did."
"Are there any secrets?" asked Christine. "It'd seem a pity to waste anything by making a secret of it. One can always get a little comfort by thinking of the pleasure one's sins have given. It's really your duty to your neighbour to be talked about. You know Harriet Courtland's begun her action? There'll be no defence, I suppose?"
"Has she actually begun? How dreadful! Poor Tom! John tried to bring her round, didn't he?"
A curious smile flickered on Christine's lips. "Yes, but that didn't do much good to anybody."
"She flew out at him, I suppose?"
"So I understood." Christine was smiling oddly still.
"And what will become of those unhappy children?"
"They have their mother. If nature makes mistakes in mothers, I can't help it, Kate."
"Is she cruel to them?"
"I expect so—but I daresay it's not so trying as a thoroughly well-conducted home."
"Really it's lucky you've no children," laughed Kate.
"Really it is, Kate, and you've hit the truth," Christine agreed.
Kate Raymore looked at the pretty and still youthful face, and sighed.
"You're too good really to say that."
Christine shrugged her shoulders impatiently.
"Perhaps I meant lucky for the children, Kate," she smiled.
"And I suppose it means ruin to poor Tom? Well, he's been very silly. I met him with the woman myself."
"Was she good-looking?"
"As if I noticed! Why, you might be a man! Besides it was only decent to look away."
"Yes, one looks on till there's a row—and then one looks away. I suppose that's Christianity."
"Now really, I must beg you, Christine——"
"Well, Eva's not in the room, is she, Kate?"
"You're quite at your worst this afternoon." She came and touched her friend's arm lightly. "Are you unhappy?"
"Don't! It's your business to be good and sympathetic—and stupid," said Christine, wriggling under her affectionate touch.
"But John's affairs are ever so much better, aren't they?"
"Yes, ever so much. It's not John's affairs. It's—— Good gracious, who's this?"
Something like a tornado had suddenly swept into the room. It was Jeremy in a state of high excitement. He had a letter in his hand, and rushed up to Kate Raymore, holding it out. At first he did not notice Christine.
"I've had a letter from Sibylla——" he began excitedly.
"Any particular news?" asked Christine quickly.
"Oh, I beg your pardon, Mrs. Fanshaw! I—I didn't see you." His manner changed. Christine's presence evidently caused him embarrassment. "No; no particular news. It's—it's not about her, I mean."
"I'll go if you like, but I should dearly like to hear." She looked imploringly at Jeremy; she was thinking that after all he was a very nice boy.
"Give me the letter, Jeremy. Show me the place," said Kate Raymore.
Jeremy did as she bade him, and stood waiting with eager eyes. Christine made no preparations for going; she thought that with a little tact she might contrive to stay and hear the news. She was not mistaken.
"Dora Hutting engaged!" said Kate, with a long breath.
Jeremy nodded portentously.
"Good gracious me!" murmured Kate.
"To a curate—a chap who's a curate," said Jeremy. His tone was full of meaning.
"Wasn't she always High Church?" asked Christine sympathetically.
"Why, you never knew her, Mrs. Fanshaw?"
"No, but most curates are High Church now, aren't they?"
"It's very curious, isn't it, Jeremy?" asked Mrs. Raymore. "Met him at her aunt's, I see Sibylla says."
Jeremy stood before the fire with knitted brows. "Yes, at her aunt's," he repeated thoughtfully.
"Why is it curious, Kate?"
"Oh, you know nothing about it, Christine."
"I'm trying to learn—if Mr. Chiddingfold would only tell me."
"It's nothing. It's—it's just a girl I used to know, Mrs. Fanshaw."
"Ah, those girls one used to know, Mr. Chiddingfold!"
Jeremy laughed—he laughed rather knowingly.

"And she's consoled herself?" pursued Christine.

"Oh, come now, I say, Mrs. Fanshaw!"

"It's no use trying to be serious with her, Jeremy. We'll read all about it when she's gone."

"Yes, all right. But to think——! Well, I'm dining here, aren't I?"

"Oh, yes," said Christine reassuringly.

"Christine, you're very impertinent. Yes, of course, Jeremy, and we'll discuss it then. Why don't you find Eva? She's in the library, I think."

"Oh, is she? Then I—I might as well, mightn't I?" He spoke listlessly, almost reluctantly. And he did not leave the room by a straight path, but drifted out of it with an accidental air, fingering a book or two and a nick-nack or two on his devious way. Christine's eyes followed his erratic course with keen amusement.

"You wicked woman!" she said to Kate as the door closed. "You might have given him one afternoon to dedicate to the memory of Miss Dora—what was her name?"

"She was the rector's daughter down at Milldean. Well, I'm really glad. I fancy she was a flighty girl, Christine."

"Oh dear me, I hope not," said Christine gravely. "What an escape for the poor dear boy!"

"You shan't put me out of temper," beamed Kate Raymore.

"I should think not, when your machinations are triumphing!"

"He's too nice a boy to be thrown away. And I don't think he was quite happy about it."

"I don't suppose he deserved to be."

"And now he can——"

"Oh, I won't hear any more about it! As it is, I've heard a lot more than anybody meant me to, I suppose." She got up. "I must go home," she said, with a little frown. "I'm glad I came. I like you and your silly young people, Kate."

"Oh, no, stay a little," Kate begged. "I want to ask you about a frock for Eva."

Christine was glad to talk about frocks—it was the craft whereof she was mistress—and glad too to stay a little longer at the Raymores'. There was youth in the air there, and hope. The sorrow that was gradually lifting seemed still to enrich by contrast the blossoming joy of the young lives which had their centre there. Her chaff covered so keen a sympathy that she could not safely do anything except chaff. The thought of the different state of things which awaited her at home did as much to make her linger as her constitutional dislike of leaving a cheery fire for the dreary dusk outside. Once she was near confiding the whole truth to Kate Raymore, so sore a desire had she for sympathy. But in the end her habit of reticence won the day, and she refused to betray herself, just as she had declined to be false to Sibylla's secret. What would Kate Raymore do for her? To speak of her trouble would only be to cast a shadow over the joy of a friendly heart.

When she did go, chance tempted her to a very mean action, and she fell before the temptation without the least resistance. The lights were not yet turned up on the staircase or in the hall, and Christine, left by her own request to find her way downstairs, found the library door open—it gave on to the hall. The room was not lighted either, except by a bright fire. She saw two figures sitting by the fire, and drew back into the gloom of the hall with a smile on her lips.

Eva was wondering at Jeremy. Of course he had said nothing of the news to her; indeed she knew nothing explicit of Dora Hutting—she had heard only a hint or two from her mother. But this evening there was a difference in Jeremy. Hitherto an air of hesitation had hung about him; when he had said anything—well, anything rather marked—he would often retreat from it, or smooth it down, or give it some ordinary (and rather disappointing) explanation in the next sentence. He alternated between letting himself go and bringing himself up with a jerk. This demeanour had its interesting side for Eva, but it had also been rather disquieting; sometimes it had seemed almost to rebuke her for listening to the first sentence without displeasure, since the first had been open to the interpretation which the second so hastily disclaimed. In fact Jeremy's conscience had kept interposing remarks between the observations of another faculty in Jeremy. The result had not been homogeneous. Conscience spoils love-making; it should either let it alone, or in the proper cases prevent it altogether.

This evening things had changed. His chagrin and his relief—his grudge against Dora and her curate, and his sense of recovered liberty—joined forces. He did not let the grass grow under his feet. He engaged in the primeval art of courting without hesitation or reserve. His eyes spoke in quick glances, his fingers sought excuses for transient touches. He criticised Eva, obviously meaning praise where with mock audacity he ventured on depreciation. Eva had been sewing embroidery; Jeremy must have the process explained, and be shown how to do it. To be sure, it was rather dark—they had to lean down together to get the firelight. His fingers were very awkward indeed, and needed a lot of arranging. Eva's clear laugh rang out over this task, and Jeremy pretended to be very much hurt. Then, suddenly, Eva saw a line on his hand, and had to tell him what it meant. They started on palmistry, and Jeremy enjoyed himself immensely. The last Christine saw was when he had started to tell Eva's fortune, and was holding her hand in his, inventing nonsense, and not inventing it very well.

Well or ill, what did it matter? Old or new, it mattered less. The whole thing was very old, the process as well ascertained as the most primitive method ever used in Jeremy's dyeing works. "Poor children!" breathed Christine, as she stole softly away towards the hall door. She could not stand there and look on and listen any more. Not because to listen was mean, but because it had become intolerable. She was ready to sob as she let herself out silently from the house of love into the chilly outer air. She left them to their pleasure, and set her face homewards. But her mind and her heart were full of what she had seen—of the beauty and the pity of it; for must not the beauty be so short-lived? Had not she too known the rapture of that advancing flood of feeling—yes, though the flood flowed where it should not? How the memories came back—and with what mocking voices they spoke! Well had it been for her to stand outside and look. For of a surety never again might she hope to enter in.

A man came full beneath the light of a street-lamp. It was a figure she could never forget nor mistake. It was Frank Caylesham. He saw her, and raised his hat, half-stopping, waiting her word to stop. She gave an involuntary little cry, almost hysterical.

"Fancy meeting you just now!" she gasped.

CHAPTER XIX
IN THE CORNER

Christine had neither desire to avoid nor strength to refuse the encounter. Her emotions had been stirred by what she had seen at Kate Raymore's; they demanded some expression. Her heart went forth to a friend, forgetting any bitterness which attached to the friendship. The old attraction claimed her. When Caylesham said that it was quite dark and there was no reason why he should not escort her, she agreed readily, and was soon babbling to him about Eva and Jeremy. She put her arm in his, talked merrily, and seemed very young and fresh as she turned her face up to his and joked fondly about the young people. None of the embarrassment which had afflicted her visit to his flat hung about her now. She had somebody she could talk to freely at last, and was happy in his society. It was a holiday—with a holiday's irresponsibility about it. He understood her mood; he was always quick to understand at the time, though very ready to forget what the feeling must have been and what it must continue to be when he had gone. He shared her tenderness, her pity, and her amusement at the youthful venturers. They talked gaily for a quarter of an hour, Christine not noticing which way they went. Then a pause came.

"Are we going right?" she asked.

"Well, not quite straight home," he laughed.

"Oh, but we must," she said with a sigh. He nodded and took a turn leading more directly to her house.

"I hear things are much better with John. I met Grantley and he told me they were in much better shape."

"Thanks to Grantley Imason and you. Yes, and you."

"I was very glad to do it. Oh, it's nothing. I can trust old John, you know."

"Yes; he'll pay you back. Still it was good of you." She lifted her eyes to his. "He knows, Frank," she said.

"The devil he does!" Caylesham was startled and smiled wryly.

"I don't know why I told you that. I suppose I had to talk to somebody. Yes; Harriet Courtland told him—you remember she knew? He made her angry by lecturing her about Tom, and she told him."

"He knows, by Jove, does he?" He pulled at his moustache; she pressed his arm lightly. "But, I say, he's taken the money!" He looked at her in a whimsical perplexity.

"So you may imagine what it is to me."

"But he's taken the money!"

"How could he refuse it? It would have meant ruin. Oh, he didn't know when he sent me to you—he'd never have done that."

"But he knew when he kept it?"

"Yes, he knew then. He couldn't let it go when once he'd got it, you see. Poor old John!"

"Well, that's a rum thing!" Caylesham's code was infringed by John's action—that was plain: but his humour was tickled too. "How did he—well, how did he take it?"

"Awful!" she answered with a shiver.

"But I say, you know, he kept the money, Christine."

"That makes no difference—or makes it worse. Oh, I can't tell you!"

"It doesn't make it worse for you anyhow. It gives you the whip hand, doesn't it?"

She did not heed him; she was set on pouring out her own story.

"It's dreadful at home, Frank. Of course I oughtn't to talk to you *of* all people. But I've had two months and more of it now."

"He's not unkind to you?"

"If he was, what do I deserve? Oh, don't be fierce. He doesn't throw things at me, like Harriet Courtland, or beat me. But I——" She burst into a little laugh. "I'm stood in the corner all the time, Frank."

"Poor old Christine!"

"He won't be friends. He keeps me off. I never touch his hand, or anything."

A long-dormant jealousy stirred in Caylesham.

"Well, do you want to?" he asked rather brusquely.

"Oh, that's all very well, but imagine living like that! There's nobody to speak to. I'm in disgrace. He doesn't talk about it, but he talks round it, you know. Sometimes he forgets for five minutes. Then I say something cheerful. Then he remembers and—and sends me back to my corner." Her rueful laugh was not far from a sob. "It's awfully humiliating," she ended, "and—and most frightfully dull."

"But how can he——?"

"One good scene would have been so much more endurable. But all day and every day!"

Caylesham was amused, vexed, exasperated.

"But, good heavens, it's not as if it was an ordinary case. Remember what he's done! Why do you stand it?"

"How can I help it? I did the thing, didn't I?"

His voice rose a little in his impatience.

"But he's taken my money. He's living on it. It's saved him. By gad, how can he say anything to you after that? Haven't you got your answer? Why don't you remind him gently of that?"

"That would hurt him so dreadfully."

"Well, doesn't he hurt you?"

"He'd never be friends with me again."

"He doesn't seem particularly friendly now."

"I feel quite friendly to him. I want to be friends."

"It does you credit then," he said with a sneer.

She pressed his arm lightly again, pleading against his anger and his unwonted failure to understand.

"It would be an end of all hope if I threw the money in his teeth. He's unhappy enough about it as it is." She looked up as she added: "I've got to live with him, you know, Frank."

Caylesham gave her a curious quick glance.

"Got to live with him?"

"Yes; all my life," she answered. "I suppose you hadn't thought of that?"

It was not the sort of thing which Caylesham was in the habit of thinking about, but he tried to follow her view.

"Yes, of course. It would be better to be friends. But you shouldn't let him get on stilts. It's absurd, after what he's done. I mean—I mean he's done a much queerer thing than you have."

"Poor old John! How could he help it?"

He glanced at her sharply and was about to speak, when she cried, "Why, where are we? I didn't notice where we were going."

"We're just outside my rooms. Come in for a bit."

"No, I can't come in. I'm late now, and—and—really I'm ashamed to tell even you. Well, I'm always questioned where I've been. I have to give an account of every place. I have to stand with my hands behind me and give an account of all my movements, Frank."

He whistled gently and compassionately.

"Like a schoolgirl!"

"How well you follow the metaphor, Frank! So I can't come in. I'll go home. No, don't you come."

"I'll come a bit farther with you. Oh, it's quite dark."

"Well, not arm in arm!"

"But doesn't that look more respectable?"

"You're entirely incurable," she said, with her old pleasure in him all revived.

"It's infernal nonsense," he went on. "Just you stand up for yourself. It's absolute humbug in him. He's debarred himself from taking up any such attitude—just as much as he has from making any public row about it. Hang it, he can't have it both ways, Christine!"

"I've got to live with him, Frank."

"Oh, you said that before."

"And I'm very fond of him."

"What?" He turned to her in a genuine surprise and an obvious vexation.

"Yes, very. I always was. We used to spar, but we were good friends. We don't spar now; I wish we did. It's just iciness. But I'm very fond of him."

"Of course, if you feel like that——"

"I always felt like that, even—even long ago. I used to tell you I did. I suppose you thought that humbug."

"Well, it wouldn't have been very strange if I had."

"No, I suppose not. It must have looked like that. But it was true—and it is true. The only thing I've got left to care much about in life is getting to be friends with John again—and I don't suppose I ever shall." Her voice fairly broke for a moment. "That's what upset me so much when I saw those silly children at Kate Raymore's."

Caylesham looked at her. There was a roguish twinkle in his eye, but he patted her hand in a very friendly sympathy.

"I say, old John's cut me out after all!" he whispered.

"You're scandalous! You always were," she said, smiling. "The way you put things was always disreputable. Yes, it was, Frank. But no; it's not poor old John who's cut you out—or at least it's John in a particular capacity. Life's cut you out—John as life. John, as life, has cut you out of my life—and now I've got to live with John, you see."

Caylesham screwed up his mouth ruefully. Things certainly seemed to shape that way. She had to live with John. John's conduct might be unreasonable and unjustifiable, but people who must be lived with frequently presume on that circumstance and behave as they would not venture to behave if living with them were optional. John really had not a leg to stand on, if it came to an argument. But arguing with people you have to live with does not conduce to the comfort of living with them—especially if you get the better of the argument. He was exceedingly sorry for Christine, but he didn't see any way out of it for her.

"Of course there's a funny side to it," she said with a little laugh.

"Oh, yes, there is," he admitted. "But it's deuced rough luck on you."

"Everything's deuced rough luck." She mimicked his tone daintily. "And I don't suppose it's ever anything worse with you, Frank! It was deuced rough luck ever meeting you, you know. And so it was that John wanted money and sent me to you. And that Harriet's got a temper, and, I suppose, that we've got to be punished for our sins." She took her arm out of his—she had slipped it in again while she talked about John as life. "And here I am, just at home, and—and the corner's waiting for me, Frank."

"I'm devilish sorry, Christine."

"Yes, I'm sure you are. You always meant to be kind. Frank, if ever I do make friends with John, be glad, won't you?"

"I think he's behaved like a——"

"Hush, hush! You've always been prosperous—and you've never been good." She laughed and took his hand. "So don't say anything against poor old John."

"I tell you what—you're a brick, Christine. Well, good-bye, my dear."

"Good-bye, Frank. I'm glad I met you. I've got some of it out, haven't I? Don't worry—well, no, you won't—and if I succeed, do try to be glad. And never a word to show John that I've told you he knows!"

"I shall do just as you like about that. Good-bye, Christine."

He left her a few yards from her house, and she stood by the door watching his figure till it disappeared in the dark. He had done her so much harm. He was not a good friend. But he was good to talk to, and very kind in his indolent, careless way. If you recalled yourself to him, he was glad to see you and ready to be talked to. A moment of temptation came upon her—the temptation to throw up everything, as Tom Courtland had thrown everything up, to abandon the hard task, to give up trying for the only thing she wanted. But Caylesham had given her no such invitation. He did not want her—that was the plain English of it—and she did not want him in the end either. She had loved the thing and still loved the memory of it; but she did not desire it again, because in it there was no peace. She wanted a friend—and John would not be one. Nobody wanted her—except John; and because he wanted her, he was so hard to her. But Frank Caylesham had been in his turn too hard on John. She was the only person who could realise John's position and make allowances for him. Yet all the light died out of her face as she entered her home.

John was waiting for her. His mind was full of how well things were going in the City. In the old days this would have been one of their merry, happy, united evenings. He would have told her of his success, and "stood" a dinner and a play, and brought her home in the height of glee and good companionship, laughing at her sharp sayings, and admiring her dainty little face. All this was just what he wanted to do now, and his life was as arid as hers for want of the comradeship. But he would not forgive; it seemed neither possible nor self-respecting. That very weak point in his case, with which Caylesham had dealt so trenchantly, made him a great stickler for self-respect; nothing must be done—nothing more—to make her think that he condoned her offence or treated it lightly. It was part of her punishment to hear nothing of the renewed prosperity in the City, to know nothing of his thoughts or his doings, to be locked out of his heart. This was one side; the other was that obligation to make full disclosure of all she did, and of how her time was spent. She must be made to feel the thing in these two ways every day. Yet he considered that he was treating her very mercifully; he was anxious to do that, because he was all the time in his heart afraid that she would throw Caylesham's money—the money which was bringing the renewed prosperity—in his face.

She faced the punishment with her usual courage and her unfailing humour. There was open irony in the minuteness with which she catalogued her day's doings; she did not sit down, but stood on the other side of his writing-table, upright, and with her hands actually behind her—because she liked the schoolgirl parallel which Caylesham had drawn. John saw the humour and felt the irony, but he was helpless. She did what she was told; he could not control the manner in which she did it.

"And then I walked home—yes, walked. Didn't take a bus, or a tram, or a steam-engine. I just walked on my two legs, going about three miles an hour, and oh, yes, taking one wrong turn, which makes me five minutes later than I ought to be. Quite a respectable turn—just out of the way, that's all. May I go and get myself some tea?"

He did so want to tell her about the successes in the City. And in fact he admired the courage and liked the irony. They were her own, and of her. Doing justice was very hard, with that provoking dainty face at once resenting and mocking at it. But justice must be done; his grievance should not be belittled.

"I'm not stopping you getting yourself tea. Is it a crime to ask where my wife's been?"

"It's mere prudence, I'm sure. Only what makes you think I should tell you the truth?"

She had her tea now—a second tea—and was sipping it leisurely.

"At any rate I know your account, and if I heard anything different——"

"That's the method? I see." Her tone softened. "Don't let's quarrel. What's the good? Had a good day in the City?"

"Just like other days," grunted John.

"Nothing particular?"

"No."

"There never is now, is there?"

He made no answer. Opening the evening paper, he began to read it. Christine knew what that meant. Saving what was unavoidable, he would talk no more to her that evening.

The wound to her vanity, her thwarted affection, her sense of the absurdity of such a way of living together, all combined to urge her to take Caylesham's view of the position, and to act upon it—to make the one reply, the one defence, which was open to her. The very words which she would use came into her mind as she sat opposite to John at dinner. Living on Caylesham's generosity—it would be scarcely an exaggeration to say that. And from what motive came the bounty? It would not be hard to find words—stinging words—to define that. John could have no answer to them; they must shame him to the soul. At every sullen short word, at every obstinate punitive silence, the temptation grew upon her. Knowing that she knew all, how could he have the effrontery to behave in this fashion? She steeled herself to the fight, she was ready for it by the time dinner was done and they were left alone, John sitting in glum muteness as he drank his port, Christine in her smart evening frock, displaying a prettiness which won no approving glances now. It was insufferable—she would do it!

Ah, but poor old John! He had been through so many worries, he had so narrowly escaped dire calamity. He had been forced into a position so terrible. And they had been through so many things together; they had been comrades in fair and foul weather. What would be the look in his eyes when he heard that taunt from her? He would say little, since there would be little to say—but he would give her a look of such hopeless fierce misery. No; in the end she was responsible for the thing, and she must bear the burden of it. Caylesham's view might be the man's view, perhaps the right view for a man to take. It could not be the woman's; the wife was not justified in looking at it like that. No, she couldn't do it.

But neither could she go on living like this. Her eyes rested thoughtfully on him. He was looking tired and old. Poor old John! He wanted livening up, some merriment, a little playful petting to which he might respond in his roughly jocose, affectionately homely fashion—with his "old girl" and "old lady" and so on. He never called her "old girl" now. Would she hate it as much now? She longed for it extraordinarily, since it would mark happiness and forgetfulness in him. But it seemed as if she would never hear it again. Suddenly she broke out with a passionate question:

"Are we to live like this always?"

He did not seem startled; he answered slowly and ponderously; "What have you to complain of? Do I say anything? Do I reproach you? Have I made a row? Look at what I might have done! Some people would think you were very lucky."

"It makes you miserable as well as me."

"You should have thought of all that before."

He took out a cigar and lit it, then turned his chair half-way round from the table, and began to read his paper again. Christine could not bear it; she began to sob softly. He took no visible notice of her; his eyes were fixed on a paragraph and he was reading it over and over again, not following in the least what it meant. She rose and walked towards the door; he remained motionless. She came back towards him in a hesitating way.

"I want to speak to you," she said, choking down her sobs and regaining composure.

He looked up now. There was fear in his eyes, a hunted look which went to her heart. At the least invitation she would have thrown herself on her knees by him and sought every means to comfort him. She was thinking only of him now, and had forgotten Caylesham's gay attractiveness. And in face of that look in his eyes she could not say a word about Caylesham's money.

"I'm going away for a little while, John. I'm going to ask Sibylla to let me come down to Milldean for a bit."

"What do you want to go away for?"

"A change of air," she answered, smiling derisively. "I can't bear this, you know. It's intolerable—and it's absurd."

"Am I to blame for it?"

"I'm not talking about who's to blame. But I must go away."

"How long do you want to stay away?"

"Till you want me back—till you ask me to come back." He looked at her questioningly. "It must be one thing or the other," she went on.

"It's for me to decide what it shall be."

"Yes; which of the two possible things. It's for you to decide that. But this state of things isn't possible. If you don't want me back, well, we must make arrangements. If you ask me to come back, you'll mean that you want to forget all this wretchedness and be really friends." Her feeling broke out. "Yes, friends again," she repeated, holding her arms out towards him.

"You seem to think things are very easily forgotten," he growled.

"God knows I don't think so," she said. "Do you really think that's what I've learnt from life, John?"

"At any rate I've got to forget them pretty easily!"

She would not trust herself to argue lest in the heat of contention that one forbidden weapon should leap into her hand.

"We can neither of us forget. But there's another thing," she said.

He would not give up his idea, his theory of what she deserved and of what morality demanded.

"You may go for a visit. I shall expect you back in two or three weeks."

"Not back to this," she insisted.

He shrugged his shoulders and held the paper up between them.

"If you don't want me back, well, I shall understand that. But I shan't come back to this." She walked to the door, and looked back; she could not see his face for the paper. She made a little despairing movement with her hands, but turned away again without saying more, and stole quietly out of the room.

John Fanshaw dashed his paper to the ground and sprang to his feet. He gave a long sigh. He had been in mortal terror—he thought she was going to talk about the money. That peril was past. He flung his hardly lighted cigar into the grate and walked up and down the room in a frenzy of unhappiness. Yes, that peril was past—she had said nothing. But he knew it was in her heart; and he knew how it must appear to her. Heavens, did it not appear like that to him? But she should never know that he felt like that about it. That would be to give up his grievance, to abandon his superiority, to admit that there was little or nothing to choose between them,—between her, the sinner, and him, who profited by the sin, whose salvation the sin had been, who knew it had been his salvation and had accepted salvation from it. No, no; he must never acknowledge that. He must stick to his position. It was monstrous to think he would own that his guilt was comparable to hers.

He sank back into his chair again and looked round the empty room. He thought of Christine upstairs, alone too. What a state of things! "Why did she? My God, why did she?" he muttered, and then fell to lashing himself once more into a useless fury, pricking his anger lest it should sleep, setting imagination to work on recollection, torturing himself, living again through the time of her treachery, elaborating all his grievance—lest by chance she should seem less of a sinner than before, lest by chance his own act should loom too large, lest by chance he might be weak and open his heart and find forgiveness for his wife and comrade.

"By God, she had no excuse!" he muttered, striking the table with his fist. "And I—why, the thing was settled before I knew. It was settled, I say!" Then he thought that if things went on doing well he would be able to pay Caylesham sooner than the letter of his bond demanded. Then, when he had paid Caylesham off—ah, then the superiority would be in no danger, there would be no taunt to fear. Why, yes, he would pay Caylesham off quite soon. Because things were going so well. Now to-day, in the City, what a stroke he had made! If he were to tell Christine that——! For a moment he smiled, thinking how she would pat his cheek and say, "Clever old John!" in her pretty half-derisive way; how she would——

He broke off with a groan. No; by heaven, he'd tell her nothing. His life was nothing to her—thanks to what she'd done—to what she had done. Oh, he did well to be angry!—Even to think of what she had done——!

So he struggled, lest perchance forgiveness and comradeship should win the day.

CHAPTER XX

THE HOUR OF WRATH

As soon as the first shot was fired, Tom Courtland struck his flag. There was no fight in him. His career was compromised, and by now his affairs were seriously involved. He resigned his seat; he wasn't going to wait to be turned out, he said, either by divorce or by bankruptcy, or by both at once. He never went home now. As a last concession to appearances, he took a room at his club. Mrs. Bolton now urged him to fight—since things had gone so far. Of course he would have to tell lies! But there were circumstances in which everybody told lies! She was ready to back him through thick and thin. If they could get Lady Harriet into the box and cross-examine her thoroughly, they could rely on a great deal of sympathy from a jury of husbands. It was really a good fighting case—given the lies, of course. She urged fighting, which was unselfish of her from one point of view, since an undefended case would do her little real harm, while a cross-examination in open Court could not be a pleasant ordeal for her, any more than it ought to be for Harriet Courtland. But she liked Tom—although incurable habit had caused her to make his affairs so involved—and she hated that Harriet should "have a walk over." She was angry with Tom because he gave in directly, and took it all "lying down," as she said. But Tom was broken; he could only mutter that he did not "care a damn" what they did; it was all over for him. His bristly hair began to turn a dull grey in these troublesome days. When he was not with Mrs. Bolton he was haunting the streets and parks, hoping he might meet his girls taking their walk with the maid or with Suzette Bligh. Such stray encounters were his only chance of ever seeing them now—the only chance of ever seeing them in the future, he supposed, unless the Court gave him "access." And much pleasure there would be in access, with Harriet to tell them the sort of man he was before every such visit as the law might charingly dole out to him! He grumbled disconsolately about everything—the suit, his affairs, his children, the access, all of it—to Mrs. Bolton; but he did and tried to do nothing. He was in a condition of moral collapse.

Harriet Courtland's state was even worse. She was almost unapproachable by the children and Suzette Bligh—and none other tried to approach her. She had no friends left. Not one of Tom's set was on her side; she had wearied them all out. The last to keep up the forms of friendship was Christine Fanshaw. Now that was at an end too. She had heard nothing from Christine. From the day of John's visit there had been absolute silence. She knew well what that meant. She brooded fiercely over what she had done to Christine—her one remaining friend—had done not because she wanted to hurt Christine or to lose her friendship, had done with no reasonable motive at all, but just in blind rage, because in her fury she wanted to strike and wound John, and this had been the readiest and sharpest weapon. She could not get what she had done out of her head; she was driven to see what a light it cast on the history of her own home; it showed her the sort of woman she was. But she held on her way, and pressed on her suit. Realising what she was bred in her no desire to change. There was no changing such a woman as she was—a cursed woman, as she called herself again and again. So there she sat, alone in her room, save when her nervous children came perforce to cower before her—alone with the ruin she had made, in bitter wrath with all about her, in bitterest wrath with herself. She was a terror in the house, and knew it. Nobody in the house loved her now—nay, nobody in the world. It had come to this because of her evil rage. And the rage was not satiated; it had an appetite still for every misfortune and every shame which was to afflict and disgrace her husband. In that lay now her only pleasure; her sole joy was to give pain. Yet the thought that her girls had ceased to love her, or had come to hate her, drove her to a frenzy of anger and wretchedness. What had they to complain of? How dared they not love her! She exacted signs of love from them. They dared not refuse a kiss for fear of a blow being given in its place; but Harriet knew now why they kissed her and accepted her kisses. "Little hypocrites!" she would mutter when they went out, accusing the work of her own hands. But they should love her—aye, and they should hate their father. She swore they should at least hate their father, even if they only pretended to love her. The woman grew half mad at the idea that in their hearts they loved their father, pitied him, thought him ill-used, grieved because he came no more; that they were in their hearts on their father's side and against her. She wished they were older, so that they could be told all about the case. Well, they should be told even now, if need be, if that proved the only way of rooting the love of their father out of their hearts.

An evil case for these poor children! They had no comfort save in gentle colourless Suzette Bligh. To all her friends she had seemed a superfluous person. She used to be invited just to balance dinner-parties, or on a stray impulse of kindness. But fate had found other work for her now. The once useless superfluous woman was all the consolation these three children had; any love they got she gave them. She stood between them and desolation. She warned them what temper their mother was in, whether it were safe to approach her, and with what demeanour. More than once her love gave the meek creature courage, and she stood between them and wrath. Lamentable as the state of affairs was, Suzette had found a new joy in life. She took these children into her life and her heart, and became as a mother to them. Gradually they grew to love her.

But none the less—perhaps all the more—they tormented her, bringing to her all the doubts and questions which were rife in their minds. The portentous word "divorce" had come to their ears—Harriet was not careful in her use of it. They connected it quickly with their father's now continuous absence. Whatever else it might mean—and they thought it meant something bad for their father, to be suffered at the hands of their mother—they understood it at least to mean that he would be with them no more. Suzette knew nothing at all about "access," and could only fence feebly with their questions; they ventured to put none to Harriet. They grew clear that their father had gone, and that they were to be left to their mother.

One and all they declined such a conclusion. They loved Tom; they did not love Harriet. Tom had always been a refuge, sometimes a buffer. They had no doubt of what they wanted. They wanted to go to their father, and to take Suzette Bligh with them. That scheme conjured up the vision of a happy home, free from fear, where kisses would be volunteered, not exacted, and the constant dread would be no more.

"But we daren't tell mamma that," said Sophy, in a tremble at the bare idea.

Lucy shook her head; Vera's eyes grew wide. They certainly dared not go to Harriet with any such communication as that. They had been shrewd enough to see that they were expected to hate their father: Vera had been roughly turned out of the room merely for mentioning his name.

After much consultation, carried on in a secrecy to which not even Suzette was privy, a plan was laid. They would write to their father and tell him that, whether he were sentenced to divorce or not, they wanted to come and live with him—and to bring Suzette if they might.

"We won't say anything about mamma. He'll understand," Sophy observed.

Vera piped out in terror:

"But when mamma finds out?"

"We shall be gone, don't you see?" cried Lucy. "We shall ask papa to meet us somewhere, and he'll take us with him, and then just write and tell mamma."

"He can say we're sorry when he writes to tell mamma."

"Oh, yes, I see," said Vera. "It will be splendid, won't it? I wish we could tell Suzette!"

The elder girls were dead against that. Suzette was a dear, but she was too much afraid of mamma; the great secret would not be safe with her, and if it were discovered before they were out of reach—significant nods expressed that situation with absolute lucidity.

So Sophy—who wrote the best hand—squared her elbows and sat down to her task in the schoolroom. A scout was posted at the foot of the stairs, another at the top. On the least alarm the letter was to be destroyed, and the scribe would be discovered busy on a French exercise.

"Dearest Papa," Sophy wrote,—

"We all send our love, and, please, we do not want to stay here now that you have gone away. Please let us come and live with you. We promise not to be troublesome, and Suzette might come too, might not she, and look after us? Dearest papa, do not make us stay here. Because we love you, and we want to come and live with you. Please tell us where to meet you, and we will make Suzette bring us, and you can take us home with you. Please let it be soon. We do so want to see you. Please do not make us stay here. We each of us send you a kiss, and are your loving daughters."

The signatures were attached, the letter closed and addressed to Tom's club; they knew where that was, because he had taken them to see it one Sunday morning, and they had admired the great armchairs and all the wonderful big books. The same afternoon Lucy broke away from Suzette, ran across to a pillar post, and dropped the important missive in. She came back with an air of devil-may-care triumph, nodding at her sisters, frankly refusing to tell Suzette anything about it.

"You'll see very soon," she promised in mysterious triumph, and that evening the three had a wonderful talk over the letter, speaking in low cautious tones, agreeing that their manner must be carefully guarded, that meekness and affection towards their mother must be the order of the day, and that one of them must always be on the watch for the postman's coming, lest by chance Tom's answer should fall into the hands of the enemy.

"Would she open it?" shuddered Vera.

"I expect she would," said Sophy.

They saw the danger, and the hours were anxious. But they tasted some of the delights of conspiracy too. And hope was on the horizon. One more "row" could be endured if after that the doors were open to freedom.

Tom's heart was touched by the little scrawl, written on a sheet torn from a copybook. In his broken-down state he was inclined to be maudlin over it. He carried it to Mrs. Bolton, and showed it to her, saying that he could not be such a bad chap after all if the little ones loved him like that, pitying them because they were exposed to Harriet's tempers, bewailing his own inability to help them, or to comply with their artless request.

"I shouldn't be allowed to keep them," he said ruefully, trying to smooth his bristly hair.

Mrs. Bolton made a show of sympathy, and was in fact sorry for him; but she did not encourage any idea of trying to take or keep them. He suggested smuggling them out of the jurisdiction. She was firm, if kindly, in asking how he meant to support them. Anyhow Lady Harriet could feed them! Tom was very much under her influence, and had no longer the strength of will needed for any venturous plan. The conclusion that he could do nothing was not long in coming home to him.

"But I must write to the poor little things," he said, "and tell them I shall come and see them sometimes. That'll comfort them. I'm glad they're so fond of me. By Jove, I haven't been a bad father, you know!" He read Sophy's letter over again and laid it down on Mrs. Bolton's mantelpiece; when he went back to the club he forgot it and left it there.

There Mrs. Bolton's friend, Miss Pattie Henderson (she was not married to Georgie Parmenter yet—negotiations were pending with his family), found it, and it was from her that a suggestion came which appealed strongly to Mrs. Bolton. As she drank her glass of port, Miss Henderson opined that it would be "a rare score" to send the letter to Harriet Courtland. "It'll make her properly furious," said Miss Pattie, finishing her port with hearty enjoyment.

Mrs. Bolton caught at the notion. Harriet was putting her to a great deal of annoyance, and so was Tom's refusal to stand up to Harriet. It was meet and right that any person who was in a position to give Harriet a dig should give it. Neither of them thought of what might be entailed on the little folk who had dared to send the letter; in the end they had a very inadequate idea of the terror Harriet inspired. Mrs. Bolton laughed as she contemplated the plan.

"Just stick in a word or two of your own," Miss Pattie advised. "Something spicy!"

Mrs. Bolton at once thought of several spicy little comments which would add point to Sophy's letter. One was so spicy, so altogether satisfying to Mrs. Bolton's soul, and to Miss Pattie Henderson's critical taste, that it was irresistible. It—and Sophy's letter—were posted to Harriet before lunch that day; and Mrs. Bolton's eyes were only opened at all to what she had done when she told Caylesham (who had dropped in in the afternoon), and heard him exclaim:

"But, by Jove, she'll take it out of those unhappy children, you know! I say, you don't know Harriet Courtland, or you'd never have done that!"

His concern seemed so great that Mrs. Bolton's heart was troubled. If she did not upbraid herself, at any rate she denounced Miss Henderson. But what was to be done? Nothing could be done. By now the letter must be almost in Harriet Courtland's hands. Caylesham said a few plain words about the matter, but his words could not help now. They had, however, one effect. They made Mrs. Bolton afraid to let Tom know what she had done: and she persuaded Caylesham not to betray her. When Tom next came she told him that she had accidentally burnt Sophy's letter in mistake for one of her own.

"Well, I've sent them an answer, poor little beggars—under cover to Suzette Bligh," said Tom. "But I'm sorry. I should have liked to keep that letter of theirs, Flora."

"I know. Of course you would. I'm sorry," said Mrs. Bolton, now feeling very uncomfortable, although she had not lost her pleasure at the idea of giving Harriet such a fine dig.

Tom's letter reached its destination first, and Suzette read it to the little girls. It was a kind and a good letter. He told them to behave well towards their mother, and to love her. He said he was obliged to be away from them now, but presently he would see them and hoped to see them very often, and that they were not to forget to go on loving him, because he loved them very much.

Suzette's voice broke a little over the letter, and the children listened in an intent and rather awed silence. They were divided between relief that an answer had come safely, and depression at what the answer was. But they understood—or thought they did—that if they were good they would presently be allowed to see their father very often.

"That's what he means, isn't it?" Lucy asked Suzette.

"Yes, dear, that's it," Suzette told her, not knowing what else to tell her.

"We'd better burn papa's letter," Sophy suggested.

There was no difference of opinion about that. Vera was accorded the privilege of putting it in the fire, and of stamping carefully on the ashes afterwards.

"Because," she said, justifying this precaution, "you remember the story where the man was found out just because he didn't stamp on it after he'd burnt it, Sophy!"

This was the last day on which Tom Courtland was entitled to put in a defence to his wife's suit. He had made no sign. Harriet was the fiercer against him. His ruin was not enough; she desired herself to see it made visible and embodied in a trial whose every word and proceeding should aggravate his shame and satisfy her resentment. She had nursed the thought of that, making pictures of him and of the woman undergoing the ordeal and being branded with guilt while all the world looked on. Now Tom refused her this delight; there would be no trial, because he would not fight.

It was a fine moment for the letter to arrive. The mine was all laid, only the match was wanting. Harriet was dressing for dinner when it came; her maid Garrett was doing her hair before the glass. As she read, Garret saw a sudden change come over her face—one quick flush, then a tight setting of her lips. Garrett knew the signs by experience. Something in that letter had upset her ladyship. Warily and gently Garrett handled her ladyship's hair; if she blundered in her task now, woe to her, for her ladyship's temper was upset.

"Dearest papa, do not make us stay here. Because we love you and want to come and live with you"——"Please do not make us stay here."

That was the truth of it, that was what they really thought, these little hypocrites who came and kissed her so obediently every morning and evening, those meek little creatures with their "Yes, mamma dear," "No, dear mamma," accepting all her commands so docilely, returning her kisses so affectionately. All that was a show, a sham, a device for deluding her, for keeping her quiet, while they laid their vile plots—none the less vile for being so idiotic—and sent their love to "dearest papa"—to that man, to Flora Bolton's lover—while they gave Flora Bolton the means of mocking and of triumphing over her.

She sat very still for awhile, but Garrett was not reassured. Garrett knew that the worst fits of all took a little time in coming. They worked themselves up gradually.

"Is that to your ladyship's satisfaction?" asked Garrett, as she put the last touches to her work.

"No, it isn't," snarled Harriet. "No, don't touch me again. Let it alone, you clumsy fool."

Garrett went and took up the evening dress. Harriet Courtland rose and stood for a moment with Sophy's letter to Tom in her hand.

"I'm going to the schoolroom for a few minutes. Wait here," she said to Garrett, and walked out of the room slowly, taking the letter with her. Another slip of paper she tore into shreds as she went; that was Mrs. Bolton's comment on the situation, as "spicy" and as vulgar as she and Miss Pattie Henderson could make it. Yet Harriet was not now thinking of Mrs. Bolton.

Garrett stood where she was for a moment, then stole cautiously after her mistress. She knew the signs, and a morbid curiosity possessed her. She would have a sensational story to retail downstairs, if she could manage to see or hear what happened—for beyond a doubt something had put her ladyship in one of her tantrums. Pity for the children struggled with Garrett's seductive anticipations of a "scene."

Suzette Bligh was reading a story aloud in the schoolroom when Harriet marched in. She held the letter in her hand. The children could make, and had leisure to make, no conjecture how the catastrophe had come about, but in a flash all the little girls knew that it was upon them. The letter and their mother's face told them. They sat looking at her with terrified eyes.

"So you don't want to stay here?" she said sneeringly. "You want to go to your dearest papa? And you dare to write that! Who wrote it? Was it you, Lucy?"

"I—I didn't write it, mamma dear," said Lucy.

Suzette rose in distress.

"Dear Lady Harriet——" she began.

"Hold your tongue. So you wrote it, Sophy. Yes, I see now it's your writing. Oh, but you were all in it, I suppose. So you love your papa?"

Garrett had stolen to within two or three yards of the door now, and it stood half open. She could hear all and see something of what happened.

"So you love your papa?"

Sophy had most courage. Desperate courage came to her now.

"Yes, we do."

"And you want to go to him?"

"Yes, mamma."

"And you don't love me? You don't want to stay with me?"

Sophy glanced for a moment at her sisters.

"Papa's so kind to us," she said.

"And I'm not kind?" asked Harriet with a sneering laugh. "When you're older, my dears, thank me for having been kind—really kind. It's really kind to teach you not to play these tricks—these mean and disgraceful little tricks."

All the children rose slowly and shrank back. They tried to get behind Suzette Bligh. Harriet laughed again when she saw the manœuvre.

"You needn't stay, Suzette," she said. "I know how to manage my own children."

Suzette was very white, and was trembling all over; it seemed as if her legs would hardly support her.

"What are you going to do?"

"It's no business of yours. They know very well. Leave me alone with them."

It was a terrible moment for timid Suzette. But love of the children had laid hold of her heart, and gave her strength.

"I can't go, Lady Harriet," she said in a low voice. "I can't leave you alone with them—not now."

"Not now?" cried Harriet fiercely.

"You're—you're not calm now. You're not fit——"

"You'd stand between me and my own children?"

"Dear Lady Harriet, I—I can't go away now." For she remembered so vividly all that the children's reminiscences, their nods and nudges, had hinted to her; she realised all the things which they had not told her; and she would not leave them now.

Her resistance set the crown to Harriet Courtland's rage. After an instant's pause she gave a half-articulate cry of anger, and rushed forward. Suzette tried to gather the children behind her, and to thrust the angry woman away. But Harriet caught Sophy by the arm and lifted her midway in the air. Garrett came right up to the door and peeped through.

"So you love papa and not me?"

Sophy turned her pale, terrified little face up to her mother's. The worst had happened, and the truth came out.

"No, we—we hate you. You're cruel to us; we hate you, and we love papa."

Harriet's grip tightened on the child's arm. Sophy's very audacity kept her still for a moment. But at the next she lifted her higher in the air. Suzette sprang forward with a cry, and Garrett dashed into the room, shrieking, "Don't, don't, my lady!"

They were too late. The child was flung violently down; her head struck the iron fender; she rolled over and lay quite still, bleeding from the forehead. Suzette and Garrett caught Harriet Courtland by the arms. A low, frightened weeping came from the other two little girls.

Harriet stood for a moment in the grasp of the two women who sought to restrain her and would have thrown themselves upon her had she tried to move. But restraint was no more necessary. Sophy had ransomed her sisters, and lay so quiet, bleeding from the head. In a loud voice Harriet Courtland cried, "Have I killed her? Oh, my God!" and herself broke into a tempest of hysterical sobbing. She fell back into Garrett's arms, shuddering, weeping, now utterly collapsed. Suzette went and knelt by Sophy.

"No, she's not dead, but it's no fault of yours," she said.

Harriet wrenched free from Garrett and flung herself on her knees by the table, stretching her arms across it and beating her forehead on the wood. The two children looked at her, wondering and appalled.

CHAPTER XXI

AN UNCOMPROMISING EXPRESSION

On the morrow of her attempted flight and enforced return a leaden heaviness had clogged Sibylla's brain and limbs. Her body was quick to recover; her thoughts were for long drowsy and numb. She seemed to have died to an old life without finding a new one. Blake was to her as a dead friend; she would see and hear of him no more; she harboured no idea of meeting him again. The bonds between them were finally rent. This attitude towards him saved his character from criticism and his weakness from too close an examination, while it left her free to brood in the security of despair on all that she had thought to find in him and on the desolation his loss had made. The instinctive love for her child, which had asserted itself while her intellect was dormant, could not prevail against the sullen preoccupation of re-awaking thoughts, or, if it could penetrate into them, came no more fresh and pure, but tainted with the sorrow and the anger which circled round that innocent head. She was tender, but in pity, not in pride; she loved, but without joy. The shadows hung so dark about the child's cot. They hid from her eyes still the sin of her own desertion, and hindered the remorse which might best lead her back to love unalloyed. Still she arraigned not herself but only Grantley and the inevitable. Grantley was the inevitable; there stood the truth of it; she bowed her head to the knowledge, but did not incline her heart to the lesson it had to teach.

Yet the knowledge counted; she looked on Grantley with different eyes. The revelation of himself, wrung from him by overpowering necessity, did its work. The resolve he had then announced, presumptuous beyond the right of mortal man, less than human in its cruelty, almost more than human in its audacity of successful revolt against destiny, might leave him hateful still, but showed him not negligible. He could not be put on one side, discarded, eliminated from her life. He was too big for that. Against her will he attracted her attention and constrained her interest. The thought of what lay beneath his suave demeanour sometimes appalled, sometimes amused, and always fascinated her now. She saw that her old conception had erred; it had been too negative in character; what he could not do or be or give had seemed the whole of the matter to her. In the light of the revelation that was wrong. The positive—a very considerable positive—must be taken into account. The pride she had loathed was not a barren self-conceit, nor merely a sterile self-engrossment. It had issue in an assurance almost supernatural and a courage above morality. Sibylla's first relief came in the reflection that though she might have married a monster, at least she had not given herself to a stick or a stone; she was clear as to her preference when the choice was reduced to that alternative.

His behaviour appealed to her humour too—that humour which could not save her from running away with Blake under the spell of her ideas, but would certainly have made her want to run away from him when the glamour of the ideas had worn off. The old perfection of manner found a new ornament in his easy ignoring of the whole affair. He referred to it once only, then indirectly and because he had a reason. He suggested apologetically that it would be well for them to exchange remarks more freely when the servants were waiting on them at meals.

"It will prevent comment on recent events," he added, as though that were his only reason.

Sibylla was deceived at first, but presently detected another and more important motive. The suggestion marked the beginning of a new campaign on which his inexhaustible perseverance engaged. He understood that his wife accused him of not taking her into his confidence, and of not making her a partner in his life. He was no more minded than before that she should have even plausible grounds for complaint. Starting, then, from general topics and subjects arising out of the journals of the day, he slid placidly and dexterously into frequent discussions of his own plans and doings, his business, his work on the County Council, his Parliamentary ambitions, his schemes for improving the property at Milldean. Sibylla acknowledged the cleverness of these tactics with a rueful smile. She had claimed to share his life; yet most of these topics happened to seem to her rather tedious. But she was debarred from saying that to Grantley; his retort was so obvious. She was often bored, but she was amused that boredom should be the first result of the new method.

"I hope all this interests you?" Grantley would inquire politely.

"Of course, since it concerns you," equal politeness obliged her to reply—and not politeness only. She had to be interested; it had been her theory that she would be, her grievance that she had been denied the opportunity of being. Nor could she make out whether Grantley had any inkling of her suppressed indifference to the County Council and so forth. Was he exercising his humour too? She could not tell, but curiosity and amusement tempered the coldness of her courtesy. They got on really very well at dinner, and especially while the servants were in the room; there was sometimes an awkward pause just after they were left alone. But on the whole the trifling daily intercourse went better than before Sibylla's flight—went indeed fairly well, as it can generally be made to if people are well bred and moderately humorous.

The great quarrel remained untouched, no span bridged the great chasm. Grantley might consent to talk about his County Council; that was merely a polite concession, involving no admission of guilt, and acknowledging no such wrong to his wife as could for a moment justify her action. When it came to deeper matters, he was afflicted with a shame and helplessness which seemed to paralyse him. To gloss over the absence of love, or even of friendship, was a task at which he was apt and tactful; to gain it back was work of the heart—and here he was as yet at a standstill. His instinct had told him to work through the child. But if he caressed the child in order to conciliate Sibylla, he would do a mean thing, and yet not succeed in his deception; he would admit a previous fault and gain no absolution by a calculated and interested confession. He could not bring himself to it. His manner to the child was as carelessly kind as ever; and when Sibylla was there the carelessness was almost more apparent than the kindness. Grantley's nature was against him; to do violence to it was a struggle. Ever ready to be kind, he disliked to show emotion. He felt it was being false to himself; being a sham and a hypocrite. To be gushing was abhorrent to him; to pretend to gush surely touched a more profound depth? His efforts achieved no success; and he did not let Sibylla perceive even the efforts themselves. For once his will, strong as it was, and his clear perception were both powerless before his temper and the instincts of his nature. The result was a deadlock. Matters could not move.

Such was the juncture of affairs when Christine Fanshaw came to Milldean. Her resolve to escape from the atmosphere of disgrace at home perhaps alone could have brought her; for she came in some trepidation, rather surprised that Sibylla had welcomed her, wondering whether the welcome was of Sibylla's own free will. Had she not betrayed Sibylla? Was she not responsible for the frustration of the great plan? Yet an acute curiosity mingled with and almost overpowered her apprehensions, and she was prepared to defend herself. The rumours about Walter Blake would be a weapon, if she needed one—a weapon effective, if cruel. As regards her own treachery, she made haste to throw herself on Sibylla's mercy.

"Of course you must have known it was through me?" she ended.

"Oh, yes, I knew that, of course."

"Here's your letter—the one you sent me to hand on to Grantley. He wired me not to send it."

"Oh, I thought he'd read it," said Sibylla thoughtfully.

She took it and put it in her pocket.

Christine looked at her with a smile.

"And yet you ask me to stay!" she remarked.

Sibylla smiled mockingly.

"Since this household owes all its happiness to you, it's only fair that you should come and look on at it."

"That's not at all a comfortable thing to say, Sibylla."

"No, it isn't, and it departs from our principle, which is to say nothing."

"That's not always very comfortable either."

Christine was giving a thought to her own affairs here.

"And we won't say anything more about what you did," Sibylla went on. "We won't discuss whether you were right, or whether I'm grateful, or anything of that sort."

"You ought to be."

"Or even whether I ought to be—though, of course, you'd want to think that."

Christine was disappointed. In her heart she had rather hoped to be put on her defence just enough to entitle her to use her weapon, and to tell some of the truth about Walter Blake. Sibylla's attitude gave her no excuse.

Though she would say nothing more about what Christine had done, Sibylla was easily persuaded to break the principle of silence about the main affair. Christine's curiosity lost the zest of difficult satisfaction; she had the whole history for the asking. She heard it, marvelling at the want of reticence her friend displayed, seeking how to reconcile this seeming immodesty with the rest of her impression of Sibylla. She recollected being very shy and ashamed (in the midst of her exultation) when she had let Harriet Courtland worm out the secret of her love for Caylesham. Sibylla was not ashamed—she was candid. Sometimes she was excited, sometimes she played the judge; but she was never abashed. Christine's wits sought hard for an explanation of this. Suddenly it came to her as she gazed on Sibylla's pure face and far-away eyes.

"My dear, you were never in love with him!" she cried.

If she hoped to surprise, or even to win a compliment on her penetration, she was utterly deceived.

"Oh, no!" said Sibylla. "In the way you mean I've never been in love with anybody except Grantley."

"Then why did you? Oh, tell me about it!" Christine implored.

"He appealed to my better feelings," Sibylla smiled back to her, mocking again. "I'd give the world that we hadn't been stopped! No, I can't say that, because——"

"Well?"

"I think Grantley would have done what he said."

Christine was the last woman in the world to rest ignorant of what Grantley had said. Sibylla was again disappointingly ready to tell the whole thing without any pressure worth mentioning.

"And you really believe he would have?" Christine half whispered when she had heard the story.

"If I didn't believe it with my whole heart, I shouldn't be here. I should be—well, somewhere—with Walter Blake."

"Thank God you're not!"

"Why do you say that? The proprieties, Christine?"

"Oh, only partly; but don't you think lightly of them, all the same. And the rest of the reasons don't matter." Christine got up and walked across the room and back again before she came to a stand opposite Sibylla. "I call that a man worth being in love with," she said.

"Walter?"

"Heavens, no! Grantley Imason! Oh, I know he's your husband! But still——"

Sibylla broke into a gentle laugh.

"It has the attraction of the horrible," she admitted. "He'd have done it, you know."

"It's mediæval," said Christine fondly. "And you were going away with Walter Blake!" She drew her little figure up straight. "Sibylla, you're no woman if you don't manage a man like that in the end. He's worth it, you know."

"You mean—if I don't let him manage me?" Sibylla was a little contemptuous. "I don't care about tyranny, even tempered by epigrams," she explained.

"Well, not when you only do the epigrams," smiled Christine.

"That's not true. I only ask a real partnership."

"You must begin by contributing all you have."

"I did. But Grantley——"

"Paid a composition? Oh yes, my dear; men do. That's as old as Byron anyhow." She came suddenly to Sibylla and kissed her. "And you'd be adorable, properly deluded."

"You shan't put it like that, Christine."

"Yes, I will—and I know he loves you."

"He can't love anything—not really."

"I shall watch him. Oh, my dear, what a comfort to watch anybody except John! Oh yes, yes, I suppose you'd better have my story too. You've had most of it before—without the name. But look away. I've no theories, you know—and—well, I was in love."

She laughed a little, blushing red. But her composure returned when she had finished her confession.

"And now what do we think of one another?" she asked, with her usual satirical little smile. "You don't know? Oh yes! You think me rather wicked, and I think you very silly; that's about what it comes to."

"I suppose that is about it," Sibylla laughed reluctantly.

"But I've repented, and you're only going to repent."

"Never!"

"Yes, you are. I take no credit for having done it first. It's much easier to repent of wickedness than of nonsense. The wickedness is much pleasanter at the time, and so seems much worse afterwards."

"And now you're in love with John?"

"Good heavens, no!" She pulled herself up. "Well, I don't know. If I'm in love now, it's not what I used to mean by it. One gets to use words so differently as time goes on."

"I don't think I shall ever learn that."

Destiny assumed Christine's small neat features for a moment in order to answer sternly:

"But you must!"

It was the worst way of dealing with Sibylla.

"I won't!" she answered in overt rebellion, her cheek flushing now as her confession had not availed to make it flush.

Christine did not fail to perceive the comic element in the case—strong enough, at all events, to serve as a relief to conversation, almost piquant when Grantley conscientiously related all manner of uninteresting things in order that Sibylla might be at liberty to take an interest in them. But this aspect did not carry matters very far or afford much real consolation. Substantially no progress was made. The failure endured, and seemed to Christine as complete as the devastation wrought in her own life. Nay, here there was an aggravation. In her home—she almost smiled to use the word now—there was no child. Here there was the boy. Her thoughts flew forward to the time when he would wonderingly surmise, painfully guess, at last grow into knowledge.

And already the mind stirred in little Frank. His intelligence grew, his affection blossomed as the first buds of a flower. He was no more merely a passive object of love and care. He began to know more than that he was nursed and fed, more than that his right was to these ministrations. The idea of the reason dawned in him. He stretched forth his hand no longer for bounty only, but for the inspirer of bounty—for love. Strung to abnormal sensitiveness, Christine deluded herself with the fancy that already he felt the shadow over the house, that his young soul was already chilled by the clouds of anger, and vainly cried for the sunshine of sympathy. If she did not truly see, yet she foresaw truly. Seeing and foreseeing, then, she asked where was the hope. And on this, with a bound, her thoughts were back to her own sorrow, and back to poor lonely old John in London, all by himself, with nobody to talk to, nobody to congratulate him on the success of his business, nobody to open his heart to, alone with his grievance against her, alone with the thought that, notwithstanding his grievance, he had taken Frank Caylesham's money, and grew prosperous again by the aid of it.

When Christine had been at Milldean a fortnight or so, business carried Grantley to town. The change his departure made was instantaneous and striking. A weight was off the house, the clouds dispersed. Sibylla was full of gaiety, and in that mood she could make all about her share her mirth. Above all, her devotion to Frank was given full rein. The child was always with her, and she knew no happiness save in evoking and responding to his love. She was now open and ostentatious about it, fearing no frigid glances and no implied criticism of her fond folly. Christine might well have found new ground for despair, so plainly did Sibylla display to her the blighting influence of Grantley's presence. He it was who froze up love—so Sibylla declared with an impetuous aggressive openness. But Christine would not despair. A wholesome anger rose in her heart and forbade despair. Her manner took on a coldness exceeding Grantley's indifference. She would not be a sharer in the games, a partner in the merriment, a sympathiser in the love. Sibylla was not slow to see how she stood off and drew herself away. Quickly she sought for reasons. Was it that Christine would not join in what seemed to be a league against Grantley; or was there another reason? She had told Christine how it was through Walter Blake's weakness and not through her scruples that little Frank had not been left to his fate. Did her love then seem hypocrisy? That was not true—though it might be true that remorse now had a share in it. The more the child grew to life, the more horrible became the thought that he might have died. After a day or two of smouldering protest, she broke out on Christine.

"You think I've no right to love him," she asked, "after what I was ready to do? Is that what you think? Oh, speak out plainly! I see you've got something against me."

Christine was cold and composed. Never had her delicately critical manner been more pronounced.

"I'm sure I hope you repent," she observed meditatively; "and I hope you thank heaven that man was what he turned out to be."

"Well, call it repentance, then. I suppose I've a right to repent? You can't understand how I really feel. But if it is repentance, why need you discourage it?"

"I don't discourage repentance, and I'm glad you're beginning to see that you ought to repent. But it's not that I'm thinking of."

"What are you thinking of, then?" cried Sibylla in unrestrained impatience.

"You're prepared for an open quarrel?"

"Oh, I shan't quarrel with you!" Her smile was rather disdainful.

"No, you won't quarrel with me; I'm not of enough importance to you! I'm very glad I'm not, you know. Being important to you doesn't seem to be consistent with being an independent creature."

Sibylla glanced at her in arrested attention.

"What do you mean by that?" she asked in low quick tones. The charge was so strangely like that which she was for ever formulating against Grantley. Now Christine levelled it at her.

"You call Grantley selfish," Christine went on. "You're just as bad yourself—yes, worse! He is trying to be different, I believe. Oh, I admit the poor man doesn't do it very well: he gets very little encouragement! But are you trying? No! You're quite content with yourself. You've done no wrong—— Well, perhaps it was a little questionable to be ready to leave Frank to die! But even that would be all right if only I could understand it!"

"You'd better go on now," said Sibylla quietly.

"Yes, I will go on; I am going on. You were ready to leave the child to die sooner than go on living as you'd been living. Isn't that how you put it? You were willing to give his life to prevent that? Well, are you willing to give any of your own life, any of your way of thinking, any of what you call your nature, or your temperament, or what not? Not a bit of it! You can love Frank when there's no danger of Grantley's thinking it may mean that you could forgive him! As soon as there's any danger of that, you draw back. You use the unhappy child as a shield between Grantley and yourself, as a weapon against Grantley. Yes you do, Sibylla. Whenever you're inclined to relent towards Grantley, you go and sit by that child's cot and use your love for him to fan your hatred against Grantley. Isn't that true?"

Sibylla sat silent, with attentive frightened eyes. This was a new picture—was it a true one? One feature of it at least struck home with a terribly true-seeming likeness of her own mind. She used her love for her child to fan her hatred against Grantley!

"You complain," Christine went on in calm relentlessness, "of what Grantley is to the child. That's a sham most of the time. You're thinking of what he is to you. And even where it's true, don't you do all you can to make him feel as he does? How is he to love what you make the stalking-horse of your grievances?" She turned on Sibylla scornfully, almost fiercely now. "Your husband, your son, the whole world, aren't made for your emotions to go sprawling over, Sibylla! You must have caught that idea from young Blake, I think."

She walked off to the window and stood there, looking out. No sound came from Sibylla. Presently Christine looked round rather nervously. She had gone a little too far perhaps. That phrase about emotions "sprawling" was—well, decidedly uncompromising. She met Sibylla's eyes. They wore a hunted look—as though some peril walled her in and she found no way of escape. Her voice trembled as she faltered:

"Is that what you really think of me, Christine?"

"A bruised reed thou shalt not break." Christine had the wisdom to remember that. Remorse must fall short of despair, self-knowledge of self-hatred, or there remains no possibility of a rebound to hope and effort. Christine came across to her friend with hands outstretched.

"No, no, dear," she said, "not you—not yourself! But this mood of yours, the way you're going on. And, true or false, isn't it what you must make Grantley think?"

Sibylla moved her hands in a restless gesture, protesting against the picture of herself—even thus softened—denying its truth, fascinated by it.

"I don't know," she murmured, "I don't know. Christine, it's a horrible idea!"

Christine fell on her knees beside her.

"If only you hadn't been so absurdly in love with him, my dear!" she whispered.

CHAPTER XXII

ASPIRATIONS AND COMMON SENSE

Rumour spoke truly. Young Walter Blake was back in town with an entirely new crop of aspirations maturing in the ready soil of his mind. The first crop had not proved fortunate. It had brought him into a position most disagreeable and humiliating to reflect upon, and into struggles for which he felt himself little fit. He had been given time to meditate and to cool—to cool even to shuddering when he recalled that night in the Sailors' Rest, and pictured the tragedy for which he had so nearly become responsible. His old desires waning, his aspirations were transfigured at the suggestion of a new attraction. He had been on the wrong tack—that was certain. Again virtue seemed to triumph in this admission. He no longer desired to be made good—it was (as he had conceived and attempted it) such a stormy and soul-shaking process. Now he desired to be kept good. He did not now want a guiding star which he was to follow through every peril, over threatening waves and through the trough of an angry sea. The night at the Sailors' Rest disposed of that metaphor and that ideal. Now he wanted an anchor by whose help he might ride out the storm, or a harbour whose placid bosom should support his gently swaying barque. Strength, constancy, and common sense supplanted imagination, ardour, and self-devotion as the requisites his life demanded.

Again Caylesham showed tact. He would not ask the lady's name. But when Blake next dined with him, he enjoyed the metamorphosis, and silently congratulated Grantley Imason.

"So it's St. George's, Hanover Square, and everything quite regular this time, is it?" he asked, with an indulgent humour. "Well, I fancy you're best suited to that. Only take care!"

"You may be sure that the woman I marry will be——" Blake began.

"Perfection? Oh, of course! That's universal. But it's not enough." He lay back comfortably in his armchair, enjoying his cigar. "Not enough, my boy! I may have two horses, and you may have two horses, and each of my horses may be better than either of your horses; but when we come to driving them, you may have the better pair. Two good 'uns don't always make a good pair." He grew quite interested in his subject—thanks, perhaps, to the figure in which he clothed it. "They've got to match—both their paces and their ways. They've got to go kindly together, to like the feel of one another, don't you know? Each of 'em may be as good as you like single, but they may make—by Jove, yes!—the devil of a bad pair! It's double harness we're talking about, Blake, my boy. Oh, you may think I know nothing about it, but I've seen a bit—— Well, that's not a thing I boast about; but I have seen a bit, you know."

"That's just what I've been thinking," said young Blake sagaciously. He referred to Caylesham's doctrines, not his experiences.

"Oh, you've been thinking, have you?" smiled Caylesham. "Come a mucker then, I suppose?"

"I—I miscalculated. Well, we must all learn by experience."

"Devilish lucky if we can!"

"There's no other way," Blake insisted.

"Have I said there is?" He looked at Blake in an amused knowledge. "Going in for the straight thing this time?"

Half in pride, half in shame, Blake answered:
"Yes."
"Quite right too!" Caylesham was very approving.
"Well, if you say so——" began Blake, laughing.
"Quite right for you, I mean." There was a touch of contempt somewhere in his tone. "But don't forget what I've been saying. It's double harness, my boy! Pace, my boy, and temper, and the feel—the feel! All the things a fellow never thinks about!"
"Well, you're a pretty preacher on this subject!"
"I've heard a lot of things you never have. Oh, well, you may have once, perhaps." His glance was very acute, and Blake flushed under it. "You're well out of that affair," Caylesham went on, dropping his mask of ignorance. "Oh, I don't want to know how it happened. I expect I can guess."
"What do you mean?" Blake's voice sounded angry.
"You funked it—eh?"
It was a strong thing to say to a man in your own house. But a sudden gust of impatience had swept Caylesham away. The young man was in the end so contemptible, so incapable of strength, such a blarney over his weakness.
"Now don't glare at me; I'm not afraid. You tackled too big a job, I fancy. Oh, I'm not asking questions, you know." He got up and patted Blake's shoulder. "Don't mind me. You're doing quite right. Hope you won't find it devilish dull!"
Blake's bad temper vanished. He began to laugh.
"That's right," said Caylesham. "I'm too old to convert, and nearly too old to fight; but I'll be your best man, Walter."
"It'll keep me straight, Caylesham."
"Lord bless you, so it will!"
He chuckled in irrepressible amusement.
"The other thing's no go!"
"No more it is. It needs—— No, I'm not going to be immoral any more. Go ahead! You're made for double harness, Walter. Choose her well! you'll have to learn her paces, you know."
"Or she mine?"
Blake was a little on his dignity again.
"Have another whisky and soda," said Caylesham, with admirable tact.
His advice, meant as precautionary, proved provocative. Memory worked with it—the carking memory of a failure of courage. Blake might blarney as he would about awakened conscience, but Caylesham had put his finger on the sore spot. Pleasure's potentiality of tragedy had asserted itself. It had been supremely disconcerting to discover and recognise its existence. Young Blake was for morality now—not so much because its eyes were turned upwards as for the blameless security of its embrace. He had suffered such a scare. He really wondered how Caylesham had managed to stand the strain of pleasing himself—with the sudden tragic potentialities of it. He paid unwilling homage to the qualities necessary for vice—for candid unmasquerading vice; he knew all about the other species.
Yet he was not hard on Sibylla. He recognised her temperament, her unhappy circumstances, and his own personal attractions. What he did not recognise was the impression of himself which that night in the Sailors' Rest would leave on her. He conceived an idea of his own magnanimity resting in her mind—yes, though such a notion could gain no comfortable footing in his.
Caylesham let him go without more advice—though he had half a mind to tell him not to marry a pretty woman.
"Oh, well, in his present mood he won't; and it would do him lots of good if he did," the impenitent, clear-sighted, good-humoured sinner reflected, with all the meaning which his experience could put into the words. He was of opinion that for certain people the only chance of salvation lay in suffering gross injustice. "If what a fellow brings on himself is injustice," he used to say. He always maintained that fellows brought it on themselves—an expiring gasp of conscience, perhaps.
Gossip and conjecture had played so much with Walter Blake's name that Mrs. Selford had at first been shy of his approaches and chary of her welcome. "We must think of Anna," she had said to her husband. But thinking of or for Anna was rapidly becoming superfluous. The young woman took that department to herself. Her stylishness grew marvellously, and imposed a yoke of admiring submission. It was an extraordinary change from the awkward, dowdy, suppressed girl to this excellently appointed product. The liberty so tardily conceded was making up for lost time, and bade fair to transform itself into a tyranny. The parents were ready subjects, and cast back from the theories of to-day a delusive light on the practices of the past. They concluded that they had always indulged Anna, and that the result was most satisfactory. Then they must indulge her still. So Blake's visits went on, and the welcome became cordial. For Anna was quite clear that she at least had nothing against Blake. His attraction for her was not what had been his charm in Sibylla's eyes. Her impulse was not to reform; it was to conquer. But gossip and conjectures as to his past life were as good incentives to the one task as to the other. His good looks, his air of fashion, his comfortable means, helped the work. He widened the horizon of men for her, and made her out of conceit with her first achievements. She was content that Jeremy should disappear from her court; she became contemptuously impatient of Alec Turner's suit. She was fastidious and worldly-wise.
Again Mrs. Selford rejoiced. She had been in some consternation over Alec Turner's now obvious attachment, coming just at the time when Anna had established the right to please herself. Suppose her first use of liberty had been to throw herself away? For to what end be stylish if you are going to marry on a hundred and fifty pounds a year? But Anna was quite safe—strangely safe, Mrs. Selford thought in her heart, though she rebuked the wonder. Almost unkindly safe, she thought sometimes, as she strove to soften the blows which fell on poor Alec—since, so soon as he ceased to be dangerous, he became an object of compassion.
"Anna is so sensible," she said to Selford. "She's quite free from the silliness that girls so often show"; but she sighed just a little as she spoke.
"She'd make a good wife for any man," declared Selford proudly—a general declaration in flat contradiction to Caylesham's theories about double harness.
Anna paid no heed to opinions or comments. She went about her business and managed it with instinctive skill. It sometimes puzzled poor Alec Turner to think why his presence was so often requested, when his arrival evoked so little enthusiasm. He did not realise the part

he played in Anna's scheme, nor how his visits were to appear to Walter Blake. Anna's generalship had thought all this out. The exhibition of Alec was a subsidiary move in the great strategic conception of capturing Walter Blake on the rebound from Sibylla.

But the pawn was not docile, and objected violently so soon as its function began to be apparent. Anna precipitated what she did not desire—a passionate avowal in which the theme of her own gifts and fascination was intermingled with the ideal of influencing the trend of public opinion from a modest home and on a modest income. She was told that she could be removed from the vanities of life and be her true, her highest self. When she showed no inclination to accept the path in life thus indicated, Alec passed through incredulity to anger. Had he cast his pearls before—— Well, at inappreciative feet? At this tone Anna became excusably huffy; to refuse a young man is not to deny all the higher moral obligations. Besides Alec annoyed her very much by assuming persistently that the dictates of her heart called her towards him, and that worldly considerations alone inspired her refusal.

"Oh, you're silly!" she cried. "I tell you it's nothing of the sort."

The dusk of the afternoon softened her features; the light of the fire threw up in clear outline the stylish well-gowned figure. Poor Alec, in his shabby mustard suit, stood opposite her, his hands in his pockets, in dogged misery and resentment, with all the helpless angry surprise of a first experience of this kind, fairly unable to understand how it was that love did not call forth love, obstinate in clinging to the theory of another reason as the sole explanation. Things did not exist in vain. For what was his love?

"But—but what am I to do?" he stammered.

Rather puzzled—after all rather flattered, Anna prayed him to be sensible and friendly. He consented to hope for her happiness, though he was obviously not sanguine about it. For himself all was over! So he said as he flung out of the room, knowing nothing of what lay before him on the path of life; discerning nothing of a certain daughter of a poor old political writer—a little round woman who made her own gowns, was at once very thrifty and very untidy, was inclined to think that the rulers of the earth should be forcibly exterminated, and lavished an unstinted affection on every being, human or brute, with which she was ever brought into contact. And if she did not greatly influence the trend of public opinion—well, anyhow she tried to. Just now, however, Alec knew nothing about her; he was left to think hopelessly of the trim figure and the lost ideals—the two things would mix themselves up in his mind.

To his pathetic stormy presence there succeeded Walter Blake, with all his accomplishment in the art of smooth love-making, with his aspirations again nicely adjusted to the object of his desires (he was so much cleverer than poor Alec over that!), with his power to flatter not only by love but still more by relative weakness. He, of course, did not run at the thing as Alec had done. That would be neither careful of the chances nor economical of the pleasure. Many a talk was needed before his purpose became certain or Anna could show any sign of understanding it.

He dealt warily with her; he was trying, unconsciously perhaps, to perform the task Caylesham had indicated to him—the task of learning her paces and adapting his thereto. It was part of his theory about her that she must be approached with great caution; and of course he knew that there was one very delicate bit of ground. How much had she heard about himself and Sibylla? It was long before he mentioned Sibylla's name. At last he ventured on throwing out a feeler. Anna's unruffled composure persuaded him that she knew nothing of the facts; but her shrewd analysis of Sibylla showed, in his judgment, that she quite understood the woman. It was the dusk of the afternoon again (Anna rather affected that time of day), and Blake, with a sigh which might be considered in the nature of a confession, ventured to say:

"I wish I could read people as you can. I should have avoided a lot of trouble."

"You can read yourself anyhow, can't you?" asked Anna.

"By Jove, that's good—that's very good! No, I don't know that I can. But I expect you can read me, Miss Selford. I shall have to come to you for lessons, shan't I?"

"I'll tell you all the hard bits," she laughed.

"You'll have to see a lot of me to do that!"

Anna was not quite so sure of the need, but she did not propose to stop the game.

"Do I seem so very reluctant to see a lot of you?" she inquired.

Blake's eyes caught hers through the semi-darkness. She was aware of the emotion with which he regarded her. It found an answer in her, an answer which for the moment upset both her coolness and her sense of mastery. She had a revelation that her dominion, not seriously threatened, yet would be pleasantly chequered by intervals of an instinctive submission. This feeling almost smothered the element of contempt which had hitherto mingled in her liking for him and impaired the pride of her conquest.

"I was judging you by myself. Compared with me, you seem reluctant," he said in a low voice, coming a little nearer to her. "But then it does me such a lot of good to come and see you. It's not only the pleasure I come for, though that's very great. You keep up my ideals."

"I'm so glad. The other day I was told I'd ruined all somebody's ideals. Well, I oughtn't to have told you that, I suppose; but it slipped out."

Things will slip out, if one takes care to leave the door open.

She was standing by the table, and Blake was now close by her.

"Since I've known you——"

"Why, you've known me for years, Mr. Blake!"

"No, I only knew a little girl till—till I came back to town this time." He referred to that yachting cruise on which he had ultimately started alone. "But since then I've been a different sort of fellow. I want to go on being different, and you can help me." His voice trembled; he was wrapped up in his emotion, and abundantly sure of its sincerity.

Anna moved away a little, now rather nervous, since no instinct, however acute, can give quite the assurance that practice brings. But she was very triumphant too, and, moreover, a good deal touched. That break in young Blake's voice had done him good service before: it never became artificial or overdone, thanks to his faculty of coming quite fresh to every new emotional crisis; it was always most happily natural.

"Anna!" he said, holding out his hands, with those skilfully appealing eyes of his just penetrating to hers.

With a long-drawn breath she gave him her hand. He pressed it, and began to draw her gently towards him. She yielded to him slowly, thinking at the last moment of what she had decided she would never think about and would show no wisdom in recalling. The vision of another woman had shot into her mind, and for a few seconds gave her pause. Her hesitation was short, and left her self-confidence unbroken. What she had won she would keep. The dead should bury its dead—a thing it had declined to do for Christine Fanshaw.

"Anna!" he said again. "Do you want me to say more? Isn't that saying it all? I can't say all of it, you know."

She let him draw her slowly to him; but she had spoken no word, and was not yet in his arms, when the door opened, and she became aware of a man standing on the threshold. Young Blake, all engrossed, had noticed nothing, but he had perceived her yielding.

"Ah, my Anna!" he whispered rapturously.

"Hush!" she hissed, drawing her hand sharply away. "Is that you, Richards?"

Richards was the Selfords' manservant.

The man laughed.

"If you'd turn the light on, you couldn't mistake me for anybody so respectable as Richards," he said. "I've been with your father in the study, and he told me I should find your mother here."

Anna recognised the voice.

"Mr. Imason! I didn't know you were in London."

"Just up for the day, and I wanted to see your father."

Anna moved to the switch, and turned on the light. She glanced hastily at young Blake. He had not moved; his face was rather red, and he looked unhappy. Anna's feeling was one of pronounced anger against Grantley Imason. His appearance had all the effect of purposed malice; it made her feel at once jealous and absurd. But it was on her own behalf that she resented it. She was not free from a willingness that Blake should be made uncomfortable; so much discipline would be quite wholesome for him. For her own part, though, she wanted to get out of the room.

"May I ring for the real Richards, and—— Oh, I beg your pardon, Blake, how are you? May I ring for the real Richards, and send word to your mother, Anna?"

Grantley was, as usual, urbane and unperturbed.

"I'll go and find her for you. I think she's lying down."

"Oh, well, then——"

"No, I know she'll want to see you," and Anna ran lightly out of the room.

Grantley strolled to an armchair and sank into it. He did not look at Blake, nor, his formal greeting given, appear conscious of his presence.

Young Blake was in a turmoil. He hated to see Grantley; all the odious thought of his failure and defeat was brought back. He hated that Grantley should have seen him making love to Anna Selford, for in his heart he was conscious that he could not cheat an outside vision as he could manage to cheat himself. But both these feelings, if not swallowed up in fear, were at least outdone by it. His great desire had been to settle this matter finally and irrevocably before a hint of it came to the ears either of Grantley or of Sibylla. What would Grantley do now?

"You saw us?" he asked in a sullen anxious voice.

"I couldn't help it. I'm sorry," said Grantley in colourless politeness.

"Well?"

"I really don't understand your question, Blake. At least, you seem to mean it for a question."

"You do know what I mean. I'm not going to ask any favours of you. I only want to know what you intend to do?"

"About what?"

"About what you saw—and heard too, I suppose?"

Grantley rose from his chair in a leisurely fashion, and stood with his back to the fire. He was looking at young Blake with a slight smile; Blake grew redder under it.

"Oh, I can't beat about the bush!" Blake went on impatiently. "You might, if you chose, tell Miss Selford what you know."

"Well?" said Grantley in his turn.

"And—and—— Oh, you see what might happen as well as I do. I—I meant to—to explain at my own time; but——"

"I shouldn't let the time come in a hurry, Blake. It'll be a very awkward quarter of an hour for both of you, and quite unnecessary."

"Unnecessary?"

There was a ring of hope in Blake's voice; he liked to be told that any such confession was unnecessary, and would have welcomed such an assurance even from Grantley's hostile lips.

"Certainly; and equally unnecessary that I should tell Anna anything." He paused a moment, and then went on. "In a different case I might think I had a different duty—though, being what you might call an interested party, I should consider carefully before I allowed myself to act on that view. But as matters stand, you yourself have made any action on my part superfluous."

"I have?"

"Oh yes! You so far injured the fame of the woman for whom you hadn't afterwards the pluck to fight, that it's not necessary for me to tell Selford that you were in love with her a few months before you made love to his daughter, nor that you tried to run away with her, but that in the end you funked the job. I needn't tell him, because he knows—and his wife knows. You took care of that."

Young Blake said nothing, though he opened his lips as if to speak.

"And I needn't tell Anna either. That's unnecessary, for the same reason. She knows just as well as her father and mother know."

"She knows nothing, I tell you. She hasn't an idea——"

"Did you see her face when she saw that I wasn't Richards?"

"I tell you—— She was embarrassed, of course—— But——"

"She knows quite well, Blake. Oh, not the details, but the main thing. She knows that quite well. And she will have made her decision. There's no duty incumbent on me."

"You'll say nothing then?"

"I shall say nothing at all."

Grantley relapsed into silence—a most easy self-possessed silence. His eyes were on young Blake no more, but rested placidly on one of Selford's best pictures on the opposite wall. Blake cleared his throat, and shifted uneasily from one foot to the other.

"Why do you stay?" asked Grantley mildly. "Wouldn't it be better to continue your interview with Anna elsewhere? Mrs. Selford's coming in here, you see."

Blake broke out:

"God knows, Imason, it's difficult for me to say a word to you, but——"

Grantley raised his hand a little.

"It's impossible," he said. "There can be no words between you and me about that. And what does it matter to you what I think? I shall hold my tongue. And you'll feel sure I've no real cause of complaint—quite sure if only I hold my tongue. And I think Anna will hold her tongue. Then you'll forget she knows, and go on posturing before her with entire satisfaction to yourself." He turned his eyes on him and laughed a little. "As long as you can humbug yourself or anybody else, or even get other people to let you think you're humbugging them, you're quite happy, you know."

Blake looked at him once and twice, but his tongue found no words. He turned and walked towards the door.

"Wait in the dining-room," said Grantley.

Blake went out without turning or seeming to hear. After a moment or two Anna's step came down the stairs.

"Mamma'll be down directly, Mr. Imason," she called as she reached the door. Then her eyes took in the room. "Mr.—Mr. Blake?" she asked, with a sudden quick rush of colour in her cheeks.

"I think you'll find him in the dining-room," said Grantley gravely.

She understood—and she did not lack courage. She had enough for two—for herself and for Blake. She met Grantley's look fair and square, drawing up her trim stylish figure to a stiff rigidity, and setting her lips in a resolute line. Grantley admired her attitude and her open defiance of him. He smiled at her in a confidential mockery.

"Thanks, Mr. Imason, I'll look for him. You'll be all right till mamma comes?"

"Oh yes, I shall be all right, thanks, Anna."

He smiled still. Anna gave him another look of defiance.

"I intend to go my own way; I know what I'm about. I don't care a pin what you think." The glance seemed to Grantley as eloquent as Lord Burghley's nod. And no more than Lord Burghley did she spoil its effect by words. She gave it to Grantley full and square, then turned on her heel and swung jauntily out of the room.

Grantley's smile vanished. He screwed up his lips as if he had tasted something rather sour.

CHAPTER XXIII

A THING OF FEAR

Grantley Imason had intended to go down to Milldean that same evening, but a summons from Tom Courtland reached him, couched in such terms that he could not hesitate to obey it. He sought Tom at his club the moment he received the message. Tom had been sent for to his own house in the morning, and had heard what had happened there. He had seen the wounded child and the other two terrified little creatures. Suzette Bligh gave him her account. The doctor told him that Sophy was no longer in danger, but that the matter was a grave one—a very serious shock and severe local injury; the child would recover with care and with quiet, but would always bear a mark of the wound, an ineffaceable scar. That was the conclusion, half good, half bad, reached after a night of doubt whether Sophy would not die from the violence and the shock.

"Did you see your wife?" Grantley asked.

"See her? I should kill her if I saw her," groaned Tom.

"But—but what's being done?"

"She's in her room—she's been there ever since it happened. Suzette's seen her—nobody else. Nobody else will go near her. Of course, while there was a doubt about Sophy—well, the doctor made it a condition that she should confine herself to her room till the thing took a definite turn. I hope she's frightened at last. I don't know what to do. The woman ought to be hanged, Grantley."

But wrath and horror at his wife were not the only feelings in Tom's mind; the way the thing had happened raised other thoughts. He was prostrate under the sense that the fury which had smitten poor little Sophy had been aimed at him; his acts had inspired and directed it. He had made his children's love for him a crime in their mother's eyes. All his excuses, both false and real, failed him now. His own share in the tragedy of his home was heavy and heinous in his eyes.

"I ought to have remembered the children," he kept repeating desperately. He ought to have stayed and fought the battle for and with them, however hard the battle was. But he had run away—to Mrs. Bolton, and left them alone to endure the increased fury of Harriet's rage. "I've been a damned coward over it," he said, "and this is what comes of it, Grantley."

It was all true. Tom had not thought of the children. Even though he loved them, he had deserted them treacherously, because he had considered only his own wrongs, and had been wrapped up in his personal quarrel with his wife. What he had found unendurable himself he had left those helpless little creatures to endure. All the arguments which had seemed so strong to justify or to palliate his resort to the Bolton refuge sounded weak and mean to him now—and to Grantley too, who had been used to rely on them, lightly accepting them with a man of the world's easy philosophy. His friends had almost encouraged Tom in his treacherous desertion of his children; they too had looked at nothing but the merits of his quarrel with Harriet, putting that by itself in a false isolation from the total life of the family, of which it was in truth an integral indivisible part. So Grantley meditated as he listened to Tom's laments; and the meditation was not without meaning and light for him also.

Tom had a request to make of him—that he would go round to the house and spend the evening there.

"I daren't trust myself near Harriet," he said, "and I'm uneasy with only the servants there. They're all afraid of her. She was cowed, Suzette says, while there was danger; but she may break out again—anything might start her again. If you could stay till she's safely in bed——"

"I'll stay all night, if necessary, old fellow," said Grantley promptly.

"It'll take a weight off my mind—and I've got about enough to bear. I'm going to stay here, of course; so you'll know where to find me if I'm wanted, though I don't see what can happen now."

Terror brooded over the Courtlands' house. Grantley rejoiced to see how his coming did something to lift the cloud. The two children left Suzette's side (they loved her, but she seemed to them a defence all too frail), and came to him, standing on either side of his knee and putting their hands in his. The listening strained look passed out of their eyes as he talked to them. Presently little Vera climbed up and nestled on his knee, while Lucy leant against his shoulder, and he got them to prattle about happy things, old holidays and bygone treats, to which Tom had taken them. At last Lucy laughed merrily at some childish memory. The sound went straight to Grantley's heart; a great tenderness came upon him. As he kissed them, his thoughts flew to his own little son—the child who had now begun to know love, to greet it and to ask for it. How these poor children prized even a decent kindness! Grantley seemed to himself to have done a fine day's work—as fine a day's work as he had ever done in his life—when he sent them off to bed with smiling lips and eyes relieved of dread.

"You won't go away to-night, will you?" Lucy whispered as she kissed him good-night.

"Of course he's not going!" cried little Vera, bravely confident in the strength of her helplessness.

"No, I'll stay all night—all the whole night," Grantley promised.

He made his camp in the library on the ground floor, and there presently Suzette Bligh came to see him. She gave a good account of the wounded child. Sophy slept; the capable cheery woman who had come as nurse gave her courage to sleep.

"We must get her away to the seaside as soon as possible, and she'll get all right, I think; though there must be a mark always. And of course the permanent question remains. Isn't it all hopeless, Mr. Imason?"

"It's a terrible business for you to be involved in."

"Oh, I can only thank heaven I was here! But for me I believe she'd have killed the child."

"What state is she in now?"

"I really don't know. She won't speak to me. She sits quite still, just staring at me. I try to stay with her, but it's too dreadful. I can't help hating her—and I think she knows it."

Grantley had some experience of coming to know what people felt about him.

"I expect she does," he nodded.

"What will happen, Mr. Imason?"

"I don't know—except that the children mustn't stay with her. Is she afraid of being prosecuted, do you think?"

"She hasn't said anything about it. No, she doesn't seem afraid; I don't think that's her feeling. But—but her eyes look awful. When I had to tell her that the doctor had forbidden her to come near the children, and said he would send the police into the house if she tried to go to them—well, I've never seen such an expression on any human face before. She looked like—like somebody in hell, Mr. Imason."

"Ah!" groaned Grantley with a jerk of his head, as though he turned from a fearful spectacle.

"I've just been with her. I persuaded her to go to bed—she's not slept since it happened, I know—and got her to let me help her to undress. Her maid won't go to her; she's too frightened. I hope she'll go to sleep, or really I think she'll lose her senses." She paused and then asked: "Will this make any difference in—in the proceedings?"

"Well, it gives Tom something to bargain with, doesn't it? But you can't tell with her. The ordinary motives may not appeal to her, any more than the natural feelings. I hope it may be possible to frighten her."

"Anyhow the children won't have to stay—you're sure of that?"

"We must try hard for that," said Grantley.

But Tom had made even that more difficult, because he had considered only his own quarrel, and, not thinking of the children, had run away to refuge with Mrs. Bolton, saving his own skin by treacherous flight.

Suzette bade Grantley good-night. She too must sleep, or her strength would fail.

"You'll keep the door open?" she asked. "And her room is just over this. You'll hear if she moves, though I don't think she will. It is good of you, Mr. Imason. We shall all sleep quietly to-night. Oh, but how tired you'll be!"

"Not I!" he smiled. "I've often sat up till daylight on less worthy occasions. You're the hero! You've come through this finely."

Suzette's cheeks flushed at his praise.

"I do love the poor children," she said, as Grantley pressed her hand.

He sat down to his vigil. The house became very still. Once or twice steps passed to and fro in the room above; then there was silence. In a quarter of an hour, perhaps, there were steps again; then another interval of quiet. This alternation of movement and rest went on for a long time. If Harriet Courtland slept, her sleep was broken. But presently Grantley ceased to mark the sound—ceased even to think of the Courtlands or of the house where he was. Led by the experiences of the day and by the feelings they had evoked, his thoughts took their way to Milldean, to his own home, to his wife and son. How nearly tragedy had come there too! Nay, was it yet gone? Was not its shadow still over the house? And why? He looked back again at the Courtlands—at Harriet's unhallowed rage, at Tom's weakness and desertion, at the fate of the children—not thought of and forgotten by the one, ill-used and put in terror by the other. He recollected how once they used to joke about the Courtlands' being at any rate useful as a warning. That joke had taken on too keen an edge to sound mirthful now. But the serious truth in it came home to him, making plain what he had been groping after ever since that night at the Sailors' Rest at Fairhaven, ever since Sibylla had opened her mouth against him and spoken the bitterness of her heart. Yes, he thought he saw where the truth lay now. Calamity held up a torch to light his wandering feet.

No borrowed light had made plain the steps of the woman upstairs. The glare of her own ruin had been needed to illuminate the way she trod, so dense was the turbid darkness of her spirit. She saw now where she stood—and there seemed no going back. She had fallen into fits of remorse before—she had called herself cursed over her betrayal of Christine: that was nothing to this; yet she remembered it now, and it went to swell the wave of despair which overwhelmed her. Well might her eyes look like the eyes of one in hell, for she was cut off from all love and sympathy. She herself had severed all those bonds whereby a human being becomes other than a roving solitary brute. There was no re-binding them. Nobody would come near her; nobody could endure her presence; she was a thing of hatred and of fear. Even Suzette Bligh shrank while she served, and loathed while she ministered. Her husband could not trust himself in the house with her, and she could not be trusted in the room with her children. By the narrowest luck she was not a murderess; in the hearts of all, and in her own heart, she seemed a leper—a leper among people who were whole—an unclean thing—because of her bestial rage.

These thoughts had been in her mind all the night before and all the day. They did not consort with sleep nor make terms with peaceful rest. Sometimes they drove her to wild and passionate outbursts of weeping and imprecation; oftener they chained her motionless to her chair, so still that only her angry eyes showed life and consciousness. They left little room for fear of any external punishment, or for shame at any public exposure. They went deeper than that, condemning not the body but the soul, pronouncing not the verdict of the world, but of herself and of nature's inexorable law. They displayed the procession of evil—weakness growing to vice, vice turning to crime, crime throttling all the good—till she had become a thing horrible to those about her, horrible and incredible even to herself. And there was no going back, no going back at all. Her will was broken, and she had no hope in herself. The weights were on her feet, and dragged her down the abyss which now lay open and revealed before her eyes.

Suzette had persuaded her to undress and go to bed. She must sleep—yes, or she would go mad with the thoughts. But where was sleep with the agony of their sting? She had her chloral—an old ally—and had recourse to it. Then she would fling herself on the bed and try to think she could sleep. Exasperation drove her up again, and she paced the room in wrathful despair, cursing herself because she could not sleep, battling against the remorseless thoughts, exclaiming against their tortures, refusing the inquisition to which they subjected her. Then—back to bed again for another futile effort, another cry of despair, to be followed by another outburst of wild impatience, another fierce unavailing struggle against her tormentors, new visions of what she was and of what her life must be.

This was not a thing that she would endure; nobody could endure it and keep sanity. It should be ended! Her fierce defiant fury rose yet once more; the temper which had wrought all the calamity was not tamed by it in the end. She turned to her drug again. She knew there was danger in that, but she put the notion behind her scornfully. Why, the stuff would not even make her sleep! Could it hurt her when it could not even give her sleep? That was nonsense, stupid nonsense. She would have sleep! Nature fell victim to her rage now; she would beat nature down by her fury, as she had been wont to beat down all opposing wills. She had listened to nothing in her tempests. Now she rose again to the whirlwind of passion, denying what she knew, refusing to look at it. Kill herself? Not she! Yet if she did, what matter? Had she anything to look for in life? Would anybody grieve for her? It would be a riddance for all of them if she died. But she wouldn't die. No danger of that—and no such luck either! Each dose left her more pitiably wide-awake, more gruesomely alert in mind, more hideously acute to feel the sting of those torturing thoughts. An over-dose indeed! No dose, it seemed, could serve even to dull the sharpness of her mordant reflections. But she would have sleep—at all costs, sleep! She cursed herself vilely because she could not sleep.

Thus came, as of old, now for the last time, the madness and blindness of her rage, the rage which forgot all save itself, merged every other consciousness, spared nobody and nothing. It was turned against herself now, and neither did it spare herself. She drugged herself again, losing all measure, and then flung herself heavily on the bed. Ah! Yes, surely there was a change now? The horrid pictures grew mercifully dim, the sting of the torturing thoughts was drawn, the edge of conscience blunted. Her rage had had its way, it had beaten down nature. For a moment she grasped this triumph, and exulted in it in her old barbarous gloating over the victories of her fury. All things had been against her sleep. But now it came; she had won it. She ceased to move, to curse, even to think. The blessed torpor stole over her. Her life and what it must be passed from her mind; a compassionate blankness spread over her intellect. She was at peace! To-morrow—yes, to-morrow! All things could wait now till to-morrow. She would be better able to face them to-morrow—after a good night's sleep. Who had dared to say she could not sleep? Her eyes closed, and her heavy breathing sounded through the room. She stirred no more. Her rage had its way with her, as with all others. It had demanded sleep. She slept.

Dawn had broken when a hand laid on his shoulder roused Grantley Imason from an uneasy doze. He found Suzette by him in her dressing-gown and barefooted. Instinctively he listened for an instant to hear if there were any sound from the room above. There was none, and he asked her:

"Is anything wrong?"

"Yes," whispered Suzette, "Come upstairs!"

Not knowing what the evil chance might be, he followed her, and she led him into Harriet Courtland's room. She had already opened one of the shutters, and the early light streamed in on to the bed. Harriet lay on her side, with her head thrown back on the pillow and her eyes turned up to the ceiling. She lay above the clothes of the bed, and her nightgown was torn away from her throat. Suzette had thrown a dressing-gown over her body from breast to feet. She looked wonderfully handsome as she lay there, so still, so peaceful, like some splendid animal in a reaction of exhaustion after savage grand exertion. He drew near. The truth came home to him at once. The two stood and looked at Harriet. At last he turned to Suzette. He found her very pale, but quite calm.

"She's dead, Mr. Imason," Suzette said.

"How?" he asked.

"An over-dose of chloral. She often used to take it—and of course she would be very likely to want a sleeping-draught last night."

"Yes, yes, of course she would. Her nerves would be so much upset."

Their eyes met—Suzette's seemed puzzled.

"What do you think?" asked Grantley in a whisper.

"I really don't know. She would really have been quite likely to take too much. She would be impatient if it didn't act quickly, you know."

"Yes, yes, of course she would. Have you sent for a doctor?"

"Oh, yes, directly I found her—before I came to you. But I've done some nursing, and—and there's not the least——" She stopped suddenly, and was silent for several seconds. Then she said quietly and calmly: "There's not the least chance, Mr. Imason."

Grantley knew what word she had rejected in favour of "chance," and why the word had seemed inappropriate. He acknowledged the justice of the change with a mournful gesture of his hands.

"Well, we can never know whether it was accidental or not," he said, as he turned to leave the room.

"No, we can never know that," said Suzette.

How should they know? Harriet Courtland had not known herself. As always, so to the end, her fury had been blind, and had destroyed her blindly.

She had struck at herself as recklessly as at her child; and here her blow had killed. Her rage had run its final course, and for the last time had its way. She slept.

And while she slept, her home was waking to the life of a new day.

CHAPTER XXIV

FRIENDS

The calamity at the Courtlands' struck on all their acquaintance like a nip of icy wind, sending a shudder through them, making them, as it were, huddle closer about them the protecting vesture of any hope or any happiness that they had. The outrage on the child stood out horrible in the light of the mother's death: the death of the mother found an appalling explanation in the child's plight. Whether the death were by a witting or an unwitting act seemed a small matter; darkness and blindness had fallen on the unhappy woman before the last hours, and somehow in the darkness she had passed away. There was not lacking the last high touch of tragedy; the catastrophe which shocked and awed was welcome too. It was the best thing that could have happened. Any end was better than no end. To such a point of hopelessness had matters come, in such a fashion Harriet Courtland had used her life. The men and women who had known her, her kindred, her friends, and her household, all whom nature had designed to love her, while they shuddered over the manner of her going, sighed with relief that she was gone. The decree of fate had filled the page, and it was finished; but their minds still tingled from it as they turned to the clean sheet and prayed a kinder message.

Grantley Imason, so closely brought in contact with the drama, almost an eye-witness of it, was deeply moved, stirred to fresh feelings, and quickened to a new vision. The devastation Harriet had wrought, Tom's cowardly desertion, the pitiable plight of the children, grouped themselves together and took on, as another of their company, the heightened and freshened impression of stale sentimentality, and a self-delusion trivial to vulgarity, which he had carried away from his encounter with Walter Blake. To all this there seemed one clue; through it all one thread ran. He felt this in the recesses of his mind, and his fingers groped after the guiding-line. That must be found, lest, treading blindly through the labyrinth, he and his too should fall into the pit whence there was no upward way. They had been half over the brink once: a preternatural effort—so it might properly be called—had pulled them back; but they were still on the treacherous incline.

Out of his sombre and puzzled reflections there sprang—suddenly as it seemed, and in answer to his cry for guidance—an enlightening pity—pity for his boy, lest he too should bear on his brow the scar of hatred, almost as plain to see as the visible mark which was to stamp little Sophy's for evermore—and pity for Sibylla, because her empty heart had opened to so poor a tenant: in very hunger she had turned to Blake. He no longer rejected the hope of communion with the immature infantile mind of his son; he ceased to laugh scornfully at a love dedicated to such a man as Walter Blake. A new sympathy with his boy—even such as he had felt for Tom Courtland's little girls—spurred him to fresh efforts to understand. Contempt for his wife's impulsive affections gave way to compassion as his mind dwelt, not on what she had done, but on what had driven her to do it—as he threw back his thoughts from the unworthy satisfaction her heart had sought to the straits of starvation which had made any satisfaction seem so good. This was to look in the end at himself, and to the task of studying himself he was now thrust back. If he could not do that, and do it to a purpose, desolation and pitiableness such as he had witnessed and shuddered at stood designated as the unalterable future of his own home.

Then, at last, he was impatient; his slow persevering campaign was too irksome, and success delayed seemed to spell failure. The time comes when no man can work. The darkness might fall on his task still unperformed. He became afraid, and therefore impatient. He could not wait for Sibylla to come to him. He must meet her—in something more than civility, in something more than a formal concession of her demands, more than an acquiescence which had been not untouched by irony and by the wish to put her in the wrong. He must forget his claims and think of his needs. His needs came home to him now; his claims could wait. And as his needs cried out, there dawned in him a glow of anticipation. What would it not mean if the needs could be satisfied?

He stayed in London for Harriet Courtland's funeral, and in the evening went down to Milldean, a sharper edge given to his thoughts by the sight of Tom and the two little girls (Sophy could not come) following Harriet's coffin to the grave. Christine Fanshaw was in the carriage which met him at the station, and was his companion on the homeward drive. The Courtland calamity had touched her deeply too, but touched her to bitterness—if, indeed, her outward bearing could be taken as a true index of her mind. She bore herself aggressively towards fate and its lessons; an increased acidity of manner condemned the follies of her friends; she dropped no tears over their punishment. Still there was very likely something else beneath; she had not heard from John since she came down to Milldean.

"How have you all been getting on?" Grantley asked, as he took the reins and settled himself beside her.

"We've done excellently since you went away. Of course we've been upset about this horrible business, but——"

"Otherwise you've done very well?" he smiled.

"Oh, yes, very!"

"Since I went away?"

"Yes, since you went away," Christine repeated.

"Perhaps it's not a very good thing for me to come back?"

"We can hardly banish you from your own house."

The concession was grudging. Grantley laughed, and the tone of his laugh brought her eyes sharply round to his face.

"You seem very cheerful," she remarked with an accusing air.

"No, I'm not that exactly; but I've got an idea—and that brightens one up a bit, you know."

"Any change does that," Christine admitted waspishly.

"I saw John for a minute. He looked a bit worried. Does he complain?"

"He hasn't complained to me."

"Oh, then it's all right, I suppose. And he says the business is all right, anyhow. How's the boy?"

"As merry and jolly as he can be."

"And Sibylla?"

"Yes, Sibylla too, as merry as possible."

"They both have been, you mean?"

"Yes, of course I do."

"While I've been away?"
"Yes, while you've been away."
Grantley laughed again. Christine looked at him in dawning wonder. She had expected nothing from this drive but a gloom deepening—or at least a constraint increasing—with every yard they came nearer to Milldean. But there was something new. With some regret she recognised that her acidity, her harping on "Since you went away," had not been the best prelude to questioning or much of an invitation to confidence; and it had, moreover, failed in its primary purpose of annoying Grantley by its implied comment on his conduct. Her voice grew softer, and, with one of her coaxing little tricks, she edged herself closer to his side.
"Any good news among all the bad, Grantley?"
"There's no good news yet," said he.
She caught at his last word.
"Yet? Yet, Grantley?"
"I'm not going to talk any more. That off-horse is a young 'un, and——"
"It's something to have a 'yet' in life again," she half whispered. "'Yet' seems to imply a future—a change, perhaps!"
"Do you want a change too?"
"Oh, come, you're not so dull as to have to ask that!"
"You've told me nothing."
"And I won't. But I'll ask you one question—if you'll leave it at that."
"Well, what's the question?"
"Did John send his love to me?"
Grantley looked at her a moment, and smiled in deprecation.
"It would have been tactful to invent the message," smiled Christine.
"I'm getting a bit out of heart with tact, Christine."
"Quite so, my dear man. And get out of patience with some other things too, if you can. Your patience would try Job—and not only from jealousy either."
Grantley's only answer was a reflective smile.
"And what about Tom Courtland?" she went on. "Is he with the children?"
"No, he's living at the club."
"Hum! At the club officially?"
"You're malicious—and you outrage proper feeling. At the club really, Christine. He feels a bit lost, I fancy. I think it rather depends on somebody else now. He's a weak chap, poor old Tom."
"You're full of discoveries about people to-day. Any other news?"
"No, none."
"But, you see, I've heard from Janet Selford!"
"Will you consider my remarks about your remarks as repeated—with more emphasis?"
"Oh, yes, I will! You're talking more as you used to before you were married."
"That's a compliment? I expect so—coming from a woman. Christine, have you read Sibylla Janet Selford's letter?"
"Parts of it."
"I wish you hadn't. I didn't want her to know. I saw the fellow there—with Anna."
"Anna's a very clever girl. She does me great credit."
"I should wait a bit to claim it, if I were you. I'm sorry you told Sibylla."
"If you're going to be generous as well as patient, there's an end of any chance of your turning human, Grantley."
"You're quite good company to-day."
"I'm always ready to be; but one can't manage it without some help."
"Which you haven't found in my house?"
"Yes, I have—since you went away."
But she said it this time in a different way, with a hint, perhaps an appeal, in her upturned eyes, and the slightest touch of her hand on his sleeve—almost like the delicate soft pat of a kitten's paw, as quick, as timid, and as venturous. Grantley turned his head to look at her. Her eyes were bright and eager.
"We've actually begun to be pleasant," he said, smiling.
"Yes, almost to enjoy ourselves. Wonderful! But we're not at the house yet!"
"Not quite!" he said.
His face set again in firm lines.
"You'd so much better not look so serious about it. That's as bad as your old County Council!"
"Are you quite sure you understand the case?"
"Meaning the woman? Oh, no! She's difficult. But I understand that, when one thing's failed utterly, you don't risk much by trying another."
They came to the top of the hill which runs down to Milldean. Christine sighed.
"Poor old Harriet! She was a jolly girl once, you know, and so handsome! I've had some good times with Harriet. Do you think she's at peace, Grantley?"
"She has paid," said he. "She has paid for what she was and did. I hope she's at peace."
Christine's eyes grew dreamy; her voice fell to a gentle murmur.
"I wonder if it's quite silly to fancy that she's paid something for some of us too, Grantley? I was thinking something like that—somehow—when I said, 'Poor old Harriet!'"
"I daresay it's silly, but I don't know that it seems so to me," he answered.

Just once again he felt the tiny velvety touch. So they came to Milldean.

The twofold pity which had roused Grantley from a lethargy of feeling, misconceived as self-control, had its counterpart in the triple blow with which the course of events assailed Sibylla's estimate of herself. In the first place, the news about young Blake announced in Janet Selford's letter—indirectly indeed, but yet with a confident satisfaction—made her ask whether her great sacrifice had been offered at a worthy shrine, and her great offering received with more than a shallow and transitory appreciation. In the second, the thought and image of the Courtland children spoke loud to the instinct which her ideas had lulled to sleep, bitterly accusing her desertion of the child and her indifference to his fate, rousing her ever underlying remorse to quick and vengeful life. Lastly, she was stirred to see and recognise the significance of the third turn of fate—the meaning of the nemesis which had fallen on Harriet Courtland: how she had let her rage spare nothing, neither self-respect, nor decency, nor love; and how, in the end, thus enthroned in tyranny, it had not spared herself. The three accusations, each with its special import, each taking up a distinct aspect of the truth, and enforcing it with a poignant example, joined their indictments into one, and, thus united, cried out their condemnation of her, taking for their mouthpiece Christine Fanshaw's pretty lips, using her daintily scornful voice, and the trenchant uncompromising words from which the utterer herself had afterwards recoiled as too coarse and crude to be a legitimate weapon of attack. The logic of events was not so squeamish; it does not deal in glosses or in paraphrase; it is blunt, naked, and merciless, and must be, since only when all other appeals and warnings have failed does its appointed work begin. It fastened with what almost seemed malicious glee on Christine's biting word, and enforced it by a pitiless vividness of memory, an unceasing echo in Sibylla's thoughts. Her emotions had gone "sprawling" over everything. The description did not need elaboration. It was abominably expressive and sufficient. And it did not admit of pleading or of extenuation. It showed her touching, on one extreme, Blake's shallow and spurious sentiment; on the other, Harriet Courtland's licence of anger. It pointed her attention to the ruin of Tom's life, to the piteous plight of his children, to Harriet's fate, to Blake's facile forgetfulness of love too heedlessly and wantonly offered. It stripped her fantastic ideas of their garish finery, leaving them, in the revulsion of her feelings, bereft of all beauty and attractiveness. Impelled to look back, she seemed to find the same trail over everything—even in those childish days of which Jeremy Chiddingfold had once given a description that would not have reassured her; even in the beginning of her acquaintance with Grantley, in the ready rapture of her first love, in the intoxication of the fairy ride. Changing its form, now hostile to her husband instead of with him, the same temper showed in all the events which led up to the birth of little Frank: its presence proved that her madness over Blake was no isolated incident, but rather the crown of her development and the truest interpreter of a character empty of worth, strength, or stability. Many bitter hours brought her to this recognition; but when light came, the very temper which she condemned was in her still, and turned the coolness of recognition and analysis into an extravagant heat of scorn and self-contempt.

What was the conclusion? Was she to throw herself at Grantley's feet, proclaiming penitence, imploring pardon, declaring love? "No, no!" she cried. That would be so easy, so short a cut, so satisfying to her roused feelings. She put the notion from her in horror; it was the suggestion of her old devil in a new disguise. Her love for Grantley had bitten too deep into her nature to be treated like that, with that levity and frivolity of easy impulse, that violence of headstrong emotion, those tempests of feeling so remote from true sincerity of heart. The cure did not lie in pampering sick emotions into a plump semblance of healthy life. Where did it lie, if it were possible at all? It must lie in the most difficult of all tasks—a change not of other people or of their bearing and feelings towards her, but a change of herself and of her own attitude towards others and towards the world, and in her judgment and her ruling of herself. If things were to go differently with her, she must be different. The arrogance of her nature must be abated, the extravagant claims she had made must be lowered. The thought struck on her almost with despair. So hard seemed the lesson, so rough the path. And it seemed a path which must be trodden alone. It was not as the easy pleasant road of emotion, beguiled by enchanting companionship, strewn with the flowers of fancy, carpeted with pleasure. This way was hard, bleak, and solitary. Merely to contemplate it chilled her. Even that happiness with her child, which had so struck Christine and afforded matter for one of those keen thrusts at Grantley Imason, appeared to her in a suspicious guise. She could not prevent it nor forgo it—nature was too strong; but she yielded to it with qualms of conscience, and its innocent delights were spoilt by the voice of self-accusation and distrust. Could it be real, genuine, true in the woman who had deserted the child and been indifferent to his fate?

Both penitents, both roused to self-examination, Grantley Imason and his wife seemed to have exchanged parts. Each suffered an inversion, if not of character, yet of present mood. Each sought and desired something of what had appeared to deserve reprobation when displayed by the other. Their own propensities and ideals, carried to an extreme, had threatened ruin; they erected the opposite temper of mind into a standard, and thereto sought to conform their conduct at the cost of violence to themselves. It seemed strange, yet it was the natural effect of the fates and the temperaments which they had seen worked out and displayed before their eyes, in such close touch with them, impinging so sharply on their own destinies.

Sibylla had not been at home when Grantley arrived. She met him first in the nursery, when she went to see little Frank at his tea. No mood, be it what it would, could make Grantley a riotous romping companion for a tiny child: that effort was beyond him. But to-day he played with his son with a new sympathy; talked to him with a pleasant gravity which stirred the young and curious mind; listened to his broken utterances with a kindly quizzical smile which seemed to encourage the little fellow. Grantley had never before found so much answering intelligence. He forgot the quick development which even a few weeks bring at such a time of life. He set all the difference down to the fact that never before had he looked for what he now found so ready and so obvious. Anything he did not find for himself the nurse was eager to point out, and with the aid of this enthusiastic signpost Grantley discovered the road to understanding very readily. He and the boy were, without doubt, enjoying one another's society when Sibylla came in.

She stood in the doorway, waiting with an aching heart for the usual thing, for a withdrawal of even such sign of interest as Grantley had ever shown in old days. It did not come. He gave her a cheery recognition, and went on playing with Frank. Irresistibly drawn, she came near to them. Something was signalled in Frank's struggling speech and impatiently waving arms. Grantley could not follow, and now turned his eyes to Sibylla, asking for an explanation. The nurse had gone into the other room, busied about the preparations for the meal. Sibylla took Frank in her arms.

"I know what he means," she said proudly.

Her eyes met Grantley's. His were fixed very intently on her.

"I don't," he said. "Is it possible for a man to learn these mysteries?"

His tone and words were light; they were even mocking, but not now with the mockery which hurts.
She flushed a little.
"You'd like to learn?" she asked. "Shall we try to teach him, Frank—to teach him your code?"
"I'll watch you with him."
For a moment she looked at him appealingly, and then knelt on the floor and arranged the toys as Frank had wanted them. The little fellow laughed in triumph.
"How did you know?" asked Grantley.
"I've not lost that knowledge—no, I haven't," she answered almost in a whisper.
The scene was a spur to his newly stirred impulses. He had rejoiced in his wife before now; but the clouds had always hung about the cot, so that he had not rejoiced nor gloried in the mother of his child. His heart was full as he sat and watched the mother and the child.
"You've got to watch him very carefully still; but he's getting ever so much more—more——"
"Lucid?" Grantley suggested, smiling.
"Yes," she laughed, "and, if possible, more imperious still. I believe he's going to be like you in that."
"Oh, not like me, let's hope!"
He laughed, but there was a look of pain on his face.
Sibylla turned round to him and spoke in a low voice, lest by chance the nurse should hear.
"You mustn't be sure I agree altogether with that," she said, and turned swiftly away to the child again.
Grantley rose.
"Lift him up to me and let me kiss him," he said.
With grave eyes Sibylla obeyed.
But the natural man is not easily subdued, nor does he yield his place readily. In the end Grantley was not apt at explanations or apologies. The evening fell fair and still, a fine October night, and he joined Sibylla in the garden. Christine remained inside—from tact perhaps, though she was very likely chilly too. Grantley smoked in silence, while Sibylla looked down on the little village below.
"This thing has shaken me up dreadfully," he said at last. "The Courtlands, I mean."
"Yes, I know." She turned and faced him. "And isn't there something else that concerns you and me?"
"I know of nothing. And you can hardly say the Courtlands concern us exactly."
"They do; and there is something else, Grantley. I know what Janet Selford wrote."
"That's nothing at all to me."
"But it is something to me. You know it is."
"I won't talk of that. It's nothing." He put his hand out suddenly to her. "Let's be friends, Sibylla."
She did not take his hand, but she looked at him with a friendly gaze.
"We really ought to try to manage that, oughtn't we? For Frank's sake, if for nothing else. Or do you think I've no right to talk about Frank?"
"Suppose we don't talk about rights at all? I'm not anxious to."
"It'll be hard; but we'll try to be friends for his sake—that he may have a happy home."
Grantley's heart was stirred within him.
"That's good; but is that all?" he asked in a low voice full of feeling. "Is it all over for ourselves? Can't we be friends for our own sakes?"
"Haven't we lost—well, not the right—if you don't like that—but the power?"
"I'm an obstinate man; you know that very well."
"It'll be hard—for both of us; but, yes, we'll try."
She gave him her hand to bind the bargain; he gripped it with an intensity that surprised and alarmed her. She could see his eyes through the gloom. Were they asking friendship only? There was more than that in his heart and in his eyes—a thing never dead in him. It had sprung to fresh vigour now, from the lessons of calamity, from the pity born in him, from the new eyes with which he had looked on the boy in his mother's arms. She could not miss the expression of it.
"Is that the best we can try for?" he whispered. "There was something else once, Sibylla."
He had not moved, yet she raised her hands as though to check or beat off his approach. She was afraid. All that the path he again beckoned her on had meant to her came to her mind. If she followed him along it, would it not be once more to woo disillusion, to court disaster, to invite that awful change to bitterness and hatred?
"You are you, and I am I," she protested. "It—it is impossible, Grantley."
His face assumed its old obstinate squareness as he heard her.
"I don't want that," she murmured. "I'll try to be friends. We can understand one another as friends, make allowances, give and forgive. Friendship's charitable. Let's be friends, Grantley."
"You have no love left for me?" he asked, passing by her protests.
"For months past I've hated you."
"I know that. And you have no love left for me?"
She looked at him again, with fear and shrinking in her eyes.
"Have you forgotten what I did? No, you can't have forgotten! How can you wish me to love you now? It would be horrible for both of us. You may forgive me, as I do you—what I may have to forgive; but how can we be lovers again? How can we—with that in the past?"
"The past is the past," he said calmly.
She walked away from him a little. When she came back in a minute or so, he saw that she was in strong agitation.
"That's enough to-night—enough for all time, if you so wish," he said gently. "Only I had to tell you what was in my heart."
"How could you, Grantley?"
"I haven't said it was easy. I'm coming to believe that the easy things aren't worth much."
"You could love me again?"

"I've never ceased to love you—only I hope I know a bit more about how to do it now."

She stood there the picture of distress and of fear. At last she broke out:

"Ah, I've not told you the real thing! I'm afraid Grantley, I'm afraid! I dare not love you. Because I loved you so beyond all reason and all—all sanity, all this came upon us. And—and I daren't love you again now, even if I could. Yes, I ought to have learnt something too; perhaps I have. But I daren't trust myself with my knowledge." She came a step nearer to him, holding out her hands beseechingly. "Friends, friends, Grantley!" she implored. "Then we shall be safe. And our love shall be for Frank. You'll get to love Frank, won't you?"

"Frank and I are beginning to hit it off capitally," said Grantley cheerfully. "Well, I shall go in now: we mustn't leave Christine alone all the evening." He took her hand and kissed it. "So we're friends?" he asked.

"I'll try," she faltered. "Yes, surely we can manage that!"

He turned away and left her again gazing down on the village and Old Mill House. He lounged into the drawing-room where Christine sat, with an easy air and a smile on his face.

"A beautiful evening, isn't it?" asked Christine with a tiny shudder, as she hitched her chair closer to the bit of bright fire and threw a faintly protesting glance at the open window.

"Beautiful weather—and quite settled. I shall enjoy my holiday down here."

"Oh, you're going to stay down here, and going to have a holiday, are you?" she asked with a lift of her brows.

"Well, hardly a holiday, after all. I've got a job to do," he answered as he lit his cigarette—"rather a hard job at my time of life."

"Is it? What is the job?"

"I'm going courting again—and a very pretty woman too," he said.

A rather tremulous smile came on Christine's face as she looked at him.

"It's rather a nice amusement, isn't it?" she asked. "And you always had plenty of self-conceit."

"Why, hang it, I thought it was just the opposite this time!" exclaimed Grantley in whimsical annoyance.

Christine laughed.

"I won't be unamiable. I'll call it self-confidence, if you insist."

He took a moment to think over her new word.

"Yes, in the end I suppose it does come to that. Look here, Christine; I wish the people who tell you you ought to change your nature would be obliging enough to tell you how to do it."

Christine's answer might be considered encouraging.

"After all there's no need to overdo the change," she said. "And there's one thing in which you'll never change: you'll always want the best there is."

"No harm in having a try for it—as soon as you really see what it is," he answered, as he strolled off to the smoking-room.

CHAPTER XXV

PICKING UP THE PIECES

Mrs. Bolton was very much upset by what had happened at the Courtlands'. An unwonted and irksome sense of responsibility oppressed her. She discussed the matter with Miss Henderson and made Caylesham come to see her—Miss Pattie Henderson, who knew all about how Sophy's letter had reached her mother's hands; and Caylesham, whom Mrs. Bolton had made a party to the joke. It did not seem so good a joke now. She and Pattie were both frightened when they saw to what their pleasantry had led. Little Sophy's suffering was not pleasant to think of, and there was an uncomfortable uncertainty about the manner of Harriet's death. A scheme may prove too successful sometimes. Caylesham had warned Mrs. Bolton that she was playing with dangerous tools. He was not now inclined to let her down too easily, nor to put the kindest interpretation on the searchings of her conscience.

"You always time your fits of morality so well," he observed cynically. "I don't suppose poor old Tom's amusing company just now, and he's certainly deuced hard up."

Mrs. Bolton looked a very plausible picture of injured innocence, but of course there was something in what Frank Caylesham said; there generally was, though it might not be what you would be best pleased to find. Tom was not lively nor inclined for gaiety, and he had just made a composition with his creditors. On the other hand, Miss Henderson was in funds (having completed her negotiations with the Parmenter family), and had suggested a winter on the Riviera, with herself for hostess. There are, fortunately, moments when the good and the pleasant coincide; the worst of it is that such happy harmonies are apt to come rather late in the day.

"It's all different now that woman's gone," observed Mrs. Bolton. "It's the children now, Frank."

"Supposing it is, why am I to be dragged into it?"

"We must get him to go back to them."

Various feelings combined to make Mrs. Bolton very earnest.

"He wants to stay here, does he?"

"No, he hates being here now. Yes, he does. He only comes because he's got nobody else to speak to. And he's in awful dumps all the time. It's not very cheerful for me."

"I daresay not, Flora. But why doesn't he go back then?"

Mrs. Bolton had been moving about the room restlessly. Her back was to Caylesham as she answered:

"He won't. He says he can't. He says——"

Caylesham threw a glance at her, his brows raised.

"What does he say, Flora?"

"Oh, it's nonsense—and he needn't say it to me, anyhow. It really isn't particularly pleasant for me. Oh, well, then, he says he's not fit to go near them." She turned round to him; there was a flush on her face. "Such nonsense!" she ended impatiently.

Caylesham pulled his moustache, and smiled reflectively.

"I suppose it might take him like that," he observed, with an impartial air.

"Oh, I know you're only laughing at me! But I tell you, I don't like it, Frank."

"These little incidents are—well, incidental, Flora. Innocent children, you know! And I shouldn't be surprised if he even made excuses for Harriet now?"

"No, he doesn't do that. It's the children. Stop smiling like that, will you?"

"Certainly, my dear Flora. My smile was a pure oversight."

"It was all I could do to get him to go to the funeral. Do you think she killed herself, Frank?"

"I've not the least intention of examining the question. What can it matter?"

Mrs. Bolton shrugged her shoulders impatiently. It did seem to her to matter, but she would not let Caylesham think that it mattered much. She returned to her point about the children.

"He's miserable thinking about them, and yet he won't go near them. I call it idiotic."

"So do I. But then they aren't our children."

"Well, I'm not going to stand his saying it again and again to me."

"I really agree. There can't be any reason for saying such a thing more than once."

She broke into a vexed laugh.

"When you've had all the fun you can get out of me, perhaps you'll begin to help me. You see, I want it settled. I want to be off to Monte with Pattie."

"I see. You want to go with Pattie and——?"

Mrs. Bolton shook her head.

"Just you and Pattie?"

"She's going to stand it to me: I haven't got a farthing. And, I say, Frank, he ought to go back to those poor little wretches now. You can make him do it if you like, you know."

"I? Well, I'm an odd sort of party for such a job."

"Not a bit. He'll listen to you just because—well, because——"

"I haven't spared your feelings, Flora, don't mind mine."

"Because he knows you don't talk humbug or cant."

"You're being complimentary after all—or at any rate you're meaning to be. And you'd never see him again?"

"He'll never want to see me." She was facing Caylesham now. "I've been fond of poor old Tom. Come, you know I have? Say that for me."

"Yes, I know you have. I've reproved you for it myself."

"But he'll not want to see me—and soon I shan't want to see him either."

She looked a little distressed for a minute, then shrugged her shoulders with a laugh.

"That's the way of the world."

"Of part of it," Caylesham murmured as he lit a cigar.

But he was really sorry for Mrs. Bolton. Notwithstanding a notable mixture of motives, in which the condition of her purse and the opportunity of going to the Riviera figured largely, she was grieved at the way in which her friendship with Tom was ending—grieved that it must end, and hurt that Tom should desire to have it ended. She had always suffered from this unfortunate tendency to kindly emotions which the exigencies of her position did not permit her to indulge. Indeed it was very likely the kindly emotions which had originally produced the position. That did not make the matter any better; the ultimate incongruity was none the less undesirable. With his indifference to accepted codes, Caylesham thought it rather lamentable too. Still she did want, above all things, to go to the Riviera with Pattie Henderson. One must compromise with life, and it was not clear that she was getting the worst of the bargain.

With Flora Bolton set aside (and of course she had no reasonable title to consideration), the case seemed a simple one to Caylesham, and his mission an obvious utterance of common sense. He could not enter fully into Tom Courtland's mind. Tom was not naturally a lawless man; desperation had made him break loose. The bygone desperation was forgotten now in pity for his children and for the woman whom, after all, he had once loved; and he looked with shame on the thing he had done, attributing to it all the results which Harriet's fury had engrafted on it. Broken in fortune and in career, broken too in self-respect, he had been likely to drift on in a life which he had come to abhor. He felt his presence an outrage on his children. If the death of his wife had seemed to save him from a due punishment, here was a penalty different, but hardly less severe. While he was in this mood Caylesham was the best man to carry the message to him. The only chance with Tom was to treat what he had done as natural, but to insist that the sequence of events was utterly unexpected and essentially unconnected with it. To urge the gravity of his offence would have been to make reparation and atonement impossible. Caylesham took a very strong and simple line. He declined to discuss the state of Tom's conscience, or the blackness of Tom's mind, or even the whiteness of the minds of the children. Everybody was very much alike, or would be in a few years anyhow, and Tom was not to be an ass. The line of argument was not exalted, but it was adapted to the needs of the case.

"My dear chap, if you come to that, what man is fit to look his children in the face?" he asked impatiently.

But then it occurred to him that he was idealising—a thing he hated.

"Not that children aren't often wicked little beggars themselves," he added cheerfully. "They steal and lie like anything, and torment one another devilishly. I know I did things as a boy that I'd kick any grown man for doing, and so did my brothers and sisters. I tell you what it is, Tom, the devil's there all the time; he shows himself in different ways—that's all."

Tom could not swallow this gospel; he would give up neither his own iniquity nor the halo of purity to which his mind clung amid the sordid ruin of his life and home.

"If I could pull straight——" he murmured despairingly.

"Why shouldn't you? You're getting on in life, you know, after all."

"They—they guess something about it, I expect, Frank. It's not pleasant for a man to be ashamed before his own children. And Miss Bligh—I thought she looked at me very queerly at the funeral."

"You'll find they'll be as nice as possible to you. The children won't understand anything, and Suzette's sure to be on your side. Women always are, you know. They're not naturally moral—we've imposed it on them, and they always like to get an excuse for approving of the other thing."

Tom grew savage.

"I know what I've done, but anyhow I'm glad I don't think as you do."

"Never mind my thoughts, old chap. You go home to your kids," said Caylesham cheerfully.

He was very good-humoured over the matter; neither all the unnecessary fuss nor Tom's aspersions on his own character and views disturbed him in the least; and he did not leave Tom until he had obtained the assurance that he desired. This given, he went off to his club, thanking heaven that he was quit of a very tiresome business. If he did his bad deeds without misgiving, he did his good without arrogance; perhaps they were not numerous enough to give that feeling a plausible excuse for emergence.

"It's all right," he wrote to Mrs. Bolton in reporting his success. "I made him promise not to be an ass. So you can go off with Pattie with a mind free of care. Good luck to you, and lots of plunder!"

The immoral friendliness of this wish for her success quite touched Mrs. Bolton.

"Frank's a really good-hearted fellow," she told Miss Henderson as she settled herself in the train and started on her journey, the fortunes of which it is not necessary to follow.

For days Lucy and little Vera had crept fearfully through the silent house, knowing that a dreadful thing had happened, not allowed to put questions, and hardly daring to speculate about it between themselves. When Sophy began to be about again, pale and shaken, with the bandage still round her head, she took the lead as she was wont to do, and her bolder mind fastened on the change in the situation. There was no need to be afraid any more; that was the great fact which came home to her, and which she proclaimed to her sisters. It might be proper to move quietly and talk low for a little while, but it was a tribute to what was becoming, not a sign of terror or a precaution against danger. It was Sophy too who ventured to question Suzette, and to elicit instructions as to their future conduct. They were to think very kindly of mamma and love her memory, said Suzette, but they were not to talk about her to papa when he came back, because that would distress him. And they were not to ask him why he had gone away, or where he had been. Of course he had had business; and, anyhow, little girls ought not to be inquisitive. A question remained in Sophy's mind, and was even canvassed in private schoolroom consultations. What about that portentous word which had been whispered through the household—what about the divorce? None of them found courage to ask that, or perhaps they had pity on poor Suzette Bligh, who was so terribly uncomfortable under their questioning. At any rate nothing more was heard about the divorce. Since it had appeared to mean that papa was to go away, and since he was coming back now, presumably it had been put on the shelf somehow. All the same, their sharp instincts told them that their father would not have come back unless their mother had died, and that he was coming back now—well, in a sort of disgrace; that was how they put it in their thoughts.

A committee consisting of Kate Raymore, Janet Selford, and John Fanshaw (a trustee under the Courtland marriage settlement, and so possessing a status), had sat to consider Suzette Bligh's position. Suzette loved the children, and it would be sad if she had to leave them; moreover she was homeless, and a fixed salary would be welcome to her. Lastly—and on this point Janet Selford laid stress—she was not exactly a girl; she was just on thirty. John nodded agreement, adding that nobody outside of an asylum could connect scandal with the name of Suzette Bligh. So it was decided that she should stay, for the present at all events, in the capacity of companion or governess. The children wondered to find Suzette so gently radiant and affectionate one evening. She had not told them of the doubt which had arisen, nor how great a thing it was to her to stay. They had never doubted that she would stay with them now.

It was late one afternoon when Tom Courtland slunk home. He had sent no word of his coming, because he did not know till the last minute whether he would have courage to come. Then he had made the plunge, given up his room at the club, packed his luggage, and left it to be called for. But the plunge was very difficult to him—so that his weak will would not have faced it unless that other door at Mrs. Bolton's had been firmly shut in his face. He was uncomfortable before the man who let him in; he was wretchedly apprehensive of Suzette Bligh and of the children. He needed—very badly needed—Caylesham at his elbow again, to tell him "not to be an ass." But Caylesham had gone back to employments more congenial than he ever professed to find works of benevolence. Tom had to endure alone, and he could find no comfort. Against Harriet he could have made a case—a very good case in the judgment of half the world. But he seemed to have no excuse to offer to the little girls, nor any plea to meet the wondering disapprobation of Suzette Bligh.

He was told that the children were in the schoolroom with Suzette, and thither he bent his steps, going slowly and indecisively. He stopped outside the door and listened. He could hear Suzette's mild voice; apparently she was reading to them, for nothing except the continuous flow of her words was audible, and in conversation she was not so loquacious as that. Well, he must go in; perhaps it would be all right when once the ice was broken. He opened the door and stood on the threshold, blushing like a schoolboy.

"Well, my dears, here I am," he said. "I've come home."

He caught Suzette's eye. She was blushing too, blushing a very vivid pink—rather a foolish pink somehow. He felt that both he and Suzette were looking very silly. For quite a long time, as it seemed, he looked at Suzette before he looked at the little girls. After that there was, or seemed to be, another long silence while the little girls looked first at him, then at Suzette, then at one another. Tom stood there through it all—in the doorway, blushing.

The next moment all the three were upon him, clinging to his hands and his coat, kissing him, crying out their gladness in little excited exclamations, the two elder taking care to give Vera a fair chance to get at him, Vera insisting that the chance was not a fair one, all the three dragging him to an armchair, and sitting him down in it. Two of them got on his knees, and Lucy stood by his side with her arm round his neck.

"My dears!" Tom muttered, and found he could say no more.

His eyes met Suzette Bligh's. She was standing by the table, looking on, and her eyes were misty.

"See how they love you, Mr. Courtland!" she said.

Yes! And he had forsaken them, and the bandage was about Sophy's head.

"You won't go away again, will you?" implored Lucy.

"No, I shan't go away again."

"And Suzette'll stay too, won't she?" urged Vera.

"I hope she will, indeed!"

"You will, Suzette?"

"Yes, dear."

"We shall be happy," said Sophy softly, with a note of wonder in her voice.

It really seemed strange to have the prospect of being happy—permanently, comfortably, without fear; the prospect of happiness, not snatched at intervals, not broken by terror, but secure and without apprehension.

Tom Courtland pressed his little children to him. Where were the reproaches he had imagined, where the shame he had feared? They were annihilated by love and swallowed up in gladness.

"We do love you so!" whispered Lucy.

Vera actually screamed in happiness.

"Oh, Vera!" said Suzette, rather shocked.

That set them all laughing, the little girls, Tom, presently even Suzette herself. They were all laughing, though none of them could have told exactly why. Their joy bubbled over in mirth, and the sound of gladness was in the house. Tom Courtland held his head up and was his own man again. Here was something to live for, and something to show that even his broken life had not been lived in vain. The ghosts of the past were there; he could not forget them. But the clasp of the warm little arms which encircled him would keep their chilling touch away from his heart. Freed from torments that he had not deserved, rescued from pleasures that he had not enjoyed, he turned eagerly to the delights of his home which could now be his. His glad children and kindly Suzette were a picture very precious in his eyes. Here were golden links by which the fragments of his life could be bound together, though the fractures must always show—even as the scar would show always on Sophy's brow, however much her lips might smile or her eyes sparkle beneath it.

They were roused by a voice from the door.

"It's not hard to tell where you all are! Why, I heard you at the bottom of the stairs! What a hullabaloo!"

John Fanshaw's bulky figure stood there, solid and bowed with weight and his growing years. He looked on the scene—on the happy little folk in their gloomy black frocks—with a kindly smile, and the mock reproof of his tone hid more tenderness than he cared to show.

"Papa's come back—back to stay!" they cried exultantly. "Isn't that splendid, Mr. Fanshaw?"

"I hoped I should find you here, Tom; but I came to call on Miss Bligh."

"I hope you'll always find her here too," said Tom.

Suzette was flattered, and fell to blushing again. She was acutely grateful to anybody who wanted her. She took such a desire as a free and lavish gift of kindness, never making out any reason which could account for it.

"I'm only too happy to stay if—if I can be of any use," she murmured.

John sat down and made one of the party. They all chattered cheerfully till the time grew late. Sophy, still treated as an invalid, had to go to bed. She kissed John, who held her closely for a moment; then threw herself in Tom's arms, and could hardly be persuaded to let him go.

"I shall write to Mr. Imason and tell him you've come back," she whispered as a great secret. "He was so kind to Lucy and Vera when——You know, papa?"

Tom passed his hand over her flaxen hair.

"Sleep quietly, darling," he said.

For quiet and peace were possible now.

There had been no expectation that Tom would be home to dinner; and though Suzette assured him that something could easily be prepared (and that homely sort of attention was new and pleasant to Tom), he accepted John Fanshaw's invitation to take pot-luck with him. They walked off together, rather silent, each full of his own thoughts. They did not speak until they had almost reached John's door.

"That's the sort of sight that makes a man wish he had children," said John slowly.

"I've often wished I had none. Poor Harriet!"

"But you're glad of them now?"

"Why, I've nothing else! It just makes the difference to life." He paused a moment, and then broke out: "And they've nothing but love for me. Not a word, not a thought of reproach! Just because I've never been cruel to them, whatever else I've been! Poor little beggars! We can't keep like that when we grow up. We're too fond of our grievances—eh?"

John looked at him for a moment, but said nothing. They went into the house in renewed silence. It seemed very large, empty, and dreary.

"Your wife not back yet? I heard she was staying with the Imasons."

"She's there still. I don't know when she's coming back."

"Rather dull for you, isn't it? You know you always depended on her a lot."

John made no answer, but led the way into his study. He gave Tom an evening paper, and began to open his letters. But his thoughts were not on the letters. They were occupied with what he had seen that afternoon and with the words which had fallen from Tom Courtland's lips. The children forgave with that fine free forgiveness which will not even recognise the need for itself or the existence of any fault towards which it should be exercised. It is there that forgiveness rises to and is merged in love. But when people grow up, Tom had said, they are too fond of their grievances. John had been very fond of his grievance. It was a fine large one—about the largest any man could have, everybody must admit that; and John had declined to belittle it or to shear off an inch or two of its imposing stature. All it demanded he had given. But had he? What about Frank Caylesham's money? Had it not demanded there something which he had refused? But he had given all it asked so far as the sinner who had caused it was concerned. Against her he had nursed and cosseted it; for its sake he had made his home desolate and starved his heart. Aye, he had always depended on Christine. Tom was right. But because of his grievance he had put her from him. He was fond of his grievance indeed! If Tom's children had been old enough to recognise the true value and preciousness of a big grievance, they would never have received Tom as they had that afternoon; they would have made him feel what he had been guilty of. He would have been made to feel it handsomely before he was forgiven. Children were different, as Tom Courtland said.

John got up and poked the fire fiercely.

"The house is beastly cold!" he grumbled.

"Ah, it wouldn't be if Mrs. John was at home!" laughed Tom. "She always looks after the fire, doesn't she?"

John Fanshaw bitterly envied him his peace and happiness. He forgot how hardly they had been achieved. The vision of the afternoon was before his eyes, and he declared that fate was too kind to Tom. A heavy dulness was over his face, and a forlorn puzzled look in his eyes. He must have done right, he must be doing right! How could a self-respecting man do otherwise? And yet he was so desolate, so starved of human love, in the end so full of longing for Christine—for her gracious presence and her dainty little ways.

With an effort he collected his thoughts from these wanderings, and began to read his letters. Tom was still occupied with his paper and his cigar; but he looked up at the sound of an "Ah!" which escaped from John's lips. John had come on a letter which set his thoughts going again—a letter from Sibylla. She upbraided him playfully for not having come down to see them and Christine.

"I'm sure Christine must be hurt with you, though she's much too proud to say so. We want to keep her over Christmas. Will you come as soon as you can and stay over Christmas and as long as possible? I've not told her I'm asking you, so that she mayn't be disappointed if you can't come."

There was diplomacy in Sibylla's letter, since she knew the state of the case far better than her references to Christine implied. But John was not aware of this. His attention was fixed only on the invitation, and on the circumstances in which it came. He could not go to Milldean and take his grievance with him; it was too big and obtrusive for other people's houses—it could flourish properly only in a domestic *tête-à-tête*. So he must stay at home. He sighed as he laid down the letter. Then his fingers wandered irresolutely to it again as he looked across at Tom Courtland, who had now ceased reading and was smoking with a quiet smile on his face.

"Anything up, old fellow?" asked Tom, noting the gravity of his expression.

"No. It's only from Mrs. Imason, asking me to go down there at Christmas."

"You go!" counselled Tom. "Better than bringing your wife back here."

There was a third course—the course favoured by the grievance. John did not speak of it, but it was present in his thoughts. He shook his head impatiently, and began to talk of general topics; but all the evening Sibylla's letter was in his mind, ranging itself side by side with the scene which he had witnessed at Tom Courtland's.

The gloomy idol he had set up in his heart was not yet cast down. But the little hands of the children had given its pedestal a shake.

CHAPTER XXVI

THE GREAT WRONG

The Raymores were lodging over the post-office at Milldean, in the rooms once occupied by the curate. The new curate did not need them; he was staying at the rectory, and meant, after his marriage with Dora Hutting, to build himself a little house, go on being curate, and ultimately be rector. He had a well-to-do father who had bought the advowson for him as a wedding present. His path in life was clear, visible to the very end, and entirely peaceful—unless Dora decided otherwise. So the rooms came in handy for the Raymores; and it suited Jeremy's inclination and leisure to stay the while with his sister on the hill. He had a bit of work to finish down at Milldean, while the Raymores were there. However assiduous you may be, love-making in London is liable to interruption; it must be to a certain degree spasmodic there: business, society, and such-like trifles keep breaking in. A clear week in the country will do wonders. Thus thought Jeremy, and it was his brilliant suggestion that brought the Raymores to Milldean for a month. What more obvious, since Charley was to land at Fairhaven and to stay a month in England? Spend that month in London, where things interrupted, and people stared, and old-time talk was remembered? No! Kate Raymore jumped at the idea that this wonderful month should be spent in the country, in quiet and seclusion, among old friends whose lips would be guarded, whose looks friendly, whose hearts in sympathy.

When Jeremy made this arrangement—so excellent a one that he may be pardoned for almost forgetting the selfish side of it—he had not failed to remember Dora Hutting. There had always been alternative endings to that story. Jeremy's present scheme was a variation from both of them. None the less, he had come decidedly to prefer it to either. But he had not allowed for the presence of the curate; and this circumstance, casually brought to his knowledge by Grantley Imason on the evening of his arrival, had rather disturbed him. There was another feature in the case for which he was quite unprepared. The name of the curate was a famous one—actually famous through the length and breadth of the land! This was rather a staggerer for Jeremy, who might deride, but could not deny, the curate's greatness. Certain forms of glory may appeal more to one man than to another, but all are glorious. The curate was Mallam of Somerset.

"The Mallam?" asked Jeremy.

"Yes, the Mallam," said Grantley gravely.

"By Jove!" Jeremy murmured.

"I think you ought to forgive her," Grantley suggested. "He's played twice for England, you know, and made a century the first time."

"I remember," Jeremy acknowledged, looking very thoughtful.

This was quite a different matter from the ordinary curate. Ritualistic proclivities, however obnoxious to Jeremy in their essence, became a pardonable eccentricity in a man whose solid reputation had been won in other fields.

It was not surprising that Dora carried her head very high, or that the cold politeness of her bow relegated Jeremy to a fathomless oblivion. Knowing the ways of girls, and reluctantly conscious of Mr. Mallam's greatness—conscious too, perhaps, that his own riches and fame were not as yet much in evidence—he was prepared for that. But, alas, Charlie was a cricketer too, and had infected Eva with his enthusiasm for the game. She was quite excited about Mallam. Jeremy did not appreciate this feeling as generously as he might have; yet Eva made no attempt to conceal it. She rather emphasised it; for she had come to the stage when she sought defences. After the first eager spring to meet the offered and congenial love, there comes often this recoil. The girl would have things stay as they are, since they are very pleasant, and the next step is into the unknown. She loves delay then, and, since the man will not have it for its own sake (not knowing its sweetness nor the fear that aids its charm), she enforces it on him by trickery, and makes him afraid of losing the draught altogether by insisting on his sipping it at first. She will use any weapon in this campaign, and an ardent admiration for Mr. Mallam was a very useful weapon to Eva Raymore. She said more than once that she considered Dora Hutting a very lucky girl. She thought Dora must be charming, since Mallam was in love with her. She held Mallam to be very handsome, and refused to believe—well, that his talent was so highly specialised as Jeremy tried to persuade her in words somewhat less gentle than these.

Jeremy's knowledge of girls gave out before this unexpected call upon it. He recollected how Dora had served him, and how Anna Selford had trifled with Alec Turner. He grew apprehensive and troubled—also more and more in love. He forecast complicated tragedies, and saw Mallam darkening his life wherever he turned. But the women understood—Kate Raymore, Christine, even Sibylla. They glanced at one another, and laughed among themselves. They were rather proud of Eva, who played their sex's game so well.

"Thank goodness, she's learnt to flirt!" said Christine. "A woman's nowhere without that, my dear, and I don't care whether she's married or not."

"She just adores Jeremy," Kate assured Sibylla. "Only men can't see, you know."

Sibylla laughed. She understood now better than in the days when she herself was wooed. But she blushed a little too, which was strange, unless, perchance, she found some parallel to Eva's conduct which she was not inclined to discuss with her friends. Jeremy was not the only man who went courting just now in Milldean. Nor was Kate Raymore the only woman whose heart expected a wanderer home, and trembled at the joy of a long-desired meeting. The period of Mrs. Mumple's expectation was almost done. In two or three weeks she was to go on a journey; she would come back to Old Mill House not alone. The house was swept and garnished, and Mrs. Mumple had a new silk gown. The latter she showed to Kate, and a new bonnet too, which was a trifle gayer than her ordinary wear; it had a touch of youth about it. Mrs. Mumple knew very well who was the best person to show these treasures to, who the best listener to her speculations as to the manner of that meeting. And she, in turn, was eager to listen to Kate when the news came that Charley's ship was to be in quite soon. Kate could not say much about that to anybody except to Mrs. Mumple; but she was sure that Mrs. Mumple would understand.

When on the top of all this came the announcement that Dora Hutting's wedding was fixed for that day three weeks, Christine Fanshaw was moved to protest.

"Really, Grantley," she exclaimed, "this village is a centre of love-making, of one sort or another!"

"All villages are," said Grantley, suavely tolerant, "or they couldn't go on being villages. It's life or death to them, Christine."

"That's a contemptible evasion. The atmosphere is horribly sentimental. I don't think I'm in sympathy with it at all."

"Don't talk to me then," said Grantley. "I like it, you know. Oh, you needn't fret, my dear friend! There's been lots of trouble—and there'll be lots more."

"Yes, trouble—and hatred too?"

"Oh, well, suppose we suppose there won't be that?" he suggested. "But the trouble, anyhow."

"Then everybody oughtn't to pretend that there won't! The way people talk about marriages is simply hypocrisy."

"When the bather is on the bank, it's no moment for remarking that the water is cold. And the truth is in our hearts all the time. Am I likely to forget it, for instance? Or are you likely to forget poor old Tom and that unhappy woman?"

"Or am I likely to forget myself?" Christine murmured, looking out of the window. As she looked, Dora passed by, and broad-shouldered young Mallam with her. "Oh, well, bless the children!" she said, laughing.

"It doesn't do, though, to be too knowing—too much up to all nature's little tricks," Grantley went on, as he came and stood beside her. "We oughtn't to give the old lady away. She seems a bit primitive in her methods sometimes, but, if we don't interfere, she usually gets there in the end. But we mustn't find out all her secrets."

Christine looked up with a smile and the suspicion of a blush.

"Oh, well, one can always forget them again," she said.

"With the proper assistance," he agreed, smiling. "And after all she's very accommodating. If you do what she wants, she doesn't care a hang about your private reasons."

"I call that unscrupulous," Christine objected.

"Oh, yes, the most immoral old hussy that ever was!" he laughed. "I love her for that. In her matrimonial advertisement the woman is always rich, beautiful, and amiable!"

"And the man handsome, steady, and constant!"

"So we pay the fees—and sometimes get the article."

"Sometimes," said Christine. "Of course we always suit the description ourselves?"

"A faith in one's self—secure, impregnable, eternal—is the one really necessary equipment."

"So you've found?"

"Don't be personal—or penetrating, Christine. The forms of faith vary—the faith remains."

Christine looked up at him again. Something in her eyes made him pat her lightly on the shoulder.

"Oh, it's all very well," she murmured in rueful peevishness, "but I shan't be able to stand too much happiness here."

"Think of the others," he advised, "and you'll regain the balance of your judgment."

To think of the others was decidedly a good thing. Reason dictated the survey of a wider field, the discovery and recognition of an average emerging from the inequalities. The result of such a process should be either a temperate self-satisfaction or a clear-sighted resignation; you would probably find yourself not much above nor much below the level thus scientifically demonstrated. But the ways of science are not always those of the heart, and that we are less miserable than some people is not a consolation for being more unhappy than others—least of all when the happy are before our eyes and the wretched farther off. Neither the preacher of Grantley's doctrine nor its hearer was converted. Grantley still wanted the best, and Christine, asking nothing so very great, was the more aggrieved that she was denied even what she demanded.

Kate Raymore's day came. Only Jeremy accompanied the family to meet the boat. Kate said they would want somebody to bustle about after the luggage. In truth, Jeremy seemed to her already as one of her own house. But he did not seem so to himself. Eva had been very wayward, full of admiration for Mr. Mallam, and on the strict defensive against Jeremy's approaches. He was so distressed and puzzled that he might have comforted even Christine Fanshaw, and that he was in fact exceedingly bad company for anybody. But the party did not ask for conversation. A stillness fell on them all as they waited for the boat, Kate clasping her husband's arm tight while her eyes were fixed on the approaching ship.

The boy came down the gangway and saw them waiting. He was a good-looking young fellow, tall and slim, with curly hair. Joy and apprehension, shame and pride, struggled for mastery on his face. Kate saw, and her heart was very full. His fault, his flight, his banishment, were vivid in his mind, and, to his insight, vivid in theirs too. But there was something else that his eyes begged them to remember—the struggle to retrieve himself, the good record over-seas, the thought that they were to be together again for a while without fear and without a cloud between them. Their letters had breathed no reproach, and had been full of love. But letters cannot give the assurance of living eyes. He still feared reproach; he had to beg for love, and to fear to find it not unimpaired.

"My boy!" whispered Kate Raymore as she clasped him to her arms.

"You're looking well, Charley," said Raymore, "but older, I think."

Yes, he was older; that was part of the price which had fallen to be paid, and the happiness of reunion could not avail against it. His own hand had overthrown the first glory of his youth; it had died not gradually, but by a violent death—the traces were on his face. There was a touch of awe in Eva's eyes as she kissed her brother—the awe evoked by one who had fallen, endured, and fought. He had to pay the uttermost farthing of his debt.

Yet the joy rose supreme, deeper and tenderer for the grief behind it, for the struggle by which it was won, because it came as a victory after a heavy fight. To Kate it seemed as though he had suffered for their sakes as well as for his own sin, since in sorrow over him and his banishment their hearts had come closer together, and love reigned stronger in their home. A strange remorse struck her and mingled with her compassion and her gladness as she held her son at arm's length and looked again in his eyes. It was hard to keep track of these things, to see how the good and the evil worked, to understand how no man was unto himself alone, and not to accuse of injustice the way by which one paid for all, while all sorrowed for one.

As they turned away to the carriage, Eva touched Jeremy on the arm. He turned to find her smiling, but her lips trembled.

"If I drive back with them, I shall cry, and then I shall look a fright," she whispered. "Besides they'd rather have him to themselves just now. Will you walk back with me?"

"All right," said Jeremy curtly.

His feelings, too, had been touched, so that his manner was cool and matter-of-fact almost to aggressiveness. He preferred to make nothing at all of walking back with Eva, though the way was long, and the winter sun shone over the sea and the downs, the wind was fresh and crisp, and youthful blood went tingling through the veins.

"It's cold driving, anyhow," he added, as an after-thought.

It was not cold walking, though, or Jeremy did not so find it. It was in his mind that now he had his chance, if he could find courage to use it and to force an issue. For him too Charley and Charley's sorrow had done something. They had induced in Eva a softer mood; the armour of her coquetry was pierced by a shaft of deep feeling. As they walked she was silent, forgetting to torment him, silently glad of his friendship and his company. She said nothing of Dora Hutting's good-fortune or of Mallam's good looks now. She was thinking of her mother's face as she welcomed Charley, and was musing on love. It was Jeremy's moment, if he could make use of it. But in this mood she rather frightened him, raising about herself defences different from the gleaming barrier of her coquetry, yet not less effective. He feared to disturb her thoughts, and it seemed to him that his wooing would be rude and rough.

Suddenly she turned to him.

"You'll be friends with Charley, won't you? Real friends, I mean? You won't let what—what's happened stand in the way? You see, he'll be awfully sensitive about it, and if he fancies you're hanging back, or anything of that kind——"

Her eyes were very urgent in their appeal.

"Of course I shall be friends with him; I shouldn't dream of——"

"I'm sure you'll like him for his own sake, when you know him. And till then, for mother's sake, for our sake, you'll be nice to him, won't you?"

"Do you care particularly about my being nice to him?"

"Of course I do! We're friends, you see."

Jeremy's fear wore off; excitement began to rise in him; the spirit of the game came upon him. He turned to his work.

"Are we friends?" he asked. "You've not been very friendly lately."

"Never mind me. Be friendly with Charley."

"For your sake?"

"For our sake, yes."

"I said, for your sake."

A smile dimpled through Eva's gravity.

"'Your' is a plural, isn't it?" she asked.

"Then—for thy sake?" said Jeremy. "That's singular, anyhow."

"Oh, for my sake, then, if you think it worth while."

"I don't think anything worth while except pleasing you, Eva. I used to manage it, I think; but somehow it's grown more difficult lately."

He stopped in his walk and faced her. She walked on a pace or two, but he would not follow. Irresolutely she halted.

"More difficult? Pleasing me grown more difficult?"

"Well, pleasing you as much as I want to, I mean." Jeremy in his turn smiled for a moment; but he was in deadly earnest again as he stepped up to her and caught hold of her hands. "Now's the time," he said. "You've got to say yes or no."

"You haven't asked me anything yet," she murmured, laughing, her eyes away from him and her hands in his.

"Yes, I have, dozens of times—dozens and dozens. And I'm not going to ask it again—not in words, anyhow. You know the question."

"It's horribly unfair to—to do this to-day—to-day, when I'm——"

"Not a bit. To-day's the very day for it, and that's why you must answer to-day." A deeper note came into his words, deeper than he had commanded when he made love to Dora Hutting on these same downs not so very long ago. "I make love to you to-day because love's in your heart to-day. You're wanting to love; it's round about us, Eva."

For an instant she saw in him a likeness she had never noticed before—a likeness to Sibylla: Sibylla's ardent all-demanding temper seemed to speak in his words.

"Yes, this is the day—our day. And this day shall be the beginning or the end. You know the question. What's the answer, Eva?"

He let go of her hands, and drew back two or three paces. He left her free; if she came to him, it must be of her own motion.

"How very peremptory you are!" she protested.

Her cheeks were red now, and the look of sorrow had gone out of her eyes. Her breath came quick, and when she looked at the sea the waves seemed to dance to the liveliest music. At sea and land she looked, at the sky and at the wintry sun; her glance touched everywhere save where Jeremy stood.

"The answer!" demanded Jeremy.

For a moment more she waited. Then she came towards him hesitatingly, her eyes not yet seeking his face. She came up to him and stood with her hands hanging by her side. Then slowly she raised to his face the large trustful eyes which he had known and loved so well.

"The answer is Yes, Jeremy," she said. "For all my life and with all my heart, dear!"

"I knew this was the right day!" cried Jeremy.

"Oh, any day was right!" she whispered as she sought his arms.

A couple of hours later he burst into Grantley Imason's room, declaring that he was the happiest man on earth. This condition of his, besides being by no means rare in young men, was not unexpected, and congratulations met the obvious needs of the occasion. Sibylla, who was there, was not even very emotional over the matter; the remembrance of Dora Hutting inclined her mind towards the humorous aspect—so hard is it to appreciate the changeful processes of other hearts. But Jeremy himself was excited enough for everybody, and his excitement carried him into forgetfulness of a solemn pledge which he had once given. He wrung Grantley's hand with a vigour at once embarrassing and painful, crying:

"I owe it all to you! I should never have dared it except for the partnership that's coming, and that was all your doing. Without your money——"

"Damn you, Jeremy," said Grantley in a quiet whisper, rescuing his hand and compassionately caressing it with its uninjured brother.

The imprecation seemed to be equally distributed between Jeremy's two causes of offence, but Jeremy allocated it to one only.

"Oh, good lord!" he said, with a guilty glance at Sibylla.

"What money?" asked Sibylla.

She had been sitting by the fire, but rose now, and leant her shoulder against the mantelpiece.

Jeremy looked from her to Grantley.

"I'm most awfully sorry. I forgot. I'm a bit beside myself, you know." Grantley shrugged his shoulders rather crossly. "I won't say another word about it."

"Oh, yes, you will, Jeremy," observed Sibylla with a dangerous look. "You'll tell me all about it this moment, please."

"Shall I?" Jeremy turned to Grantley again.

"I expect the mischief's done now; but you needn't have lost your memory or your wits just because you're going to marry Eva Raymore."

"Marrying does make people lose their wits sometimes," said Sibylla coldly. Grantley's brows lifted a little as he plumped down in a chair with a resigned air. "Tell me what you mean, Jeremy."

"Well, I had to put money into the business if I was ever to be more than a clerk—if I was ever to get a partnership, you know."

"And Grantley gave you the money?"

"I'm going to pay it back when—when——"

"Yes, of course, Jeremy dear. How much was it?"

Grantley lit a cigarette, and came as near looking uncomfortable as the ingrained composure of his manner allowed.

"Five thousand," said Jeremy. "Wasn't it splendid of him? So, you see, I could afford——"

"Five thousand to Jeremy!" said Sibylla. She turned on Grantley. "And how much to John Fanshaw?"

"You women are all traitors. Christine had no business to say a word. It was pure business; he pays me back regularly. And Jeremy's going to pay me back too. Come, I haven't done any harm to either of them."

"No, not to them," she said. And she added to Jeremy: "Go and tell Christine. She'll be delighted to hear about you and Eva."

"By Jove, I will! I say, I'm really sorry, Grantley."

"You ought to be. No, you may do anything except shake my hand again."

"I can't help being so dashed jolly, you know."

With that apology he darted out of the room, forgetting his broken pledge, intent only on finding other ears to hear his wonderful news.

"It's very satisfactory, isn't it?" asked Grantley. "I think they'll get on very well, you know. He's young, of course, and——"

"Please don't make talk, Grantley. When did you give him that money?"

"I don't remember."

"There are bank-books and so on, aren't there?"

"How businesslike you're getting!"

"Tell me when, please."

Grantley rose and stood opposite to her, even as they had stood in the inn—at the Sailors' Rest at Fairhaven.

"I don't remember the date." He paused, seemed to think, and then went on: "Yes, I'll tell you, because then you'll understand. He came to me the morning of the day you—you went over to Fairhaven. While he was there, Christine's letter came. And I gave him the money because I wanted to put you in the wrong as much as I could. Oh, I liked Jeremy, and was willing to help him—just as I was ready to help old John. But that wasn't my great reason. My great reason was to get a bigger grievance against you—for the way you had treated me, and were going to treat me, you know."

"If it had been that, you'd have told me—you'd have told me that night in the inn. You must have known what it would have been to me to hear it then; but you never told me."

"I wouldn't part with the pleasure of having it against you—of nursing it against you secretly. I want you to understand the truth. Are you very angry?"

Sibylla appeared to be angry; there was a dash of red on her cheeks.

"Yes, I'm angry," she said; "and I've a right to be angry. You're good to John Fanshaw; you're good to Jeremy. Have you been good to me?"

"It was done in malice against you—and in petty malice, I think now, though I didn't think that then."

"Doing it was no malice to me. You did it in love of me!" Her words were a challenge to him to deny; and, looking at her, he could not deny. He had never denied his love for her, and he would not now. "The wrong you did me was not in doing it, but in not telling me; yes, not telling me about that, nor about what you did for John Fanshaw either."

"I couldn't risk seeming to try to make a claim, especially when——"

"Especially when making a claim on me might have saved me! Is that what you mean? When it might have made all the difference to me and to Frank? When it might have turned me back from my madness? All was to go to ruin sooner than that you should risk seeming to make a claim!"

He attempted no answer, but stood very still, listening and ready to listen. Her voice lost something of its hardness, and became more appealing as she went on.

"They're allowed to know your good side, the kind things you do, how you stand by your friends, how you help people, how you lavish gifts on my brother for my sake. You don't hide it from them. They know you can love, and love to give happiness. There are only two people who mayn't know—the two people in all the world who ought to know, whose happiness and whose trust in themselves and in one another lie in knowing. They must be hoodwinked and kept in the dark. They're to know nothing of you. For them you find the bad motive, the mean interpretation, the selfish point of view. And you're so ingenious in finding it for them! Grantley, to those two people you've done a great wrong."

He was silent a moment. Then he asked:

"To you and the little boy, you mean?"

"No: he's too young. Anyhow, I didn't mean him; I wasn't thinking of him. You know that sometimes I don't think of him—that sometimes, in love or in hatred, I can think of nothing in the world but you, but you and me. And it's to me and to yourself that you've done the wrong."

"To you—and myself?"

"Yes, yes! Oh, what's the use of doing fine things if you bury them from me, if you distort them to yourself, if you won't let either me or yourself think them generous and good? Why must you trick me and yourself, of all the world? Oughtn't we to know—oughtn't we of everybody in the world to know? What's the good of kindness if you dress it up as selfishness? What's the good of love if you call it malice?"

"I've spoken the truth as I believed it."

"No, I say no, Grantley! You've spoken it as you would have me believe it, as you try to make yourself believe it. But it's not the truth!" She came one step nearer to him. "I used to pray that you should change," she said imploringly. "I don't pray that now. It's impossible. And I don't think I want it. Don't change; but, oh, be yourself! Be yourself to me and to yourself. You haven't been to either of us. Open your heart to both of us; let us both know you as you are. Don't be ashamed either before me or before yourself. I know I'm difficult! Heavens, aren't you—even the real you—difficult too? But if you won't be honest in the end, then God help us! But if you'll be yourself to me and to yourself, then, my dear, I think it would be enough."

He came to her and took her hand.

"No man ever loved woman more than I love you," he said.

"Then try, then try, then try!" she whispered, and her eyes met his.

There seemed in them a far-off gleam of the light which once had blazed from them on the fairy ride.

CHAPTER XXVII

SAMPLES OF THE BULK

"You do think they'll be happy?" Mrs. Selford asked a little apprehensively. Her manner craved reassurance.

"Why put that question to me—to me, of all people? Is it on the principle of knowing the worst? If even a cynic like me thinks they'll be happy, the prospect will be very promising—is that it?"

"Goodness knows I don't expect the ideal! I've never had it myself. Oh, I don't see why I need pretend with you, and I shouldn't deceive you if I did. I've never had the ideal myself, and I don't expect it for Anna. We've seen too much in our set to expect the ideal. And sometimes I can't quite make Anna out." Mrs. Selford was evidently uneasy. "She gets on better with her father than with me now; and I think I get on better with Walter than Richard does."

"Young Walter has a way with him," smiled Caylesham.

"I hope we shan't get into opposite camps and quarrel. Richard and I have been such good friends lately. And then, of course——" She hesitated a little. "Of course there may be a slight awkwardness here and there."

Caylesham understood the covert allusion; the marriage might make matters difficult with the Imasons.

"The young folks will probably make their own friends. Our old set's rather broken up one way and the other, isn't it? Not that I was ever a full member of it."

"We've always been glad to see you," she murmured absently.

"On the whole I feel equal to encouraging you to a certain extent," he said, standing before the fire. "Anna will be angry pretty often, but I don't think she will be, or need be, unhappy. She doesn't take things to heart too readily, does she?"

"No, she doesn't."

The assent hardly sounded like praise of her daughter.

"Well, that's a good thing. And she's got lots of pluck and a will of her own."

"Oh, yes, she's got that!"

"From time to time he'll think himself in love with somebody. You're prepared for that, of course? But it's only his way. She'll have to indulge him a little—let the string out a little here and there; but she'll always have him under control. Brains do count, and she's got them all. And she won't expect romance all the time."

"You said you were going to be encouraging."

"I am being encouraging," Caylesham insisted.

"Oh, I shouldn't think it so bad if we were talking about myself. But when it's a question of one's child——"

"One is always unreasonable? Precisely. The nature of the business isn't going to change in the next generation. But I maintain that I'm encouraging—for Anna, anyhow. I rather fancy Master Blake will miss his liberty more than he thinks. But that'll be just what he needs. So from a moral point of view I'm encouraging there too."

"Of course you don't understand the feeling of responsibility, the fear that if she's the—the least bit hard, it may be because of her bringing up."

"Don't be remorseful, Mrs. Selford. It's the most unprofitable of emotions."

He had preached the same doctrine to Christine.

"When it's too late to go back?"

"And that's always." He looked down at her with a cheerful smile. "That's for your private ear. Don't tell the children. Walter Blake's quite great on remorse."

Mrs. Selford laughed rather ruefully.

"I suppose it'll turn out as well as most things. Do you know any thoroughly happy couples?"

"Very hard to say. One isn't behind the scenes. But I'm inclined to think I do. Oh, ecstasies aren't for this world, you know—not permanent ecstasies. You might as well have permanent hysterics! And, as you're aware, there are no marriages in heaven. So perhaps there's no heaven in marriages either. That would seem to be plausible reasoning, wouldn't it? But they'll be all right; they'll learn one another's paces."

"I can't help wishing she seemed more in love."

"Perhaps she will be when she flirts with somebody else. Don't frown! I'm not a pessimist. If I don't always look for happiness by the ordinary roads, I often discern it along quite unexpected routes."

"It's pleasant to see people start by being in love."

"How eternally sentimental we are! Well, yes, it is. But capacities differ. I daresay she doesn't know she's deficient, and she certainly won't imagine that her mother has given her away."

"I suppose I deserve that, but I had to talk to somebody. And really it's best to choose a man; sometimes it stops there then."

"Why not your husband? No? Ah, he has too many opportunities of reminding you of the indiscretion! You were quite right to talk to me. We shall look on at what happens with all the greater interest because we've discussed it. And, as I've said, I'm decidedly hopeful."

"We might have developed her affections when she was a child. I'm sure we might."

"Oh, I shall go! You send for a clergyman!"

Mrs. Selford shook her head sadly, even while she smiled. She could not be beguiled from her idea, nor from the remorse that it brought. The pictures, the dogs, and sentimental squabbling with her husband had figured too largely in the household; she connected with this fact the disposition which she found in Anna.

"Being a bit hard isn't a bad thing for your happiness," Caylesham added as a last consolation.

Anna herself came in. No consciousness of deficiency seemed to afflict her; she felt no need of a development of her affections or of being more in love with Walter Blake. On the contrary she exhibited to Caylesham's shrewd eyes a remarkable picture of efficiency and of contentment. She had known what she wanted, she had discerned what means to use in order to get it, and she had achieved it. A perfect self-confidence assured her that she would be successful in dealing with it; her serene air, her trim figure and decisive movements gave the impression that here at least was a mortal who, if she did not deserve success, could command it. Caylesham looked on her with admiration—rather that than liking—as he acknowledged her very considerable qualities. The thing which was wanting was what in a picture he would have called "atmosphere." But here again her luck came in, or, rather, her clear vision; it was not fair to call it luck. The man she had pitched upon—that was fair, and Caylesham declined to withdraw the expression—at the time when she pitched upon him, was in a panic about "atmosphere." He had found too much of it elsewhere, and was uneasy about it in himself. He was not asking for softness, for tenderness, for ready accessibility to emotion or to waves of feeling. Her cleverness had turned to account even the drawback which made Caylesham, in the midst of his commendation, conscious that he would not choose to be her husband—or perhaps her son either.

"You'll make a splendid head of the family," he told her cheerfully. "You'll keep them all in most excellent order."

She chose to consider that he had exercised a bad influence over Walter Blake, and treated him distantly. Caylesham supported the entire injustice of her implied charge with good-humour.

"You're not fond of excellent order, I suppose?" she asked.

"In others," said he, smiling. "May I come and see it in your house sometimes? I promise not to disturb it."

"I don't think you could."

"She taunts me with my advancing years," he complained to Mrs. Selford.

Anna's disapproval of him was marked; it increased his amusement at the life which lay before Walter Blake. Blake would want to disturb excellent order sometimes; he would be indulged in that proclivity to a strictly limited extent. If Grantley Imason were a revengeful man, this marriage ought to cause him a great deal of pleasure. Caylesham, while compelled to approve by his reason, could not help deploring in his heart. He saw arising an ultra-British household, clad in the very buckram of propriety. Who could say that morality did not reign in the world when such a nemesis as this awaited Walter Blake, or that morality had not a humour of its own when Walter Blake accepted the nemesis with enthusiasm? Yet the state of things was not unusual—a fair sample of a bulk of considerable size. Caylesham went away smiling at it, wondering at it, in the depths of his soul a trifle appalled at it. It seemed to him rather inhuman; but perhaps his idea of humanity had gone a trifle far in the opposite direction.

And, after all, could not Walter Blake supply the other element? There was plenty of softness about him, and the waves of feeling were by no means wanting in frequency or volume. Considering this question, Caylesham professed himself rather at a loss. He would have to wait and look on. But would he hear or see much? Anna had evidently put him under a ban, and he believed that her edicts would obtain obedience in the future. So far as he could see now, he had a vision of the waves stilled to rest, of the gleam of frost forming upon them, of an ice-bound sea. Now he felt it in his heart to be sorry for young Blake. Not because there was any injustice. The nemesis was eminently, and even ludicrously, just. He felt sorry precisely because it was so just. He was always sorry for sinners who had to pay the penalty of their deeds; then a fellow-feeling went out to them. Of course they were fools to grumble. The one wisdom he claimed for himself was not grumbling at the bill.

He paid another visit that day, under an impulse of friendliness, and perhaps of curiosity too. He went to Tom Courtland's, and found himself repaid for his trouble by Tom's cordiality of greeting. The Courtland family was in the turmoil of moving; they had to go to a much smaller house, and to reduce the establishment greatly. But the worries of a move and the prospect of comparative poverty—there was very little left besides Harriet's moderate dowry—were accepted by Tom very cheerfully, and by the children with glee; they were delighted to be told that there would be no more menservants and fewer maids, and that they would have to learn to shift for themselves as much and as soon as possible. They were glad to be rid of "this great gloomy house," over which the shadow of calamity still brooded.

"The children don't like to pass Lady Harriet's door at night," Suzette whispered in an aside to Caylesham.

Tom himself seemed younger and more sprightly; and he was the slave of his little girls. His grey hair, the lines on his face, and the enduring scar on Sophy's brow spoke of the sorrow which had been; but the sorrow had given place to peace—and it might be that some day peace would turn to joy. For there was much youth there, and, where youth is, joy must come, if only it be given a fair chance.

"We're rather in narrow circumstances, of course," Tom explained when Suzette and the children were out of earshot. "That's because I made such an ass of myself."

"Well, don't be hard on Flora. She was a good friend to you."

"I'm not blaming her; it's myself, Frank. I ought to have remembered the children. But we can rub along, and perhaps I shall get a berth some day."

Caylesham did not think that prospect a very probable one, but he dissembled and told Tom that his old political friends ought certainly to do something for him:

"Because it never came to an absolute public row, did it?"

"Everybody knew," sighed Tom, with a relapse into despondency.

"Anyhow you won't starve," Caylesham said with a laugh. "I reckon you must have above a thousand a year?"

"It's not much; but—well, I tell you what, Frank, Suzette Bligh's pretty nearly as good as another five hundred, and I only pay her seventy pounds a year. You wouldn't believe what a manager that little woman is! She makes everything go twice as far as it did, and has the house so neat too. Upon my soul, I don't notice any difference, except that I've dropped my champagne."

"Well, with champagne what it mostly is nowadays, that's no great loss, my boy, and I'm glad you've struck it rich with Miss Bligh."

"We should be lost without her. I don't know what the children would do, or what I should do with them, but for her. One good thing poor Harriet did, anyhow, was to bring her here."

Yes; but if Harriet had known how it was to fall out, had foreseen how Suzette was to reign in her stead, and with what joy the change of government would be greeted! Caylesham imagined, with a conscious faintness of fancy, the tempest which would have arisen, and how short a shrift would have been meted out to Suzette and all her adherents. He really hoped that poor Harriet, who had suffered enough for her faults, was not in any position in which she could be aware of what had happened; it would be to her (unless some great transformation had been wrought) too hard and unendurable a punishment.

"The children are changed creatures, Frank," Tom went on. "We don't try to repress them, you know. That would be hypocrisy, wouldn't it, under the circumstances? The best thing is for them to forget. Suzette says so, and I quite agree."

Suzette, it seemed, could achieve an epitaph of stinging quality—quite without meaning it, of course. Caylesham agreed that the best thing the girls could do was to forget their mother.

"So we let them make a row, and they're to go out of mourning very soon. That's what Suzette advises."

A merciful Providence must spare even poor Harriet this! She was to be forgotten—almost by a violent process of obliteration; and this by Suzette's decree—an all-powerful decree of gentle inconspicuous Suzette's.

The man of experience foresaw. Weak kindly Tom Courtland must always have a woman to fend for him. Because Harriet had not filled that part, ruin had come. The children must have a guardian and a guide in feminine affairs. The bonds were becoming too strong to be broken—so strong that the very idea of their ever being broken would cause terror, and impel steps to make them formally permanent. Here was another sample from a bulk of goodly dimensions, one of those by no means rare cases where a woman who would not otherwise have got a husband—or perhaps taken one—passes through the stage of the indispensable spinster to the position of the inevitable wife. Caylesham saw the process begun, and he was glad to see it. It was the best thing that could happen to Tom, and for the girls the best way of piecing together the fragments of that home-life which Harriet's cruel rage had shattered. Only they were all still so delightfully unconscious of what seemed so obvious to an outsider with his eyes about him. Caylesham smiled at their blindness, and took care not to disturb Tom's mind, or to rally him about his harping on Suzette's name and Suzette's advice. He was quite content to leave the matter to its natural course. But coming, as it did, on the top of his visit to the Selfords' and of his impressions of what he had seen there, it raised another reflection in his mind. How many roads there were to Rome! And most of them well trodden. Primitive instinct or romantic passion was only one of many—anyhow if the test of predominating influence were taken. It was not the prevailing factor with Anna Selford; it would hardly count at all with Tom and Suzette. Since then the origin was so various, what wonder the result was various too! Various results were even expected, aimed at, desired. Add to that cause of variation human error and the resources of the unexpected, and the field of chance spread infinitely wide. Save for the purpose of being amusing—an end to which all is justifiable that is not actually unseemly—only a fool or a boy would generalise about the legal state which was the outcome of such heterogeneous persons, aims, and tempers. But then at the end old nature—persistent old nature—would come back and give the thing a twist in her direction, with her babies and her nursery. She made confusion worse confounded, and piled incongruity on incongruity. But she would do it, and a pretty mixture was the general result. To make his old metaphor of double harness at all adequate to the subject which it sought to express, you must suppose many breeds of horses, and a great deal of very uneven and very unsuitable pairing of them by the grooms. It was probably all necessary, but the outcome was decidedly odd.

"It's all been pretty bad. I can't bear to think of poor Harriet, and I'm not fond of thinking about myself," said Tom Courtland, rubbing his bristly hair. "But the worst of it's over now. There's peace anyhow, Frank, and at least the children were always fond of me."

"You're going to get along first-rate," Caylesham assured him. "And mind you make Miss Suzette stick to you. She's a rare woman; I can see that."

"You're a good chap, Frank. You stick to your friends. You stuck to me all through."

"Much less trouble than dropping you, old fellow."

"That's rot!"

"Well, perhaps it is. After all, if I hadn't some of the minor virtues, I should be hardly human, should I? They're just as essential as the minor vices."

"If you ever see Flora, tell her—well, you'll know what to tell her."

"I'll say something kind. Good-bye, Tom. I'm glad to find you so cheerful."

The girls came round him to say good-bye. He kissed them, and gave each of them half a crown. He used to explain that he always tipped children because in after years he was thus made sure of finding somebody to defend his character in pretty nearly any company. Since, however, this was absolutely the only step he ever took with any such end in view, the explanation was often received with scepticism. His action was more probably the outcome of one of his minor virtues.

"How kind you are to children! What a pity you're a bachelor!" smiled Suzette.

"Thanks! I don't often get such a testimonial," he said, risking a whimsical lift of his brows for Tom Courtland's eye.

He had been seeking impressions of marriage. Chance gave him one more than he had looked for or desired. Just outside Tom Courtland's, as he was going away, he ran plump into John Fanshaw, who was making for the house. There was no avoiding him this time. The men had not met since Caylesham lent John money and John learnt from Harriet Courtland the truth of what the man from whom he took the money had done. But there had been no rupture between them. Civil notes had been written—on John's side even grateful notes—as the business transaction between them necessitated. And both had a part to play—the same part, the part of ignorance. Caylesham must play it for Christine. John had to assume it on his own account, for his own self-respect. The last shred of his pride hung on the assumption that, though he knew, and though Christine was aware of his knowledge, Caylesham at least believed him ignorant.

But heavy John Fanshaw was a clumsy hand at make-believe. His cordiality was hesitating, fumbling, obviously insincere; his unhappiness in his part very apparent. Caylesham cut short his effort to express gratitude, saying, "You shall do anything in the world except thank me!" and went on to ask after Christine in the most natural manner in the world.

"She's been a little—a little seedy, and has gone down to stay with the Imasons for a bit," John explained, taking care not to look at Caylesham.

"Oh, I hope she'll be all right soon! Give her my remembrances when you write—or perhaps you'll be running down?"

"I don't know. It depends on business."

"Come, you'll take Christmas off, anyhow?"

Then John took refuge in talking about Tom Courtland. But his mind was far from Tom. He managed at last to look Caylesham in the face, and grew more amazed at his perfect ease and composure. He was acutely conscious of giving exactly the opposite impression himself, acutely fearful that he was betraying that hidden knowledge of his. Actuated by this fear, he tried to increase his cordiality, hitting wildly at the mark, and indulging in forced friendliness and even forced jocosity.

Caylesham met every effort with just the right tone, precisely the right amount of effusiveness. He had taken a very hard view of what John had done—harder than he could contrive to take of what he himself had—and had expressed it vigorously to Christine. But now he found himself full of pity for poor John. The sight of the man fighting for the remnant of his pride and self-respect was pathetic. And John did it so lamentably ill.

"You're a paragon of a debtor," Caylesham told him, when he harked back to the money again. "My money's a deal safer in your hands than in my own. I'm more in your debt than you are in mine."

"You shall have every farthing the first day I can manage it."

His eagerness told Caylesham what a burden on his soul the indebtedness was. It was impossible to ignore altogether what was so plainly shown; but he turned the point of it, saying:

"I know how punctilious you men of business are. I wish fellows were always the same in racing. I'm ready to take it as soon as you're ready to pay, and to wait till you're ready."

"I shan't ask you to wait a day," John assured him.

Enough had passed for civility; Caylesham was eager to get away—not for his own sake so much as for John's.

"By Jove, I've got an appointment!" he exclaimed suddenly, diving for his watch. "Half-past six! Oh, I must jump into a cab!" He held the watch in one hand, and hailed a cab with his stick. "Good-bye, old fellow," he said, turning away. He had seen John begin to put out his hand in a hesitating reluctant way. He would have liked to shake hands himself, but he knew John hated to do it. John made a last demonstration of ignorance.

"Come and see us some day!" he called almost jovially.

"Yes, I will some day before long," Caylesham shouted back from the step of his hansom.

As he drove off, John was still standing on the pavement, waving a hand to him. Caylesham drove round the corner, then got down again, and pursued his way on foot.

He was quite clear in his own mind that John took the thing unnecessarily hard, but he was genuinely sorry that John should so take it. Indeed John's distress raised an unusually acute sense of discomfort in him. Nor could he take any pride in the tact with which he himself had steered the course of the interview. He could not avoid the conclusion that to John he must have seemed a hypocrite more accomplished than one would wish to be considered in the arts of hypocrisy. He had hitherto managed so well that he had not been forced into such situations; he had been obliged to lie only in his actions, and had not come so near having to lie in explicit words. He did not like the experience, and shook his head impatiently as he walked along. It occurred to him that since marriage was in its own nature so difficult and risky a thing as he had already decided, it was hardly fair for third persons to step in and complicate it more. He had to get at any state of mind resembling penitence by roads of his own; the ordinary approaches were overgrown and impassable from neglect. But in view of John's distress and of the pain which had come on Christine, and on a realisation of the unpleasant perfection of art which he himself had been compelled (and able) to exhibit, he achieved the impression that he had better have left such things alone—well, at any rate where honest old duffers as John Fanshaw were involved in the case. Having got so far, he might not unnaturally have considered whether he should remodel his way of life.

But he was not the man to suffer a sudden conversion under the stress of emotion or of a particular impression. His unsparing clearness of vision and honesty of intellect forbade that.

"I shall get better when I'm too old for anything else," he told himself with a rather bitter smile. "I suppose I ought to thank God that the time's not far off now."

It was not much of an effort in the way of that unprofitable emotion against which he had warned Christine Fanshaw and Janet Selford; but it was enough to make him take a rather different view, if not of himself, at least of old John Fanshaw. He decided that he had been too hard on John; and at the back of his mind was a notion that he had been rather hard on Christine too. In this case it seemed to him that he was getting off too cheaply. John and Christine were paying all the bill—at least a disproportionate amount. The upshot of it all was expressed in his exclamation:

"I don't want the money. I wish to heaven old John wouldn't pay me back!"

He would have felt easier for a little more demerit in John. It is probable, though his philosophising did not lead him so far as this conclusion, that he too was a sample, and from a bulk not inconsiderable in quantity. Where it is possible, we prefer that the people we have injured should turn out to have deserved injury from somebody.

CHAPTER XXVIII

TO LIFE AND LIGHT AGAIN

It was the eve of Dora Hutting's wedding—a thing in itself quite enough to put Milldean into an unwonted stir. Everybody was very excited about the event and very sympathetic. Kate Raymore had come to the front; not even preoccupation with Charley could prevent a marriage from interesting her. She had given much counsel, and had exerted herself to effect a reconciliation between the bride and Jeremy Chiddingfold. Into this diplomatic effort Sibylla also had been drawn, and peace had been signed at a tea-party. With the help of Christine's accomplished manner and Grantley's tactful composure, it had been found possible to treat the whole episode as a boy-and-girl affair which could be laughed at and thus dismissed into oblivion. The two principals could not take quite this view; but they consented to be friends, to wish each other well, and to say nothing about the underlying contempt which each could not but entertain for the other's fickleness. For Jeremy would have been faithful if Dora had been, and Dora could not perceive how the fact of her having made a mistake as to her own feelings explained the extraordinary rapidity with which Jeremy had been able to transfer an affection professedly so lasting and so deep. Christine warned her that all men were like that—except Mr. Mallam; and Grantley told Jeremy that Dora was flighty, as all girls were—except Eva Raymore. So peace, though not very cordial peace, was obtained, the satirical remarks which the parties felt entitled to make privately not appearing on the face of the formal proceedings.

Important though these matters might be, they were not in Sibylla's mind as she stood at the end of the garden and looked down on Old Mill House. Twenty-four hours before, Mrs. Mumple had started on her journey. Sibylla, Eva, and Jeremy had escorted her to Fairhaven. The fat old woman was very apprehensive and tremulous; anxious about her looks and the fit of her new silk gown; full of questionings about the meeting to which she went. It was impossible not to smile covertly at some of these manifestations, but over them all shone the beauty of the love which had sustained her through the years. Sibylla prayed that now it might have its reward, half wondering that it had lived to claim it—had lived so long in solitude and uncomforted. It had never despaired, however long the waiting, however much it was starved of all satisfaction, bereft of all pleasure, condemned to seeming uselessness, even unwelcomed, as one well might fear. These things had brought pain and fear, but not despair nor death. Yet Mrs. Mumple was not by nature a patient woman; naturally she craved a full return for what she gave, and an ardent answer to the warmth of her affection. None the less she had not despaired; and as Sibylla thought of this, she accused herself because, unlike the old woman, she had allowed herself to despair—nay, had been ready, almost eager, to do it, had twisted everything into a justification for it, had made no protest against it and no effort to avoid it. That mood had led to ruin; at last she saw that it would have been ruin. Was there now hope? It was difficult to go back, to retrace the steps so confidently taken, to realise that she too had been wrong. Yet what else was the lesson? It came to her in one form or another from every side—from the Courtlands, where death alone had been strong enough to thwart the evil fate; from the Raymores, where trust, bruised but not broken, had redeemed a boy's life from evil to good; even from Christine, who waited in secret hope; above all, from the quarter whence she had least looked for it—from Grantley himself, for whom no effort was too great, who never lost confidence, who had indeed lacked understanding but had never lacked courage; who now, with eyes opened and at her bidding, was endeavouring the hardest thing a man can do—was trying to change himself, to look at himself with another's eyes, to remodel himself by a new standard, to count as faults what he had cherished as virtues, to put in the foremost place not the qualities which had been his pets, his favourites, his ideals, but those which another asked from him, and which he must do himself a violence to display. Had she no corresponding effort to make? She could not deny the accusation. It lay with her too to try. But it was hard. John Fanshaw found it sorely difficult, grossly against his prejudices, and even in conflict with principles which he held sacred, to belittle his grievance or to let it go. Sibylla was very fond of her grievances too. She was asked to look at them with new eyes, to think of them no more as outrages, as stones of stumbling and rocks of offence. She was asked to consider her grievances as opportunities. That was the plain truth about it, and it involved so much recantation, such a turning upside down of old notions, such a fall for pride. It was very hard to swallow. Yet unless it were swallowed, where was hope? And if it were swallowed, what did it mean? An experiment—only another difficult experiment. For people are not changed readily, and cannot be changed altogether. Difficulties would remain—would remain always; the vain ideal which had once governed all her acts and thoughts would never be realised. She must not be under any delusion as to that. And now, in her heart, she was afraid of delusion coming again; and again disillusion must follow.

She turned to find Grantley beside her, and he gave her a telegram addressed to her. She opened it with a word of thanks.

"From John Fanshaw!" she exclaimed eagerly. "He's coming down here to-night!"

"Well, you told him to wire whenever he found he could get down, didn't you?"

"Yes, of course. But—but what does it mean?"

He smiled at her.

"I'm not surprised. Christine had a letter from him this morning. I saw the handwriting. I'm taking a very sympathetic interest in Christine, so I look at the handwriting on her letters. And she's been in a state of suppressed excitement all the morning. I've noticed that—with a sympathetic interest, Sibylla."

"I think I ought to go and see her."

"Not just yet, please. Oh yes, I hope it'll be a good day for her! And it'll be a great day for your poor old Mumples, won't it? I hope Mr. Mumple will behave nicely."

"Oh, so do I with my whole heart!" cried Sibylla.

"I'm taking a very sympathetic interest in the Mumples also, Sibylla. Likewise in Dora and her young man, and Jeremy and his young woman. Oh, and in the Raymores and Charley! Anybody else?"

Sibylla looked at him reprovingly, but a smile would tremble about the corners of her mouth.

"You see, I've been thinking over what you said the other day," Grantley went on with placid gravity, "and I've made up my mind to come and tell you whenever I do a decent thing or have an honest emotion. I shan't like saying it at all, but you'll like hearing it awfully."

"Some people would be serious about it, considering—well, considering everything," Sibylla remarked, turning her face away.

"Yes, but then they wouldn't see you smile—and you've an adorable smile; and they wouldn't see the flash in your eyes—and you've such wonderful eyes, Sibylla."

He delivered these statements with a happy simplicity.

"You're not imposing on me," she said. "I know you mean it." Her voice trembled just a little. "And perhaps that's the best way to tell me."

"On the other hand, I shall become a persistent and accomplished hypocrite. You'll never know how I grind the faces of the poor at the bank, nor my inmost thoughts when Frank drops half his food on my best waistcoat."

"You're outrageous. Please stop, Grantley."

"All right. I'll talk about something else."

"I think I'd better find Christine. No, wait a minute. If you're going to do all these fine things, what have you planned for me?"

"Nothing. You've just to go on being what you can't help being—the most adorable woman in England."

"I don't know what you mean to do, but what you are doing is——"

"Making love to you," interposed Grantley.

"Yes, and in the most unblushing way."

"I'm doing the love-making, and you're doing the——"

"Stop!" she commanded, with a hasty merry glance of protest.

"You ought to be used to it. I've been doing it for a month now," he complained.

Sibylla made no answer, and Grantley lit a cigarette. When she spoke again she was grave and her voice was low.

"Don't make love to me. I'm afraid to love you. You know what I did before because I loved you. I should do it again, I'm afraid. I haven't learnt the lesson."

"Are you refusing the only way there is of learning it? How have I learnt all the fine lessons that I've been telling you?"

"I've not learnt the lesson. I still ask too much."

"If I give all I have, it'll seem enough to you. You'll know it's all now, and it'll seem enough. All there is is enough—even for you, isn't it?"

"You didn't give me all there was before."

"I had a theory," said Grantley. "I'm not going to have any more theories."

She turned to him suddenly.

"Oh, you mustn't ask—you mustn't stand there asking! That's wrong, that's unworthy of you. I mustn't let you do that."

"That was the theory," Grantley said with a smile. "That was just my theory. I'm always going to ask for what I want now. It's really the best way."

"We're friends, Grantley?" she said imploringly.

"Is that all there is? Would it seem to you enough?"

"And we've Frank. You do love him now, you know."

"In and through you."

She made no answer again. He stood with his eyes fixed on her for some moments. Then he took the telegram gently from her hand and went into the house with it, to seek Christine Fanshaw.

He left Sibylla in a turmoil of feeling. That she loved him was nothing new; she had always loved him, and she had never loved any other man in that fashion. The fairy ride had never been rivalled or repeated; and she had never lost her love for him, even when she hated him as her great enemy. It had always been there, whether its presence had been prized or loathed, welcomed or feared, whether it had seemed the one thing life held, or the one thing to escape from if life were to be worthy. Blake had not displaced it; he had been a refuge from it. Grantley's offence had never been that he did not love her, nor that he could not hold her love; it was that he loved her unworthily and claimed to hold her as a slave. Her case was not as Christine Fanshaw's, any more than her temper was the temper of her friend. And now he came wooing again, and she was sore beset. So memory helped him, so the unforgettable communion of bygone love enforced his suit. Her heart was all for yielding—how should it not be to the one man whose sway it had ever owned? He was to her mind an incomparable wooer—incomparable in his buoyant courage, in the humour that masked his passion, in the passion which used humour with such a conscious art, feigning to conceal without concealing, pretending to reveal without impairing the secrecy of those impenetrable sweet recesses of the heart, concerning which conjecture beats knowledge and the imagination would not be trammelled by a disclosure too unreserved. But she feared and, fearing, struggled. They were friends. Friends could make terms, bargains, treaties, arrangements. Friendship did not bar independence, absolute and uninfringed. Was that the way with love—with the love of woman for man, of wife for husband? No, old Nature came in there with her unchanging decisive word, against which no bargain and no terms, no theory and no views, no claims or pretensions, no folly and no wisdom either, could prevail. All said and done, all concessions made, all promises pledged, all demands guaranteed, they all went for little. The woman was left to depend on the trust she had, helpless if the trust failed her and the confidence were misplaced. If she were wrong about herself or about the man, there was no help for it. The love of the woman was, after all and in spite of all, surrender. Times might change, and thoughts and theories; this might be right which had been wrong, and that held wrong which had been accounted right. The accidents varied, the essence remained. The love of the woman was surrender, because old Nature would have it so. If she gave such love—or acknowledged it, for in truth it was given—she abandoned all the claims, the grievances, the wrongs, all that had been the basis of what she had done. She took Grantley on faith again, she put herself into his hands, again she made the great venture with all its possibilities. She had seemed wrong once. Would she seem wrong again?

There was a change in him: that she believed. Was there a change too in her? Unless there were, she did not dare to venture. Had all that she had suffered, all that she had seen others suffer, brought nothing to her? Yes, there was something. When you loved you must understand, and, knowing the truth, love that or leave it. You must not make an image and love that, then make another image and hate that. You must love or leave the true thing. And to do that there is needed another surrender—of your point of view, your own ideas of what you are and of how you ought to be treated. To get great things you must barter great things in return. There are seldom cheap bargains to be had in costly goods. Had not Grantley learnt that? Could not she? It took generosity to learn it. Was she less generous than Grantley? The question hit her like a blow. If Grantley had done as she had, would she still have loved, would she have come again to seek and to woo? Ah, but the case was not truly parallel. Grantley sought leave to reign again—to reign by her will, but still to reign. That was not what was asked of her.

Was it not? Eagerly stretching out after truth, seeking the bed-rock of deep truth, her mind, spurred by its need, soared above these distinctions, and saw, as in a vision, the union of these transient opposites. Was not to reign well to serve well, was not faithfully to obey the order of the universe to be a king of life? If that vision would abide with her, if that harmony could be sustained, then all would be well. The doubts and fears would die, and the surrender be a great conquest. When she had tried before, she had no such idea as this. Much had been spent, much given, in attaining to the distant sight of it. But if it were true? If Grantley, ever courageous, ever undaunted, had won his way to it and now came, in a suppliant's guise, to show her and to give her the treasures of a queen?

While she still mused, the little boy came toddling over the lawn to her side, holding up a toy for her interest and admiration. She caught him up and held him in her arms. Had he nothing to say to it all? Had he nothing to say? Why, his eyes were like the eyes of Grantley!

The clock of the old church struck five, and on the sound a cab appeared over the crest of the opposite hill. Sibylla, with Frank in her arms, watched its descent to Milldean, and then went into the house to put on her hat. In view of the ancient love between her and Mumples, it was her privilege to be the first to greet the returned wanderer; she alone would properly understand and share Mumples' feeling. For all her sympathy, Kate Raymore was a friend of too recent standing—she had not witnessed the years of waiting. Jeremy's affection was true enough, but Mumples feared the directness of his tongue and the exuberance of his spirits. Highly conscious of the honour done to her, somewhat alarmed at the threatened appeal to her ever too ready emotion, Sibylla went down the hill.

A pale frail old student with the hands of a labouring man—that was her first impression of Mumples' husband. He had the air of remoteness from the world and of having done with the storms of life which comes to men who have lived many years in a library; his face was lined, but his eyes calm and placid. Only those incongruous hands, with their marks of toil, hinted at the true story. He spoke in a low voice, as though it might be an offence to speak loud; his tones were refined and his manner respectful and rather formal. It was evidently unsafe to make any parade of sympathy with Mumples—she was near breaking-point; but the exchange of a glance, on which Sibylla ventured, showed that her agitation was of joy and satisfaction. Evidently the meeting had disappointed the worst of her fears and confirmed the dearest of her hopes.

"I have to thank you, madame," the old man said, "for the great kindness you and your family have shown to my wife during my absence."

"We owe her far more than she owes us. I don't know what we should have done without her."

"The knowledge that she had good friends did much to enable me to endure my absence," he went on. "She's looking well, is she not, madame? She appears to me less changed than I had thought possible."

Sibylla could not resist another quick glance at Mumples.

"And I haven't seen her for ten years."

He paused and looked at Sibylla in a questioning way.

"Don't worry any more about that, Luke," said Mrs. Mumples with her hand on his shoulder. "You knew what suited you best. What was the good of my coming, if it wasn't to be a comfort to you."

"It was selfish of me, madame; but you've no idea what it is to be in—in such circumstances as I was. I've been unfortunately a man of quick temper, and I couldn't trust myself in all cases. I got beside myself if I was reminded of the outside world—of all I was losing—how the years went by—of my wife, and the home and the life I might have had. It was because I loved her that I wouldn't see her——"

"Yes, yes, I'm sure of that," said Sibylla hastily.

"But it was selfish, as love sometimes is, madame. I ought to have put her first. And I never thought what it would mean to her when I did what brought me to that place. Well, I've paid for it with my life. They've taken my life from me."

"You've many years before you, dear," whispered Mrs. Mumple.

"I have so few behind me," he said. "They've blotted out two-thirds of my life. Looking back on it now, I can't see it as it was. It seems long, but very empty—a great vacant space in my life, madame."

"Ah, but you've your home and your dear wife now—and we shall all be your friends."

How dull and cold her words seemed! Yet what else was there to say in face of the tragedy?

"I'm deeply grateful to her and to Heaven; but I—I have nothing left. It seems to me that the years have taken everything."

Mrs. Mumple put her hand down to his worn hand and caressed it.

"You'll be better by-and-by, dear," she said.

"I'm deadened," he persisted sadly.

"Don't feel like that," Sibylla implored. "Your life will come back to you in the sunshine and the country air. We shan't let you feel like that. Why, it's full of life here. There's a wedding to-morrow, Mr. Mumple! And another engaged couple—my brother and Miss Raymore! And you'll like my husband, and I'll bring my baby boy to see you."

"Such a pretty little dear," exclaimed Mumples.

"You must take an interest in us," smiled Sibylla; "and then you'll be pleased when we are—won't he, Mumples? Because you're to be one of us, just as your wife is."

Mrs. Mumple suddenly turned away and, murmuring something about getting tea, escaped from the room. The old man fixed his eyes on Sibylla's face in a long inquiring gaze.

"You say that to me, madame? I don't deserve to have that said to me. You're a beautiful young lady, and very kind, I know, and good, I'm sure. Your husband is lucky, and so is your son. But I've been a convict for seventeen years, and it's only by a chance I'm not a murderer. I'm not fit to come near you nor yours—no, not near your little boy."

Sibylla came to him and took his work-worn hand. He saw that she meant to kiss it and held it back.

"A convict and in heart a murderer, madame," he said, his lips trembling a little and his calm eyes very sad. "I'm not fit for you to touch."

"I'll tell you something," said Sibylla. "You call me kind and good—you say my husband and my boy are lucky, and you tell me you're not fit for me to touch—for me to touch! I tried to run away from my husband, and I was ready to leave my little boy to his death."

A great wonder came into the old man's eyes; he asked no question, but he ceased to resist her persuading grasp. She raised his hand to her lips and kissed it.

"I thought my heart was dead, as you think yours is. But light and life have come back into mine, and you mustn't shut yours against them. You must try to be happy, if it's only for dear old Mumples' sake. She's thought of nothing but making you happy all these years." She laid her hand on his shoulder. "And love us too. For my husband's and my boy's sake keep the secret I've told you, but remember it when you feel despairing. It wasn't easy for me to speak of it, but I thought it would give you hope; and it will prevent you feeling the sort of thing you felt about me, and I hope about any of us."

He turned his eyes to hers.

"You're telling me the truth, I know, madame," he said slowly. "It's a very strange world. I'll try not to despair."

"No, no, don't despair; above all, don't despair," whispered Sibylla.

"I have a remnant of my days, and I have the love of my wife. God has left me something out of the wreck that I've made."

Sibylla stooped and kissed him on the brow. He caught her hands and looked again in her eyes for a long time.

"It is true? And your eyes are like the eyes of an angel."

He relaxed his hold on her, and sank back in his chair with a sigh.

"I'm tiring you," said Sibylla. "I'll go now, and leave you alone with Mumples. I'll call her back here. No, I can't stay to tea—you've made me think of too much. But I'll come to-morrow and bring my little boy."

"If what you say is true, you must pray for yourself sometimes? Pray for me too, madame."

"Yes, I'll pray for you the prayer I love best: 'Those things which for our unworthiness we dare not and for our blindness we cannot ask——' I will pray for those, for you and for me. And because you're an old man and have suffered, you shall give me your blessing before I go."

She knelt to receive his trembling benediction, then rose with a glad smile on her face. She saw Mumples standing now on the threshold of the room, and kissed her hand to her.

"The old is done, and the new is begun," she said to the old man as she pressed his hand in farewell.

She walked slowly up the hill in the peaceful dusk. Lights burned in the church: the village choir was laboriously practising an ambitious effort for the next day. There were lights in the windows over the post-office; one was open to the mild evening air, and Jeremy's voice in a love-ballad competed enviously with the choir's more pious strains, till it was drowned in a merry protest of youthful shouts. When she reached home, there was a light in the nursery, and the nurse was singing softly to the little boy. Her agitation was passed, her emotion was gentle now, and her face peacefully radiant. Her grievances seemed small beside the old man's suffering, her woes nothing beside his punishment, her return to life and light so much easier than his. He had but a remnant of life left—the rest had been demanded of him in ransom for his deed, and the ransom had been exacted to the uttermost farthing. He was poor, though not destitute; but she was rich. Her life lay still before her with all its meaning and its possibilities—its work and its struggles, its successes and its failures, the winning of more victories, the effort and the resolve not to lose what had been so hardly won. Soberly she looked forward to it, assessing and measuring her strength and weakness and the strength and weakness of those with whom her life was cast. She had no more of the blind and reckless confidence of her first essay; her eyes were open. Her knowledge did not forbid her soul reaching out to the joy that was to come, but it whispered that the joy was not all, and that the joy must be fairly won. Yet she welcomed the joy with the innate ardour of her mind, exultant that now she might take it, that now it could prove no delusion because she had learnt wherein lay the truth of it. The clue was in her fingers. The path might be rough sometimes, uphill sometimes, not all in pleasant valleys and soft beguiling scenes; there would be arid tracts, perhaps, and bleak uplands. Such was the Way of Life: she recognised it now. The clue was in her hand, and though she might weary and stumble, she would not be utterly lost or belated.

CHAPTER XXIX
WITH OPEN EYES

Sibylla had allotted to Christine a small sitting-room on the first floor of the house to be her private resort during her visit; they neither of them liked a drawing-room existence all day long. Here Christine sat waiting John Fanshaw's arrival. She had taken much thought wherewithal she should be clothed, but that was rather the instinct which asserted itself in her on any occasion of moment than a token of confidence in the weapon of becoming apparel. A fair appearance was never to be wholly neglected by the wise, but she did not rely on it now. The most that any charming could do would be to extort a passing admiration, which in its turn might secure a transient forgiveness; but a reaction of feeling would surely wait on it. She did not want to be forgiven in that way. In truth she hardly wanted forgiveness at all; at any rate she would greatly dislike the process. She had been put in the corner, as she said. The position was not pleasant; but being called out again with the admonitions suitable to the moment was scarcely a more agreeable situation. By parting her from him, first in spirit, then in daily life, John had hardened her heart towards him. He had made her dwell more and more not on her sin, but on his right to inflict a penalty. More and more she had remembered what Caylesham had said, and had asked if he who benefited by the act—of his own will benefited by it—had any title to despise the hand which was guilty of it. John's distress, his doubts, struggles, and forlornness, had pleaded against this judgment of him while she was with him. The idea of them had grown faint with absence; John had left himself to be dealt with by reason then, and reason saw only what he had done; the eye could no longer trace the sorrow and the struggle which had gone with his deed.

Her mind was on Caylesham too. She had just read a letter from Anna Selford. It was full of Anna and her frocks. (Much advice was needed—when was Mrs. Fanshaw coming back to town?) It had a good deal to say of Blake and his handsome presents; and it touched on Caylesham with a rather acrimonious note. He had been to see them, and had not made himself very agreeable; really Anna did not see that there was anything to criticise, nor, above all, that Lord Caylesham had any call to set up as a critic if there were. Christine smiled over the passage, picturing so well the veiled irony and the intangible banter which Caylesham would mingle with his congratulations and infuse into his praises. Anna would not shrink nor retreat, but she would be angry and rather helpless before the sting of these slender darts. Memories stamped on her very soul stood out in salient letters, and the face of Caylesham seemed to hang in the air before her eyes. To remember loving is not to love, but it may make all other love seem a second-rate thing. She loved Caylesham no longer, but she was without power to love anyone as she had loved him. Others had his vices, others his virtues such as they were. The blend in him had been for her the thing her soul asked. Time could not wither the remembrance, though it had killed the feeling itself. Not John's displeasure was the greatest price she had paid; not John's forgiveness could undo or blot out the past. John's friendship and comradeship were the best thing the world had to offer her now—and she wanted them; but she wanted them not as the best, but because there was nothing better.

She had no thought of blame for Caylesham, nor of bitterness against him. Here her fairness of mind came in—her true judgment of herself. All along she had known what he was and what he gave, as well as what she was and gave. He had given all he had ever professed to give. (She was not thinking of words or phrases, but of the essence of the attachment, well known to both.) If it had not been all she sought, still she had accepted it as enough—as enough to make her happy, enough return for all she had to offer. She would not repudiate the bargain now. Frank had been straight and fair with her, and she would cast no stone at him. Only it was just very unlucky that matters should fall out in the way they had, and that she should be the sort of person she was—a bad sinner, because she could not minimise nor forget—a bad penitent, because she could not feel remorse that the fault had been committed, nor humbly seek forgiveness for it. It had abided with her always—now as a pleasure, now as a threatening danger, as both together sometimes. Even at this moment it was at once the cause of all her sorrow and her greatest solace in the world.

Yet in the days between the end of her love for Caylesham and the discovery which had been made by John there had been another happiness—when she was on good terms with her old friend John, when things went well with them, when he admired her—yes, when he treated her as something precious, clever, and brilliant. Then she had rejoiced in his pride in her, and given of the best she had to preserve and to strengthen it. Now, in resentment against John, she sought to deny this. But in what mood would John come? The maintenance of her denial depended largely on that.

Suddenly she heard the sound of wheels stopping before the gate of the house. She sat erect and listened. The hall-door opened. She waited till she heard it close again, then sprang up, cast a glance at a looking-glass over the mantelpiece, then turned and faced the door. Her lips were a little parted; she stood very still. Expectation mingled with defiance in her bearing. A few minutes passed before there was a knock at the door. She cleared her throat to cry:

"Come in!"

John entered and closed the door carefully behind him; but he did not advance towards her at once. He stood where he was, with a curious deprecatory smile on his face. She thought he looked rather old and worn, and he was shabbily dressed, as his habit was when he had to look after his own wardrobe without advice and criticism. He carried the sense of forlornness, as he had when he sat with Caylesham's cheque before him, and the air of being ashamed too. But his manner gave now no hint of anger. Christine's heart went out to him in a quick impulse of sympathy; but she crushed the feeling down, and would give no outward sign of it. She waited in stillness and silence. It was for him to speak, for him to set the note of their interview, and of more than their interview—of their future life, and of how they were to be to one another henceforward.

"Here I am, Christine. Mrs. Grantley told me I should find you in this room; and here I am."

She nodded her head coolly, but gave him no other welcome. He came two or three steps towards her, holding out his hands in front of him in an awkward way, and with that ashamed pleading smile still on his lips.

"I can't get on without my old girl," he said.

In a flash of her quick intuition she knew his mind. The one sentence revealed anything which his manner had left doubtful. He was doing what he thought wrong, and doing it because he could not help it. He was abandoning a great and just grievance, and thereby seemed to be sacrificing the claims of morality, condoning what deserved no forgiveness, impairing his own self-respect. His position, with all its obvious weakness, had not become untenable in theory, and his reason, hard-bound in preconceptions, was not convinced. He came under the stress of feeling, because his life had become intolerable, because, as he said in one of his phrases of rough affection, he could not get on without his old girl. The need he had of her conquered the grievance that he had against her, and brought him back to her. He came with no reproaches, no parade of forgiveness, with neither references to the past nor terms for the future.

It was a triumph for Christine, and of the kind she prized and understood best—a woman's triumph. It had not been expected; it was none too well deserved. A colour came on her cheeks, and she breathed rather quickly as she realised the completeness of it. For a moment she was minded to use it to the full, and, since she was no longer the criminal, to play the tyrant in her turn. But the very perfection of the victory forbade. It inspired in her a feeling which reproaches would have been powerless to raise—a great pity for him, a new and more genuine condemnation of herself. Had she been so much as that to him, and yet had used him so ill?

"I've been lonely too, John," she said. "Come and kiss me, my dear."

He came to her diffidently, and hardly touched her cheek when he kissed her.

"That doesn't feel a bit like you, John," she said, with a nervous laugh, as she made him sit by her on the sofa. "Now tell me all about everything! I know that's what you want to do."

That was what he wanted to do—to take her back into the life which was so empty and incomplete without her—to have her again to share his interests and to be a partner in his fortunes. Yet for the moment he could not do as she bade him. He was much moved, and was very unready at expressing emotion. He sat in silence, gently caressing her hand. It was she who spoke.

"Of course there's a lot to say; but don't let's say it, John. You'll know I'm feeling it, and I shall know that about you too. But don't let's say it." She broke into a smile again. "I should argue, you know—I always argue! And then—— But if we say nothing about it, perhaps we—well, perhaps we can nearly forget it, and take up the old life where we broke it off. And it wasn't a bad old life, after all, was it, in spite of the way we both grumbled?"

"My dear old girl!" he murmured.

"I suppose you must be as vulgar as you like to-day!" said Christine, with a dainty lift of her brow and an affected resignation. Then suddenly she turned and kissed him, saying gravely: "I'm grateful, John, and don't—don't think there's anything wrong in being generous."

"I only know I've got to have you back with me," he said. "That's all I know about it anyhow."

"I think it's enough, then," she whispered softly.

Presently the gates of John's mouth were loosed, and he began to tell all his news. It was mainly about his business—how it flourished, how he had built up his credit again, of the successes he had won; that as soon as he had paid off his debts—a moment of embarrassment befell him here—they would be as well off as ever they had been; horses could be bought again, the diamonds could reappear, there would be no need to stint Christine of any of the things that she loved. All that he had longed for sympathetic ears to hear in the last months came bubbling out now. And Christine was ready to listen. As he talked and she heard, the old life seemed to revive, the old interests of every day came back, exercised anew their uniting power, and brought with them the old friendship and comradeship. Christine had said that they could "nearly forget." The words had her courage in them; they had her caution too. To forget what had come upon them and between them was impossible—in Christine's obstinate heart even at this moment hardly desired; but it was possible nearly to forget—at most times so nearly to forget as to relegate the thing to some distant chamber of the heart and not let it count in the commerce and communion of the life which they lived together and which bound them to one another with all its ties. That was the best thing which could be looked for, since the past, being irrevocable in deed, is also not to be forgotten in thought. They were picking up and piecing together the fragments. The ruin here had not been as utter as it had at poor Tom Courtland's, where the same process was being undertaken; but there had been a crash, and, though the pieces might be joined, there would be marks to show the fracture. Yet even the memory that refused to die brought its good with it. After the ruin came the love which had in the end sought restoration; if the one could not be forgotten, the other would always claim an accompanying remembrance. From this remembrance there might well emerge an affection deeper, stronger, and more proof against the worries and the friction of common life which in the old days had so often disturbed their peace and interrupted their friendship.

Before dinner Christine found an opportunity to visit Sibylla in her room. Her own brief excitement and agitation had passed off; Sibylla seemed the more eager of the two about the event of the day. Christine related it. Her comments on it and on what it meant ran very much in the foregoing vein, but was modified by her usual veneer of irony for which her friend made easy allowance. Sibylla had been prepared for an ecstasy of sympathetic congratulation; but it was evident that though congratulation might be welcomed, ecstasy would be out of place. Neither Christine's conclusions from the past nor her anticipations of the future invited it.

"How reasonable you are, Christine!" sighed Sibylla. "And how immoral!" she added, with a smile. "You're not really very sorry about it all, you know. You're just very glad the trouble is over. And you don't expect a bit more than it's quite likely you'll get! Do you know, you're very useful to me?"

"My reasonableness or my immorality?"

"One's an example and the other's a warning," laughed Sibylla.

"I don't think I'm immoral. I've had an awful lesson, and I intend to profit by it. There'll be nothing more of that sort, you know."

"Why not?" Sibylla asked, curious to probe her friend's mind.

"I don't know. No temptation—being sorry for John—being afraid—being, between ourselves, thirty-five. It all sounds rather mixed, but it results in a good resolution. And as for the future——" She frowned just a little. "Oh, it'll be all right, and a great deal better than I've been thinking lately."

"I must get more like you—not quite like you, but more like you. I must—I must!" Sibylla declared vehemently. "Has being thirty-five a great deal to do with it? Because then I can wait and hope."

"I should think it had a good deal to do with it," admitted Christine dispassionately. "Oh, well, I needn't run myself down too much. Really John has a good deal to say to it."

"I've Frank too."

"Yes, you have; and you're in love with your husband, my dear."

"That doesn't always make it easier."

"At any rate it keeps up one's interest in the whole affair," smiled Christine.

"You're happy, anyhow?"

"Happy? Yes, reasonably happy—and I suppose immorally too. At any rate, I'm settled, and that's really a comfort in its way."

"I don't know that I care so much about being settled. Perhaps I shall at thirty-five!"

The idea of years making any difference to her moods or her needs seemed rather a new one to Sibylla. Evidently she was holding it in her mind and turning it over in her thoughts.

The idea was with her still as she sat rather silent at the dinner-table that evening. They had a little party, for all the Raymores joined them, and young Mallam was there also, their guest for the night. Christine was very gay and satirical. John watched her with ready admiration, but less ready understanding. The young men were rather noisy, toasting to-morrow's wedding to the confusion of the bridegroom and the equal confusion of Eva Raymore, to whose not distant destiny both Jeremy's words and Jeremy's eyes made references by no means covert. Kate Raymore and her husband looked on with the subdued and tempered happiness which was the outcome of their great sorrow, their triumph over it, and the impending departure of their son, to complete the working out of his atonement. They talked of the Selfords with some irony, of poor Harriet Courtland, of Tom and his children with a sympathetic hopefulness and a touch of amusement at the importance their dear old Suzette Bligh was assuming and was, it seemed, to assume in the household. Sibylla's own thoughts widened the survey, embracing in it the couple down at Old Mill House—the faithful patient woman whose love made even the ridiculous touching; the broken old man who had given the best of his life in expiation for a brief madness, and now crept home to end his days, asking nothing but peace, hoping at best not to be despised or shunned. Above in his cot lay her little son, at the other end of the scale, at the beginning of all things; and opposite to her was Grantley himself, unbroken, but not unchanged; obedient to the lessons, but never put out of heart by them; doing violence to what he had held most truly and most preciously himself in order to the search and discovery of something more true and precious still. The idea of the ever-passing years and of feelings and fortunes appropriate to each stage of life helped her, but was not enough. There were differences of minds too, of tempers and of views; and every one of them implied a fitting in, perhaps a paring away here or an addition there—a harmonising; these things must be if the system was to work. Reluctantly and gradually her ardent mind, by nature ever either buoyant in the heaven of assured hope or cast down to the depths of despair, bowed to the middle conclusion, and consented to look through the eyes of wisdom and experience. Happy he who can so look and yet look without bitterness, who can see calamity without despair, and accept partial success without peevishness. There were the hopeless cases. These must be explained, or left unexplained, by what creed or philosophy you chose to hold. There were—surely there were!—the few perfect ones, where there was not even danger nor the need for effort or for guard. Of such she had deemed hers one. It had needed much to open her eyes—much sorrow and wrong in her own life—much sorrow, wrong, and calamity in the lives which passed within her view. But her eyes were open now. Yet she took courage—she took courage from Grantley, whose crest was not lowered, though his heart was changed.

So spoke reason, and to it Sibylla bowed. The array of cases, the marshalling of instances—all that the people and the lives about her had represented and typified—their moral was not to be denied. But reason is not the sole governor, nor even the only teacher. It might open her eyes; it might even moderate the arrogance of her demands; it could not change the temper of her heart. She was not even chilled, far less embittered. She went forth to meet life and love as ardently as ever. The change was that she knew more what these things were which she started forth to welcome, and perceived better to what she must attune herself. She would hope and enjoy still. But she asked no more a privilege over her fellows. She could hope as a mortal without immunity from evil, and enjoy as one to whom there is allotted a portion of sorrow—and not of her own only, nor perhaps of her making, nor of her fault, since by her own act and by nature's will her being was bound up with the being of others, and her happiness or misery, success or failure, lay in the common fortune and the common weal. For any mortal perfect independence is a vain thing fondly imagined—most vain and fond when it is demanded together with all for which any approach to it was once eagerly abandoned.

The battle was won. As John Fanshaw sacrificed his great grievance, so she hers. As old Mumple had expiated his fault and paid his price, so she hers. As Grantley schooled his heart, so she hers. She walked with him that night in the garden while the rest made merry with games and songs and jokes within, their gay laughter echoing down to the old house where the long-parted husband and wife sat at last hand in hand. She bowed her head, and put her hands in Grantley's, saying:

"At the first sign from you it was easy to forgive. How could I not forgive you? But it's hard to ask to be forgiven, Grantley?"

"It was necessary that these things should come," he answered gravely. "They have come and gone. What are they now between thee and me?"

Wisdom had made her point, and for a while now she wisely held her peace, leaving her work to another who should surely bring it to an excellent issue—to love, tempered by sorrow and self-knowledge, yet triumphant, and looking forward to new days, new births, new victories.

"The old time is done," said Grantley. "There's a new dawn. And, Sibylla, the sunrise is golden still."

"My ever true lover, we'll ride on the downs to-morrow," said she.

"Into the gold?" he asked, in loving banter.

"Yes," she answered bravely. "Haven't we found the way now?"

"It may be hard to keep it."

"We shall be together—you and I. And more than you and me. And—and—well, I intend to be unreasonable again just for this evening! I'll expect everything, and demand everything, and dream everything again, just for to-night—just for to-night, Grantley!"

She ended in a merry laugh, as she stood opposite him with dancing eyes.

"You're always thorough. I was afraid you were going to be a bit too thorough with those delusions. Need we make quite so clean a sweep of them?"

"As if I ever should!" Sibylla sighed.

"Perhaps we've been doing one or two of them a little injustice?" he suggested.

"We'll let them stay a little bit and see if they can clear their characters," said she. "There might be one great truth hidden among them."

"I rather fancy there is," said Grantley Imason, "and we'll have the fellow out of his disguise."

THE END

Made in the USA
Middletown, DE
30 June 2018